A HISTORY OF
BRITAIN

A HISTORY OF BRITAIN

THE KEY EVENTS THAT HAVE SHAPED BRITAIN FROM
NEOLITHIC TIMES TO THE 21ST CENTURY

RICHARD DARGIE

ARCTURUS

ARCTURUS

This edition published in 2010 by Arcturus Publishing Limited
26/27 Bickels Yard, 151–153 Bermondsey Street,
London SE1 3HA

ISBN: 978-1-84837-741-7
AD000246EN

Printed in China

Author: Richard Dargie
Editor: Ella Fern
Design: Zoe Mellors
Picture Research: Anya Martin

Picture credits: Pamela Adam 12; AKG Images 8, 9, 10, 11, 26, 35, 42, 65, 99, 100, 102,
107, 109, 112, 117 (bottom), 125 (top), 134, 161 (top), 170, 174, 197; Andrew and Marie
Bells 69; Art Archive cover (centre left); Bridgeman Art Library 15, 19, 24, 38, 39, 46, 53,
56 (top), 57, 58, 64, 67, 88 (top), 90, 92, 95 (top, bottom), 98, 101, 106, 108, 110, 111
(top, bottom), 115, 116, 130, 144, 148, 162 (top), 167, 168 (bottom), 169, 179, 185 (top);
Mark Burbidge 30; Clipart 40, 54, 59, 63, 105, 113, 125 (bottom), 131 (top), 171; corbis
cover (top left, top centre, top right, centre, bottom left, bottom centre, bottom right), 5,
18, 20, 21, 25, 44, 52, 55 (left, right), 62, 66, 80, 82, 84 (bottom), 87, 117 (top), 122, 135
(top), 147, 149, 151 (top, bottom), 156, 159 (top), 172, 176, 181, 182 (top) 183, 185
(bottom), 190, 193 (top), 194, 195, 201, 202, 203, 204, 205; Mark Denovich 14; Dover 73
(top), 137, 138, 139, 141, 142, 154 (top) 155, 159 (bottom), 162 (bottom), 173; Getty
Images cover (centre right), 22, 70, 72 (left), 74, 77, 81, 83, 199, 200; Rick Harrison 93;
Mary Harrsch 23; Mary Evans Picture Library 14 (top), 29, 32, 41, 61, 72 (right), 79, 85,
86, 89, 118, 119, 121, 123 (top), 136, 140 (top, bottom), 143, 145, 152, 164, 165, 191,
193 (bottom), 196; Andy Piper 76; Ian Robertson 28; Shutterstock 6, 34; Cathy Simpson
16; Martin Stewart 60; Vanda Wallace 75; Enrico Webers 120; Wessex Archaeology 13;
David Wilmot 33; www.sacred-destinations.com 36.

We have made every attempt to contact the copyright-holders of the illustrations within
this book. Any oversights or omissions will be corrected in future editions.

CONTENTS

BRITAIN: ISLANDS, PEOPLES AND IDENTITIES

SET IN THE SILVER SEA

The history of these islands has been deeply shaped by their distinctive geography. Described by Shakespeare as the 'moat defensive', the seas surrounding Britain have served as an obstacle to enemies and invaders but also as a conduit for trade and ideas in more mundane times. The Channel ensured that the cultures of Britain developed in their own ways, taking and rejecting influences from the Continental mainland. The sea acted as a barrier too for the peoples of Hibernia and the islands of the far north and west, making them less accessible to powerful, centralizing forces. Rivers were also barriers and conduits. London's position as the largest city in these islands owes much to its being the first bridgeable point on the Thames, yet lying so deep within England. In the same way Stirling, the key to controlling Scotland, lay atop the first bridging point on the broad river Forth.

LOWLANDS AND HIGHLANDS

The relative flatness and fertility of the south and centre of Britain provided the inhabitants there with weaker natural defences but great wealth, abundant food supplies and efficient communications. Here a wide variety of types of settlements prospered. Here it was easier to make paths, build roads, move resources and mobilize people, but it was also easier to invade as Roman, Saxon and Norman commanders found. Nevertheless, this wealthy land was abundant enough to absorb new peoples, new ideas and new customs. Material

Above: The dramatic white cliffs of Dover have seen the ebb and flow of invaders and settlers to Britain's shores over the centuries.

surplus also provided the possibility to gamble on change and experiment with ways of doing and thinking things. It was a different matter in the fractured geography of Scotland and Wales, the upland hills of northern England and the remoter lands of western Ireland. Here arable land was scarcer and other resources took longer to amass. Though people came together for the purposes of war, trade and belief, permanent settlements were always fewer and far between. Large tracts of northern Britain and western Ireland remained largely inaccessible until the coming of the railways in the 19th century. Physically more isolated, older ways of life and loyalties were preserved longer here. Local resistance to authority, even into Tudor and Stewart times, was always more likely to come from upland rather than lowland peoples.

THE PEOPLES

All Britons are immigrants or the descendants of immigrants. Surnames and place names throughout these islands provide rich evidence of the importance of earlier waves of migrants in shaping the development of Britain. Some of these incomers, such as the Germanic Saxons or their later Scandinavian cousins, enjoy a prominent and honoured place in our national histories. Other groups have received less historical limelight – such as the rural Italian and Eastern European poor who fetched up on these shores in the 19th century seeking work. In the later 17th century, French Huguenots saw Britain as a place of refuge from an inflexible and intolerant government. Russian Jews escaping pogroms, Poles in 1939, Hungarians in 1956, Ugandan Asians fleeing harsh policies of 'Africanization' and Chilean victims of Pinochet have all founded communities of their own here. Migration within Britain has also been a profound force for social, economic and demographic change, especially since medieval times.

IDENTITIES

From the time of Agricola onwards, the attempt to unify these islands within one polity has been one of the enduring dynamics of our history. Rome eventually failed in this quest, while in the 10th century Athelstan, the first great English king, never proved his boast to be king of all Britain. Edward Plantagenet briefly came closer than most to creating one empire in Britain and Ireland. The Welsh, secure in their linguistic identity, accepted rule from the south. The Scots however, used the memory of English incursions into their territory to forge an alternative sense of nationhood. For the Irish, a sense of separateness has been reinforced by geographical distance, language and after 1530, faith. One polity governing from London only came into existence in 1801 with the creation of the United Kingdom of Great Britain and Ireland. This situation lasted a mere 120 years, ending with the creation of the Irish Free State. Since devolution in 1997, Welsh and Scottish identities have continued to strengthen and a new revived sense of Englishness is abroad. The politics of identity look set to continue to dominate the history of these islands in years to come.

OUR EARLIEST ANCESTORS
C. 700,000–12,000 BC

When did the first human feet tread on the lands we call Britain? Recent finds suggest that hominids (the primate ancestors of humans) lived in what became our islands more than 700,000 years ago. The earliest human remains found so far are around half a million years old. Around 25,000 BC, northern Europe and most of modern Britain was plunged into a deep Ice Age that forced our ancestors to retreat southwards to warmer climes.

THE FIRST 'BRITISH' HOMINIDS

Sandwiched between the sea waves and crumbling cliffs, in April 2003 archaeologists at Pakefield on the Suffolk coast discovered the oldest evidence of human activity found in Britain. Thirty-two black worked flints were rescued from a site dating back approximately 700,000 years, proving that humans were active in northern Europe far earlier than previously believed. At this time, Britain was still joined to mainland Europe and species such as the mammoth, rhino and giant beaver roamed the East Anglian landscape.

Above: Early British hominids made their homes in natural caves which provided shelter from the elements and from predators such as wolves.

THE BOXGROVE BONES

Half a million years ago, a water hole at Boxgrove in West Sussex attracted a wide variety of thirsty herbivores. An archaic human species took the opportunity to hunt and trap the beasts that congregated there. The discovery of prehistoric horse remains at Boxgrove has revealed the skill with which these early hominids dismembered their prey before using hammerstones to crush the bones and suck out the marrow. A neat semi-circular hole in a horse shoulder blade suggests that sharpened hunting sticks were used as spears to bring down the animals. In the 1990s, a human shin-bone and two incisor teeth were discovered at the site, the oldest human remains yet found in Britain. They once belonged to a member of a species known as *homo heidelbergensis*, the ancestor of modern humans as well as the Neanderthals. The Boxgrove specimen was about 1.80 m (5 ft 10 inches) tall and around 80 kg (176 lbs) in weight. Sadly for 'Boxgrove Man', the shin-bone had been gnawed by a large carnivore, suggesting that

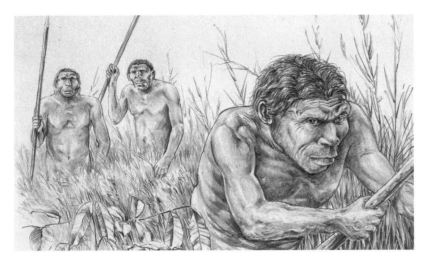

Above: *Homo heidelbergensis* and their ancestors, Neanderthal man, were of stocky stature and brutish features, built to withstand the challenges of their environment.

he was himself prey for a lion or wolf or that his unburied corpse had been scavenged after death.

NEANDERTHAL BRITAIN

In the periods when Britain was habitable between 250,000 and 30,000 BC, the dominant human species in Britain was Neanderthal man, so called after remains discovered in the Neander valley in Germany. A skull from Swanscombe in Kent and teeth found at Pontnewydd Cave in Denbighshire have distinct Neanderthal features. The Neanderthals have had a poor press, often depicted as brutish and slow. In fact, this stocky, barrel-chested creature was well adapted to the prevailing cold climate, had tool-making skills and probably some capacity for speech. The trap excavated at La Cotte de St Brelade in Jersey has provided rich evidence of Neanderthal's intelligence and success as a hunter. The pile of twenty mammoth and five rhino skulls, smashed open to get access to the nutritious brain tissues, have been described as 'prehistoric overkill' by some modern paleo-anthropologists.

ON THE EDGE

Although not always an island, for in periods of glaciation the bed of the North Sea dried up and reverted to plains, Britain was always on the extreme margin of the European mainland. Hominid numbers in Britain were never very large and for long periods they were probably concentrated in the southern and eastern areas which escaped the worst effects of the periodic ice ages. Humans retreated southwards to Europe in the last cold spell 27,000 years ago, but returned around 15,000 years ago at the first sign of a thaw. Hunters from that period, such as those who inhabited Creswell Crags in Derbyshire, lived right on the edge of the retreating glaciers. Another brief period of climatic deterioration cleared these pioneers out of Britain about 13,000 years ago. However, when the last ice age ended a thousand years or so later, humans quickly returned, following the herds of beasts that were moving north as the temperature rose. This last human re-occupation of Britain was to prove more permanent.

TIMELINE OF PALEOLITHIC BRITAIN	
c. 700,000 BC	*Date of earliest human implements found on Suffolk coast*
c. 480,000 BC	*Likely date of hominid activity at Boxgrove in West Sussex*
c. 130,000 BC	*Probable date for appearance of Neanderthals in Britain*
c. 30,000 BC	*Disappearance of Neanderthals from the archaeological record*
c. 13,000 BC	*Ice Age hunters living in caves in Derbyshire*
c. 12,000 BC	Beginning of the end *of the last Ice Age. Re-colonization of Britain by* homo sapiens.

SETTLING DOWN
c. 9,000–4,200 BC

The people who returned to Britain at the end of the last Ice Age were hunter-fisher folk. They followed the age-old custom of following their prey from place to place as the seasons unfolded. Over time however, they learned to till the land. As knowledge of farming spread after 4,000 BC, the early peoples of Britain began to settle down.

AN ISLAND AGAIN

After 8,500 BC, a warmer climate led to the growth of forests all over Britain. Thanks to higher sea levels, Ireland and Britain were now separate islands divided by the Irish Sea. The plains that formed a land bridge between Britain and Europe were gradually submerged by rising water, a process that has continued right up to modern times, as the Goodwin Sands testify. The folk and the fauna of Britain were now distanced from the mainland and a unique culture and environment would develop as a result.

THE LAST NOMADS

The people that returned to Britain in the Mesolithic or Middle Stone Age were nomads. Temporary settlements at Mount Sandel in County Derry and at Greasby in the Wirral are amongst the earliest found, dating back to between 8,000 and 7,000 BC. At Mount Sandel, a tribe of about fifteen

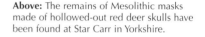

Above: The remains of Mesolithic masks made of hollowed-out red deer skulls have been found at Star Carr in Yorkshire.

A STONE AGE TIME CAPSULE

Over time, early settlements became more complex, none more so than the Neolithic village of Skara Brae in the Orkneys, occupied around 3,000 BC. Here, six dwellings with dry-stone walls, whalebone rafters and turf roofs were dug out of a midden (dunghill) left by earlier generations. Connected by passageways, these dark subterranean huts enjoyed some conveniences. The local flagstone was split to form box beds filled with heather and dressers with shelves. In the floors, stone and clay-lined tanks held shellfish in fresh water as handy snacks or ready-softened bait for fishing lines. Circular cubicles with drains may have been used as latrines. Despite these luxuries, the Skara Brae people deserted the settlement in a hurry. Scattered beads on the floor and uneaten food in a pot suggest that the inhabitants fled from an unexpected menace, perhaps a sandstorm or raiders.

TIMELINE OF MESOLITHIC AND NEOLITHIC BRITAIN

c. 9,000 BC	*End of the last Ice Age*
c. 7,500 BC	*Star Carr used by hunter-scavengers*
c. 4,200 BC	*Farming ideas begin to spread through Britain.*

people lived in seven huts, made by bending saplings into a frame over which skins and hides were probably stretched. The Greasby tent had a rectangular floor of sandstone slabs and pebbles, perhaps a sign that the hunters returned there on a regular basis.

Animal Magic

Star Carr in Yorkshire was probably a winter base for a group of about 25 to 30 people. The discovery of a wooden paddle there suggests that these nomads used canoes or coracles to travel and perhaps to fish. They hunted deer, elk and aurochs or giant wild oxen with spears and arrows, carefully culling the beasts that they depended on to maintain the strength and quality of the herd. Twenty-one deer skulls with antlers have been found at Star Carr. These had been hollowed out to lighten them and had holes bored through them so that they could be worn, perhaps as decoys in the hunt.

Above: Early Mesolithic peoples were mostly nomadic hunters living in temporary settlements. It was not until the 4th millenium BC that people began to settle down and farm the land.

They may also have played a part in magical ceremonies or been used to tell the story of great hunts in the history of the tribe.

Farming Folk

In the 4th millennium BC, the first farmers were at work in Britain. Archaeologists used to explain the change from hunting to farming as the work of new people with superior skills coming in to Britain. Migration probably played a part in spreading this new way of life, but the aboriginal people of Britain were doubtless quick to adapt to any new ideas that helped build up food reserves. The archaeological record suggests that this was the period when several amenable species – sheep, cattle, pigs and goats – were first bred in large numbers in Britain. Wheat in the south and barley in the north were the most successful farmed crops, cut by flint sickles and ground on flat stones.

A Farmed Landscape

The arrival of farming changed the British landscape forever. The dense forests that covered almost all of Britain apart from the highest peaks in North Wales and Scotland began to disappear, cleared by Neolithic farmers wielding polished axes. Reconstruction suggests that a skilled tree-feller could clear a hectare of forest in less than five weeks. Causewayed enclosures such as the 20-acre Windmill Hill in Wiltshire were built across lowland Britain. Protected by rings of ditches with earthen banks and stockades, these vast pens may have been used to control and butcher livestock. The discovery of human remains at these sites also suggests that they were used as fortifications or even had a religious function.

THE CULTS OF THE DEAD
C. 4,200–2,300 BC

The early peoples of Britain took great care when disposing of their dead. As a result, hundreds of well-preserved funerary sites have been found throughout Britain. Different habits of burying, cremating or exposing the dead may be evidence of new peoples arriving and settling in Britain, or it may be a sign that our ancestors were willing to adopt new ideas and beliefs.

Above: Trethevy Quoit in Cornwall, known locally as 'the giant's house', is a megalithic tomb with a characteristic sloping capstone.

THE GREAT BURIAL CULT
From about 4,200 BC onwards, the peoples of Britain adopted the habit of collective burial, a custom that probably spread from western Europe. After death, corpses were left to rot and stored until the dry bones could be transferred to a burial chamber. These chambers were usually lined with stone slabs, although the five corpses excavated at Foulmire Fen in Cambridgeshire were laid to rest in a fine oak-lined mortuary. In southern and eastern Britain, these chambers were often located within massive earthen barrows or long mounds as at Giants' Hills in Lincolnshire. The communal effort needed to raise these structures, and their prominent location in the landscape, suggest that they had great significance for the people who created them.

WHO WAS BURIED IN THE BARROWS?

Most barrows contain between five and fifty burials of both genders and all ages. The small numbers suggest that these people had enjoyed high status, perhaps as members of a dynasty of chieftains or an elite household that performed a ceremonial or religious function for their tribe. Most Neolithic Britons were not honoured with a long barrow burial. The jumbled collections of human remains found in the ditches of several causewayed enclosures suggest that most common folk met a less dignified end. They were probably left on 'sacred' ground or on wooden platforms and exposed to wildlife and the weather.

MEGALITHIC TOMBS
In northern and western Britain, the privileged dead were usually housed in megalithic tombs such as the portal dolmens found in Wales and Cornwall. These are stone chambers used for cremations and burials and roofed with a

A HARD LIFE

Medical research on these early remains reveal a population averaging between 160 and 170 cm (5ft 3ins to 5ft 7ins) in height and living for around thirty years. Osteoarthritis was common. Deformed shinbones suggest a life spent squatting uncomfortably. Dental remains indicate that diseased teeth and gums were another source of pain. Fractures were common but some skulls of this period bear evidence of trepanning or surgery performed in the hope of relieving pain or curing madness.

TIMELINE OF NEOLITHIC BURIALS

4,200 BC	*Earliest long barrows*
c. 3,000 BC	*Last long barrows constructed*
c. 2,750 BC	*Earliest Beaker burials.*

sloping capstone as at Dyffryn Ardudwy in Merioneth and Trethevy Quoit in Cornwall. Near the Severn estuary and in the Cotswolds, over 180 long stone tombs have been identified. These consist of an area for ritual and feasts and a separate chamber for the storage of human remains, often arranged by type, age or sex. In North Wales and parts of Ireland, the prestigious dead often ended up in passage graves such as Bryn Celli Ddu on Ynys Mon. Here, an opening in the circular earthen mound leads to an oval burial chamber. At Isbister on Orkney, a chamber containing over 340 dead was divided into stalls by stone slabs standing at intervals. The stones used in these megalithic tombs weigh up to 50 tons. Only a well-organized social group could have moved and raised slabs of this size.

MAES HOWE

The most elaborate megalithic burial site in Britain is Maes Howe in Orkney. Here the grass mound hides a complex of passages and chambers built from carefully crafted slabs. The main chamber, a rough cube of 4.5 m^2 (5 yards square), is held up by a bracketed vault. At midwinter, the rays of the setting sun travel along the entrance passage, lighting up the chamber's rear wall. Knowledge of the seasons and the skies must have been widespread around the British and Irish Isles in Neolithic times, for a similar event occurs at the winter solstice in the passage grave of New Grange in County Meath.

Below: The Beaker people who settled in Britain in Neolithic times were so called because of their distinctive pottery. They brought with them new burial practices that became known as 'Beaker burials'.

BEAKER BURIALS

A major change in British burial habits took place around 2,750 BC. Cremation, long practised in northern Britain, became more common in the south. At the same time, the tradition of collective burial in barrows was replaced by interments in single graves under small mounds. In Beaker burials, the corpse was usually laid to rest in a crouched, foetal position within a stone coffin that contained clay pottery and other grave goods.

MONUMENTS AND METALS
C. 3,000–2,300 BC

In the years after 2,500 BC, social life in Britain became more complex. The demand for new resources such as metals prompted more technical skills and more ambitious patterns of trade. The population and economy of Britain strengthened to a point where vast amounts of time and energy could be spent on building large-scale monuments.

HENGE AND CIRCLE BUILDERS

Henges, circular areas enclosed by an earthen bank and ditch, were laid out across southern and eastern Britain, often near to water features. Human remains at henge sites, such as the cleft skull of a sacrificial infant found at Woodhenge in Wiltshire, suggest that they were religious locations. Other impressive monuments appeared across Britain. Over 150,000 tons of chalk were dug out to form the earthworks at Avebury that enclose an area 365 m (1,200 ft) in diameter. In northern and eastern Britain, stone circles proliferated, with over a hundred in Aberdeenshire alone. Building on this scale suggests that the communities of prehistoric Britain now possessed unprecedented skills of leadership and organization.

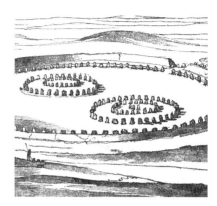

Above: A reconstruction of the earthworks and great stone circles at Avebury – built over a period of several centuries – shows the scale of the project.

STONEHENGE

The most famous henge was begun around 2,800 BC. In its first phase it was a circular earth bank and ditch facing the gigantic Heel Stone. The characteristic trilithons, made from sarsen stones hauled from the Marlborough Downs 40 km (25 miles) away, were erected around 2,000 BC. The finely shaped lintel and upright stones were held together using mortice and tenon joints. Stonehenge's builders even understood the importance of entasis – creating a slight outward curve in the upright stones to counteract the illusion of concave sagging that a straight stone would have given. The purpose of Stonehenge is unknown and may have changed during the twelve hundred years that it took for the henge to reach its final form. However, its alignment to the midsummer sunrise and midwinter sunset as well as to an eighteen-year lunar cycle has led many to suggest a religious or astro-calendrical function.

Below: Stonehenge, much of which is still standing today, was a mammoth feat of engineering and construction.

THE MYSTERIOUS BLUESTONES

In the last phase of building at Stonehenge around 1,540 BC, an

Above: When smiths discovered the tin and copper alloy bronze, the production of hardwearing tools such as these axes became widespread.

inner circle of standing bluestones was erected. It was long believed that these stones had been hauled or rolled from the Preseli Mountains in Pembrokeshire over 320 km (200 miles) away. Recent research into the movement of glaciers in the last Ice Age has suggested that the bluestones were in fact brought to the area by natural action rather than human hand. Despite this convenient deposit, paleoeconomists have calculated that two million man-hours went into the construction of Britain's most iconic prehistoric monument.

METAL MAKERS

The earliest metal objects in Britain were copper daggers first used around 2,700 BC. These may have come from Europe, but there are native sources of the metal in Wales, Derbyshire and the Isle of Man. Early copper was beaten into shape using rounded stone axes, but a wider range of objects were made once the skills of smelting and casting were mastered. Around 2,300 BC smiths in Britain began to add tin to copper to produce the alloy bronze, and so make tools and weapons that were harder and sharper still. The demand for bronze stimulated exchange between tin-rich Cornwall and the copper mines to the north. Cornish tin was also a lure for merchants from overseas.

BRONZE AGENTS

Although the ores needed for bronze were plentiful in Britain, scrap metal was valuable and it was recycled. Travelling merchants collected unwanted tools and weapons and for convenience, they stored this scrap in temporary hoards. Some of these hoards were never retrieved by their owners and now provide us with evidence of the wide range of bronze artefacts in everyday use 4,000 years ago. Other Bronze Age hoards may have been discarded intentionally. Many bronze weapons have been recovered from sites that were once bogs, wells or rivers, suggesting that these were offerings to water gods and spirits.

TRADE WITH EUROPE AND BEYOND

A series of remains found in 'Wessex' in southern England were buried in elaborate graves and are thought to have belonged to a powerful caste. Weapons, tools and treasure from these graves tell us that the early peoples of Britain had links to other peoples living far beyond their immediate locality. A grave at Bush Barrow near Stonehenge contained ornaments of gold that had probably been sourced, if not worked, in Ireland. The amber in the necklace found at Upton Lovell in Wiltshire was traded from the Baltic. The glazed faience beads prized by the Wessex elite were probably produced in the eastern Mediterranean.

TIMELINE	
3,000 BC	*Construction of earliest henges and stone circles*
2,800 BC	*First phase of building at Stonehenge*
2,700 BC	*Earliest use of copper in Britain*
2,300 BC	*Earliest use of bronze in Britain.*

IRON AGE WARRIORS
C. 650–100 BC

The first millennium BC was a period of marked change. In southern and eastern Britain the population rose sharply and the landscape filled with new settlements. Trade and the production of goods increased but so did competition for resources. Tribal rivalry intensified, prompting the building of hillforts and other fortifications in all parts of Britain.

POPULATION EXPLOSION

Estimating the population of ancient Britain is difficult, but many scholars accept that less than a million people lived in Bronze Age Britain. This figure rose sharply to around four million by 150 BC and probably rose again to about six million by 150 AD. The Roman general Julius Caesar remarked on the large number of settlements in southern Britain and its 'countless' population. Feeding these additional mouths had a huge impact on the British landscape, especially in southern areas such as Hampshire and Gloucestershire where the population pressure was greatest. Low-lying woods were cleared, more land was farmed and even less fertile upland areas were cleared for farming. However, despite the greater effort that went into food production and industry, the Iron Age in Britain was a time of increasing political and military tension.

HILLFORTS, CRANNOGS AND DUNS

Thousands of fortified sites throughout Iron Age Britain affirm that this was an age of warriors. The consolidation of regional peoples into tribal groupings provided the manpower to build impressive earthwork hillforts such as Danebury in Hampshire. These were not always places of permanent residence, for in much of southern Britain the population increasingly

MOUSA BROCH

Northern Britain was not as heavily populated as the south but defence was just as necessary. Mousa in Shetland is the best-preserved example of an Iron Age *broch* or round tower. Standing on the coast at over 13 m high (44 ft), it served as a lookout tower and a shelter from raiders. The only entrance to a *broch* was a short doorway and passage that forced incomers to stoop low, rendering them vulnerable to the defenders above. Mousa was one of over 570 *brochs* built throughout Scotland, suggesting that the instability of the late Iron Age was felt in all parts of Britain.

IRON AGE TIMELINE

c. 650 BC	*Transition from bronze to iron weaponry*
c. 600 BC	*Evidence of 'Celtic' style long swords in Britain*
c. 550 BC	*Construction of hillforts in central southern Britain*
c. 100 BC	*Construction of Mousa Broch.*

lived in sprawling lowland *oppida* or stockaded settlements, only retreating to the hills in emergencies. However, the development of fortified homesteads such as Warden Hill in Northumberland reminds us that these were unsettled times. Cliff forts in Cornwall and North Wales made good use of coastal promontories, creating safe havens protected by the sea on three sides and banks of earth to landward. In the north and west of Britain, hillforts and duns were raised with stone defences. The walls were often vitrified – fired at a high temperature to produce a hard enamel coating – as at Tap o'Noth in north-east Scotland. The peoples of Scotland and Ireland often used water features for defence, building *crannogs* or artificial islands based on wooden piles as defensive refuges. A variant of the *crannog* was the island *dun,* a stone fort built in the middle of a small loch and reached by a causeway.

THE CELTS

'Celtic' is a term loosely applied to the iron-based tribal cultures that spread from central to much of western Europe after 800 BC. Historians used to believe that Britain became part of the Celtic world after an invasion of Celtic peoples around 600 BC. However recent scholars have found little archaeological evidence of a mass movement into the British and Irish Isles at this time. Instead they argue that Iron Age Britain was populated by a diverse collection of similar cultures which were heavily influenced by ideas from Celtic Europe through trading and kinship links. These cultures shared important characteristics, such as a love of martial display and a common Druidic religion. Recent genetic studies seem to have confirmed that new ideas from overseas were absorbed by the existing inhabitants of Britain and Ireland, rather than imposed by waves of hostile invaders.

CONTACT WITH ROME

Iron Age Britons had many contacts with the Roman world before Caesar's expedition in 55 BC. The large natural harbour at Hengistbury Head in Dorset was an important port of entry for Roman goods, but the trade was in both directions. The Greek geographer Strabo recorded that the British exported 'grain, cattle, gold, silver, iron, hides, slaves and hunting dogs'. Early Roman wine amphorae dating to the 2nd century BC have been found in many sites across southern Britain. Such luxuries may have been paid for by the provision of British slaves for the Roman market.

THE COMING OF THE EAGLES
55–54 BC

In 55 BC, Julius Caesar resolved to invade the troublesome islands lying to the north-west of Gaul. The Britons were too ready to send help to their rebellious Celtic cousins in Europe. Britain was potentially rich in gold and tin, and for Caesar there was also the glorious prospect of subduing the semi-mythical lands on the edge of the known world.

BATTLE ON THE BEACH

When his fleet emerged from the Channel mists, Caesar glimpsed the cliffs of Dover lined with warriors. This was no place for a landing, as Caesar noted that 'a spear could be thrown from the clifftops to the shore'. After gathering their ships, the Romans scouted northwards, anchoring on the shore near Deal. Here too the Britons were waiting, having followed the invasion fleet along the coast in their chariots.

Above: Julius Caesar commanding his forces on the first Roman expedition to the troublesome British Isles: he encountered fierce resistance all along the coast.

Caesar ordered his reluctant troops to attempt an amphibious landing, led by the eagle-bearer of the Tenth Legion, the first Roman to leap into British waters. Without cavalry however, the heavily armed legionaries struggled to win a foothold on the beach against the more mobile Britons. The day was only saved by the British decision to call a truce and negotiate with the Roman proconsul.

ROMAN FAILURE

Not for the last time in its history, Britain was saved by the Channel winds. Transports carrying Caesar's cavalry were pushed back all the way to Gaul. Storms also damaged the ships lying at Deal. Without horsemen and secure supplies, the Romans were pinned to the Kentish coast. The Seventh Legion, sent to forage for food in the countryside, was ambushed by a large British warband. Riding to its rescue, Caesar forced the British tribes to give way, although he could not press home an advantage. This sliver of success was

Above: The second Roman invasion in 54 BC met with little organized resistance and soon established a beach base in Kent.

enough to allow the Roman general to order a dignified retreat to Gaul. For crossing the dreaded Channel, Rome granted its hero a thanksgiving of twenty days. The first invasion of Britain had lasted little longer.

CAESAR PLANS TO RETURN

The Romans had seriously underestimated the difficulty of invading Britain. The unpredictable British summer weather was as much an enemy as the British warrior in his chariot. However, Caesar had learned that southern Britain was fertile and very rich in grain. So the winter and spring were spent amassing a much larger invasion force of five legions and auxiliaries, 30,000 men in total, supported by 800 transport and supply ships. The new fleet was also adapted to ease beaching and unloading in shallow waters.

ROMAN SUCCESS

The Romans landed unopposed on a mysteriously empty beach near Sandwich. Caesar later learned that the sheer size of his fleet had made the watching Britons wary of attack. Seizing the initiative, he marched through the night to secure the ford on the river Stour at modern Canterbury. The nearby hillfort at Bigbury was taken within hours. However Caesar had to waste ten vital days repairing ships damaged by an unseasonal storm. This gave the Britons time to rally under a supreme warlord, Cassivellaunus, who ruled the Catuvellauni tribes north of the Thames.

Having finally secured their base on the Kentish coast, the Romans marched inland, fording the Thames near London. Cassivellaunus cannily avoided a set battle with the legions, preferring to harry them from the thick forest. However the Romans identified several friendly tribal leaders who led them to the main settlement of the Catuvellauni at Wheathampstead near modern Welwyn. Although well fortified, the settlement was soon taken, along with large numbers of captives and cattle.

EVACUATION

Cassivellaunus sought to negotiate with the Romans and Caesar was also eager to reach a peace. Envoys had brought news of unrest and a poor harvest in Gaul, forcing him to abandon his plans to overwinter in Britain. Hostages, tribute and guarantees of peace were quickly extracted from the tribal leaders and by early September the Roman invasion force had departed. It would be ninety-seven years before the legions and their eagles returned.

TIMELINE

55 BC	
26 Aug	*Caesar sails from Portius Itius (Boulogne)*
27 Aug	*Roman forces land at Deal beach*
31 Aug	*Channel gales scatter the Roman support fleet*
Early Sept	*British guerillas wear down Caesar's forces*
Mid Sept	*Caesar evacuates his forces to Gaul*
54 BC	
7 July	*The Romans land near Sandwich*
8 July	*Caesar captures Bigbury hillfort near Canterbury*
10 July	*Roman fleet wrecked by storms*
Late July	*Caesar crosses the Thames*
5 Aug	*Revolt in Gaul*
Early Sept	*Caesar returns to Gaul.*

THE CLAUDIAN INVASION
AD 43–60

In the early years of the 1st century, much of southern England was united under the warlord Cunobelinus. Around AD 41 his son Caratacus captured the Hampshire lands of King Verica who appealed to his Roman allies for help. The new Emperor Claudius needed a military victory to secure his unexpected elevation to the imperial purple. Verica's plea gave him the excuse to order an invasion of Britain.

IMPERIAL TRIUMPH

The Roman commander Aulus Plautius had a force of four legions and auxiliaries at his disposal, possibly 40,000 men in all, when he landed in the summer of AD 43. Two quick victories against the Catuvellauni gave Plautius control of most of England south east of the Thames. At this point he stopped and awaited his Emperor, who eventually arrived in Britain after a long sea voyage from the Mediterranean. Claudius was present in August when his legions and war elephants marched into Camulodunum, modern Colchester, the capital of the Catuvellauni. Claudius accepted the submission of the local chieftains, but after a mere sixteen days in his new province, left for Gaul and his triumphal procession in Rome.

A SHOWCASE INVASION?

Since the first explorations by Julius Caesar, much of southern Britain had been exposed to the Roman world. The advantages of trade with Rome had not been lost upon the British elite, who were happy to make alliances with the Empire and send royal hostages to Europe for a Roman education. Archaeological evidence suggests that Roman troops were present at the courts of local British rulers long before AD 43, perhaps as police or as military advisers. Even the presence of the shy and scholarly Claudius on this military adventure suggests that the events of AD 43 were very carefully stage managed. The Claudian expedition was not a sudden, brutal invasion, but part of a longer process that gradually drew Britain into the Roman world.

RESISTANCE TO ROME

Not all British tribes were happy to accept Roman power. In the south-west, the Second Augusta Legion under the future Emperor Vespasian pushed north from modern Chichester into the heartlands of the hostile Durotriges and Dumnonii tribes. The Augusta found itself in a landscape dotted with seemingly impregnable hillforts. Some of these defences fell to a simple display of Roman military devices. The defenders of Hod Hill fort in Dorset are thought to have surrendered after the opening barrage of ballista bolts

TI·CLAVDIVS·CÆS·AVG·ROM·IMP·S·

Above: The Emperor Claudius visited his troops during the campaign in southern Britain in AD 43 which laid the foundations for Roman control of England.

TIMELINE

AD 43–7	*Most of southern Britain pacified by Aulus Plautius*
44–8	*Vespasian subdues the hillfort tribes of the south-west*
49–51	*Caratacus defeated in a series of battles by Ostorius Scapula*
57	*The Silures of South Wales subdued*
68–70	*Campaigns against the Druidic tribes of Snowdonia and Ynys Mon.*

(projectiles hurled from a machine) hit their chieftain's homestead. Other strongholds were taken more forcefully. A pit at Spettisbury Ring contains more than a hundred slaughtered Britons and their shattered weapons. The spine of a Briton pierced by an iron bolt at Maiden Castle marks the point in history where the Roman war machine ended the heroic age of one-on-one warrior fighting.

More effective resistance came from Caratacus, who escaped the fall of Camulodunum to fight on further west. He battled alongside the Silures and Ordovices of modern Wales, probably from the natural fortress of limestone crags at Llanymynech. After defeat in AD 51, however, he fled to the northern Brigantes of modern Yorkshire, seeking their protection. Seeing the way that the wind was blowing, they handed him over to Rome where he featured in the processions of the Claudian triumph. With Caratacus humiliated, much of southern Britain from the Humber to the Severn was systematically garrisoned and pacified throughout the 50s.

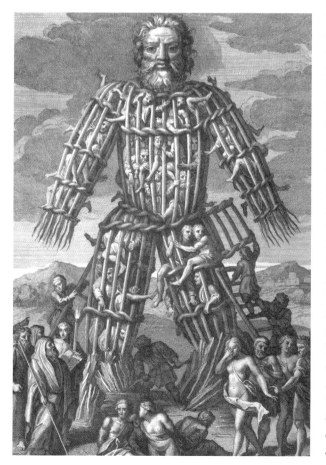

Below: The Romans were horrified by the Druid practice of building huge wicker figures which they filled with sacrificial victims before setting them alight.

THE DRUIDS

The mountains of North Wales and the island of Ynys Mon or Anglesey were the last bastions of southern British resistance. Ynys Mon, known as Mona in Latin, was a centre of the Druidic cult which horrified the Roman mind. In Gaul, Caesar had recorded the Druidic wicker giants packed with men and set alight. The Roman historian Tacitus accused the Welsh Druids of 'staining their altars with the blood of prisoners and consulting their gods by using human entrails'. Three seasons of campaigning from AD 68 to 70 were needed before the Governor of Britain, Suetonius Paulinus, could claim to have pacified Snowdonia and Ynys Mon. After a daring amphibious crossing of the Menai Straits, the legions slaughtered the Druids and destroyed their sacred groves. Paulinus' victory was only marred by news of a sudden revolt in the lands of the Iceni (modern East Anglia).

BOUDICCA'S REVOLT
AD 60–61

The revolt of the Iceni under their warrior queen Boudicca was the last serious threat to the permanent Roman annexation of southern Britain. While the Roman army campaigned in distant north Wales, the Iceni took their chance to strike at the growing settlements which symbolized the gradual Romanization of their homeland.

THE SPARK OF REBELLION

The Iceni occupied the lands of modern East Anglia. Allies of Rome, their kings were exceptionally wealthy. In AD 60, the Iceni king Prasutagus died without male issue. Prasutagus had named the Emperor Nero as his co-heir, hoping to preserve part of his kingdom for his widow Boudicca. Unfortunately this scheme ran counter to Roman policy, which was to suppress the client kingdoms of the British.

The men that Rome sent to East Anglia to supervise the takeover of Iceni land were slaves and lower ranking soldiers on the make. With the governor Suetonius Paulinus on campaign in Wales, these subordinates acted brutally towards the Iceni leadership. Boudicca was flogged and her daughters were violated. These outrages fed on deeper grievances towards Rome. British chiefs were struggling financially to pay their taxes and meet the costs of Romanization. Building the required villas and temples, educating sons in Latin and offering gifts at the imperial altar at Camulodunum; the Roman way of life was ruinously expensive. When the Iceni revolted, other tribes such as the powerful Trinovantes soon joined them on the warpath.

Below: The warrior queen Boudicca and her army were merciless in their sacking of the town of Camulodunum, a settlement for ex-Roman legionaries and their families.

MASSACRE IN EAST ANGLIA

Raising a massive warband, Boudica fell upon Camulodunum, a colony for ex-legionaries since AD 49. The Iceni and Trinovantes hated its inhabitants who had acted in a high-handed way towards local native farmers. With few ramparts, a population of ageing veterans and a guard of only 200 troops, the town was soon burned to the ground. The troops that held out for two days in the Claudian temple were butchered without mercy. A relief force sent by the Ninth Legion was ambushed en route with the loss of 2,000 infantry. News of the Iceni victory swept across Britain and the province burst aflame.

THE BRITISH AMAZON

Boudicca was tall, of terrifying appearance, with a fierce look in her eyes and a harsh tone in her voice. So said the Roman historian Dio Cassius, although he was naturally biased against a 'rebel' who had killed 80,000 Romans and their allies. More flatteringly, Dio Cassius described Boudicca's 'great mass of tawny hair falling to her hips, a golden necklace around her neck, wearing a tunic of many colours beneath a thick mantle fastened with a brooch'. At the start of her campaign against Rome, Boudicca performed an act of divination to seek the gods' approval by releasing a hare from the folds of her dress. The path taken by the hare was seen as a sign of divine support, encouraging her warriors to follow her into battle.

Right: Myths surrounding Boudicca variously describe her as a hardened warrior and as a beautiful young woman who inspired love and devotion in the hearts of her followers.

THE SACK OF LONDINIUM

Hearing of the disaster, Suetonius Paulinus in Wales set out at speed for Londinium, hoping that the Roman forces in Britain could be gathered there. Communication in the crisis proved difficult however; the bruised Ninth Legion was disorganized, while the confused commander of the Second Legion in Exeter disobeyed orders and remained behind his ramparts. Paulinus knew that he had too few troops to defend Londinium and that he would have to sacrifice the town to gain time. The writer Tacitus describes the vain pleading of those who were too old or infirm to leave the city with Paulinus before the Iceni arrived. Londinium was brutally sacked and razed. The same fate soon befell Veralumium (St Albans). In all, over 70,000 inhabitants died at the hands of the Iceni, who had no desire to take prisoners and win ransom. Roman writers were shocked by the atrocities carried out by the Iceni, who butchered and skewered their victims on stakes.

THE DEATH OF BOUDICCA

Gathering the available forces, Paulinus met the Iceni in battle somewhere near Towcester. Although greatly outnumbered, Roman discipline and tactical experience brought a decisive victory. Falling back in disarray upon their own wagons, the Iceni were trapped and systematically slaughtered. According to the Roman historian Tacitus, Boudicca took poison to avoid slavery in Rome. East Anglia was pacified by a short campaign of reprisals and the construction of new forts at key locations such as Chelmsford. However, the counsel of moderate administrators soon prevailed. British loyalty would not be won back by repression, but by encouraging the tribes to participate more in the Roman way of life.

THE CONQUEST OF BRITANNIA
AD 61–79

After the defeat of the East Anglian Iceni, southern Britain was brought wholly under direct Roman control. The Roman garrison in the province was reinforced by transferring units from the Rhine. As a symbol of Roman prestige and determination, the colony at Camulodunum was quickly restored. The key trading port of London rose from the ashes to become the centre of Roman administration. Successive Roman governors could now concentrate upon extending Roman power throughout the island.

TROUBLE IN THE NORTH

Cartimandua, queen of the northern Brigantes, had been a loyal ally of Rome since the Claudian invasion in AD 43. Her kingdom stretched across Britain from the Irish to the North Sea and her lasting friendship meant that Roman governors of the province could afford to relax their watch on their northern flank. With the Iceni completely subdued, Britain was even peaceful enough for Nero to transfer troops to Egypt in AD 66. This situation changed dramatically in AD 68–69, the Year of Four Emperors. Civil war raged throughout the Empire between army factions, draining men from the garrisons in Britain. Anti-Roman elements at the Brigantian court were encouraged by the Roman disunity to depose Cartimandua. Her place was taken by her belligerent ex-husband Venutius who had long planned war against his southern neighbours. After some inconclusive fighting, Cartimandua was rescued by her allies, but it was now clear to Rome that direct rule would have to be imposed on the entire island of Britain.

Above: The Emperor Vespasian set his sights on subjugating the rebellious tribes of the west and north of Britain, thus bringing the entire British isles under Roman control.

TIMELINE

Early 60s AD	*Roman control extended to the Dumnonii lands west of Exeter*
68–9	*Roman garrisons transferred to Europe during the civil war*
69	*Venutius deposes his former wife Cartimandua*
70	*Vespasian decides upon the complete conquest of Britannia*
70–1	*Rome makes little headway against the Brigantes*
71–3	*Brigantes defeated in a series of battles and sieges*
73	*Venutius killed in battle and Stanwick hillfort captured*
74–7	*Silures and Ordovices subdued by Governor Julius Frontinus*
75	*Network of forts throughout Wales based on Caerleon and Deva*
78	*Julius Agricola completes the conquest of Britannia.*

Below: The governor Gnaeus Julius Agricola was victorious at the battle of Ynys Mon, crushing Welsh opposition to Roman rule.

VESPASIAN'S AMBITION

The new Emperor Vespasian who emerged victorious from the Roman civil war had served as a soldier in Britain. He was convinced that the wilder, independent tribes of the west and the north had to be tamed and made to accept Roman power. The army in Britain was restored to full strength and the fort at Lincoln repaired. A new base for operations against the Brigantes was built at Eboracum or York, which become the key Roman fortress in Britain. The Brigantes were a formidable tribe, a tough nomadic people who steered their flocks across the thin pastures of the Pennines. They were led by a fierce warrior elite. Nevertheless, they were duly subdued by AD 73, probably making their last stand as a free people at the vast hillfort of Stanwick near Scotch Corner. Marching camps to the north along the Stainmore Pass are evidence of a further Roman push towards Carlisle.

THE SUBJUGATION OF WALES

A new generation of restless young warriors had grown up in Wales since the Roman action there in the late 50s. Crushing the Silures and Ordovices tribes for good was now a Roman priority. The Second Augusta Legion was stationed in a huge fortress at Caerleon near the mouth of the Usk. By AD 75, new forts at Carmarthen, Neath and Cardiff protected Roman harbours and gave access through the valleys to the heart of the tribal homelands. Once the Silurian warband had been crushed in battle, a matrix of forts within a day's march of each other sliced the tribal territories into manageable portions. The Ordovices in the north were defeated and a new castra at Deva or Chester was built to ensure their good behaviour in the future. The task of completing the subjugation of the Welsh tribes fell to a new governor, Julius Agricola. He captured Ynys Mon in AD 78 in a surprise attack, by forcing his cavalry troops to swim across the straits with their horses rather than wait for boats.

BRITANNIA AT PEACE

The following year Agricola clamped down on the Brigantes, building a network of forts to control their passes through the Pennines. By AD 78, almost all the land that is now Wales and England was securely under Roman control. In the south and east, the process of Romanization was well under way. In the north and west, opposition to Rome had been crushed and was pinned down by an extensive system of forts.

CALEDONIA – THE LIMITS OF EMPIRE
AD 79–160

*The governor Agricola campaigned in Scotland between AD 79 and 84.
In southern Scotland, the tribes were persuaded to accept the* **pax romana**
*through the usual process of fort and road building. However, the
northern tribes remained hostile, despite their defeat at Mons Graupius.
The narrow Forth-Clyde isthmus marked the natural frontier between the
governable province of Britannia and untameable Caledonia beyond.*

TERRA INCOGNITA

The first circumnavigation of Britain was probably made around 200 BC
by the Greek Pytheas of Marseilles, but by AD 85 several Roman ships
had scouted the route. The Roman author and philosopher Pliny knew of
the Orkneys, Shetlands and Hebrides, as well as the Caledonian forest.
In AD 79, the historian Tacitus accompanied the Agricolan legions on their
march into the unknown lands of northern Scotland. He described the tribes
there as 'dwelling at the utmost end of the earth...there is no-one beyond,
only waves and rocks'.

Above: The historian Gaius Cornelius Tacitus
(c.56–c.117 AD) documented the Roman
campaigns in the north of Britain.

THE TRIBES OF THE SOUTH

The rolling hills of southern Scotland were no serious barrier to Agricola's
force of 15,000 men. Roman progress was two-pronged, laying down the
routes in the east and west followed by the modern A68 and M74. The
eastern Votadini tribe quickly made peace with the invaders. Their hillfort
capital of Traprain Law in East
Lothian has yielded many pieces of
evidence that show their ready
acceptance of Roman goods and
culture. The Selgovae, based at the
Eildon Hills near Melrose, were
more reluctant to accept Roman
order, but they were soon cordoned
by a network of Roman forts, roads
and allies. In the south-west, the
broch (tower) and *crannog* (island)
dwelling Novantae were only
subdued in AD 82.

INTO THE HIGHLANDS

Beyond the narrow isthmus in
central Scotland, the geography,
vegetation, climate and people to the

TIMELINE	
AD 79	*Agricola invades southern Scotland*
80	*Roman forts built at Forth-Clyde isthmus*
82	*Tribes of southwest Scotland subdued*
83	*Roman troops operating north of the Tay*
84	*Probable date of battle at Mons Graupius*
c. 140	*Antoninus' Wall built from Forth to Clyde*
150	*Greek cartographer Ptolemy includes Scotland in his* Geographia
c. 169	*Probable date for final abandonment of Antoninus' Wall*
c. 200	*Coalescence of northern tribes into larger 'nations'*
208	*Last Roman attempt to conquer Scotland under Septimius Severus*
297	*First mention of the Picts in extant records.*

Above: The battle of Mons Graupius ended in the slaughter of thousands of the defending Caledonian warriors and victory for the Romans.

north were unremittingly hostile. Tacitus believed that the red-haired and long-limbed Caledonians were a different race, more akin to the fierce Germans than the Britons. Rather than explore the uncharted central Highland massif, Agricola chose to edge along the north-eastern lowlands, keeping in touch with his fleet. The line of Agricola's advance can still be seen in the chain of marching forts that stretch north of the Tay and into Moray. One by one, the mouths of the Highland glens were stopped with forts and a major legionary fortress was begun at Inchtuthill in Strathmore. In all, Agricola built sixty new forts and over 2,000 km (1,300 miles) of road in his six years of campaigning in Scotland.

MYSTERIOUS MONS GRAUPIUS

In AD 84, all this Roman activity prompted 30,000 Caledonian warriors to mass for battle under the leadership of a chieftain called Calgacus. This name comes to us from Tacitus, who probably witnessed the clash at Mons Graupius. While the Caledonians held to the hill, the smaller Roman force made little headway. However, once the tribesmen were lured down on to flatter ground by early successes, Roman discipline won the day. Tacitus claimed that 10,000 warriors were slain at a cost of only 360 Roman lives. Despite this, Agricola's victory meant nothing, for the tribes did not submit but simply melted away into the hills to wage guerilla war another day.

The precise location of the battlefield of Mons Graupius is lost and many places in eastern Scotland have been suggested. Of these, the Glens of Foudland near the landmark hill of Bennachie in Aberdeenshire seem the most probable suggestion, for at that point the legions were far from the sea and cut off from support from their fleet.

ANTONINUS' WALL

Recalled to Rome, Agricola's work was soon undone as legions were sent to other trouble spots in the Empire. His forts were abandoned and in the 120s the Emperor Hadrian drew the frontier along the Solway-Tyne line further south. The last serious Roman incursion into Scotland was made in the 140s, when Antoninus Pius built a wall of turf blocks and spikes from the Forth to the Clyde. He hoped to protect allies like the Votadini and make it easier to police the restless Selgovae. The wall and its forts were held by a force of 7,000 men until AD 169, when plague and disorder throughout the Empire brought about a permanent retreat to Hadrian's Wall.

THE LOST LAND OF HIBERNIA

Agricola's campaign in AD 82 against the Novantae of Galloway was supported by a fleet that took him within sight of Ireland. Merchants who traded there provided him with information about the Irish coast and Agricola carried a fugitive Irish prince in his entourage, in case a convenient excuse for a Hibernian invasion was needed. However a new Emperor, Domitian, ordered him to complete the conquest of Caledonia instead and the invasion of Ireland was indefinitely postponed.

HADRIAN'S WALL
AD 122

When the Spanish soldier Hadrian donned the imperial purple in AD 117, he inherited a vast Empire that sprawled from southern Scotland to Mesopotamia. An experienced military strategist, he believed that much of the Empire was indefensible and wanted borders that could be held. Hadrian visited Britain in AD 122, when 'he set many things right and drew a wall along a length of 130 km [80 miles] to separate barbarians and Romans.' Hadrian's Wall was to become the largest symbol of Roman power in Britain.

WHY WAS THE WALL BUILT?

The Wall was never meant to be a platform for fighting back the northern hordes. Instead the complex of forts, roads and the deep *vallum* or ditch on its southern side created a defined military zone where all traffic could be controlled. Although vulnerable to a concentrated attack, the Wall and its garrison were strong enough to prevent persistent low-level raiding. Links between the Brigantes of northern England and the Selgovae of southern Scotland, two groups who were reluctant to accept the benefits of *Romanitas,* were more easily monitored and deterred. Trade across the Wall could be channelled and tolls gathered. The existence of this impressive barrier, the most developed set of fortifications in the Roman world, probably had a psychological impact upon the inhabitants of southern Britain, encouraging the elites there to feel that their accommodation with Rome was secure. An astute commander who knew the army well, Hadrian also realized the value of keeping the army busy at a time of relative peace. Building and maintaining the Wall helped the morale and discipline of the units involved and took their mind off politics.

Below: The original Hadrian's Wall ran for 117 km (73 miles) across the hills of northern England. Built to monitor trade between rebellious tribes, it came to mark the northern boundary of Roman Britain.

MURDER MYSTERY ON THE WALL

The presence of a large military force was a boon to the economy of northern England. Civilian settlements quickly grew up around the fortifications. Here local merchants provided the army with fresh supplies to supplement the preserved foods sent from Europe. Brothel masters and

WALL NUMBERS

The original Wall ran from Segedunum or Wallsend on the Tyne to Bowness-on-Solway, a distance of 117 km (73 miles). There were 80 fortlets or milecastles built at intervals of 1,481 m (1,620 yards), a Roman mile. These held from ten to thirty men. Observation turrets stood at intervals of 494 m (540 yards). Sixteen larger forts were built along the Wall for larger garrisons of 500 men. Depending on materials and geography, the height of the Wall ranged from 4.5–6 m (15–20 ft) and varied in width from 2.5–3.5 m (8–12 ft). There were three forts north of the Wall which acted as listening posts in the tribal lands beyond the Empire. Three legions, the 2nd, 6th and 20th, completed the initial construction. Begun in AD 122, the bulk of the Wall was completed in under five years or so, but a further 32 km (20 miles) of defences along the Cumbrian coast and additions to the fort system kept the legions busy for more than a decade. Once finished, Hadrian's Wall was garrisoned by a force of around 10,000 men, mostly auxiliary troops.

tavern keepers met the other needs of the troops. At the settlement or *vicus* near Housesteads, archaeologists discovered the skeletal remains of a man and a woman in the foundations of a simple room. They seem to have been murdered with a knife and hidden away beneath the floorboards. Perhaps they were the unlucky victims of a drunken brawl in the gambling and drinking dens that sprang up on the wild frontier of Britannia.

WHAT HAPPENED TO THE WALL?

Clues from written records, and the archaeological evidence of destruction followed by hurried rebuilding, suggests that the Wall enjoyed long periods of relative peace punctuated by moments of tension. There were troubles after AD 180, especially around 195 and 205. These prompted the campaign by Severus in 209 which aimed, and failed, to teach the Caledonians a final lesson. Tension in the Wall area inevitably coincided with troubles elsewhere in the Empire. War with distant Parthia or struggles for the imperial succession diluted the army in Britain as units were posted elsewhere. These weaknesses were noted, especially by the northern Picts who launched a massive attack in AD 367 in conjunction with their Irish and Germanic allies. After AD 402, payments to the few loyal troops left on the Wall came to an end. The soldiers in the military zone probably stayed on. They had become residents more than occupiers, living on in small communities and farms in the shadow of the Wall. However, over time these faded into the landscape as the original purpose of Hadrian's great work was forgotten.

Below: The Emperor Hadrian supervised the construction of the impressive fortifications along the Wall. Observation turrets were spaced at regular intervals, with a further sixteen large forts to house legionaries.

THE ROMANIZATION OF BRITAIN
AD 43–409

The culture of Roman Britannia was deeply influenced by the geography of the British Isles. Physically separated from the rest of the Empire, Roman civilization in this distant outpost was a hybrid of native and classical traditions. Britons in the southern lowlands accommodated most readily to the lifestyle of their conquerors. In upland Britain, the new ways made less progress and the legions were the only permanent bearers of Roman culture.

Above: The Roman villa of Bignor in Sussex, dating from the 2nd century AD, contains well-preserved mosaic floors depicting dancers, gladiators and religious themes.

JOBS FOR THE BRITISH

Throughout the Empire, the Roman trick was to govern lightly and encourage the locals to carry out the burdens of maintaining public works, enforcing the law and collecting taxes. Imperial Roman officials were concentrated in the army garrison towns and the ports. Elsewhere, the daily administration of the province was largely in the hands of the local British aristocracy. They served as members of the *civitates* or self-governing tribal councils and stood for election as municipal magistrates. They shared in Roman power by sitting in the local *basilica* to carry out central directives and settle local disputes. Tacitus noted how quickly they adopted Roman ways, donning the toga when on official business and ensuring that their sons mastered Latin, the new language of social mobility. More humble Britons could also aspire to become Roman by serving in the imperial army. Around 15,000 men served in the auxiliary regiments, lured by the promise of Roman citizenship at the end of their 25-year stint in the ranks.

SPREADING WEALTH

The old British kingdoms had minted coins, but it was only in the Roman age that the use of money entered daily life. The growth of trade saw a new class of clerks, merchants, money-lenders and tax collectors come into being. Market halls and streets lined with shops were common sights in

Romano-British towns. The Roman genius for manufacturing and distribution saw a profusion of goods from all ends of the Empire on display in British markets. Wealthy British consumers acquired a taste for Roman luxuries, such as the much-prized Falernian wines from Campania. In return, British textiles found a ready market in Gaul and the Rhineland. Ingots of silver, lead and tin from the state-controlled British mines were traded throughout the Mediterranean. As ever, widening trade helped to spread new ideas. By the early 2nd century, wall-paintings, mosaics and domestic items in British homes were decorated with images from Ovid's mythological tales or from Virgil's epic of the Trojan hero Aeneas.

ROMAN OR BRITISH AFTER DEATH?

Poorer Romans often joined burial clubs to make sure that they would be given a proper funeral. Regular subscriptions paid for the necessary but expensive sacrifices and the fees of the professional mourners who were part of the Roman way of death. Funeral clubs also existed in Roman Britain. The guild of armourers at Bath raised monuments to mark the passing of their members. One club at Halton Chester on Hadrian's Wall even helped slaves to leave the world with dignity. Romano-Britons generally followed the 3rd-century preference throughout the Empire for cremation rather than burial. However, Celtic ways persisted. In one 2nd-century burial in the Roman cemetery at Brough on Humber, the corpse was sent to the next world in an iron-bound wooden bucket holding two broken sceptres, in the same way as his tribal ancestors.

THE OLD WAYS

The Roman lifestyle made little headway in the British uplands. There were fewer towns and few villas in the higher reaches of the West Country, in northern Wales, the Pennines or in Caledonia. Here, the settlements remained tribal and more Celtic in nature. The material culture of Rome was present in these wilder places as many treasure hoards prove, but Latin was seldom heard here. The only permanent reminder of Roman civilization were the distant towers and forts of the legions.

ROMAN-BRITISH GODS

Religious practices reveal the cultural compromise between British and Roman traditions. The Romans expected outward signs of compliance and received them. Temples to the Capitoline gods, Jove, Juno and Minerva, graced the public spaces of larger towns such as Wroxeter and St Albans. Colchester was the centre of Emperor worship, offering annual games and festivals to the *numen* or spiritual power of the divine ruler. However, the most popular gods in Britannia were an amalgam of British and Roman deities. The Celtic and Roman goddesses of healing merged into Sulis-Minerva who was worshipped at Bath. Mars-Teutates was worshipped by British troops in the Roman army. In later centuries, Roman trade routes brought a complex pantheon to British shores including the Phoenician Astarte, the Egyptian Serapis and the Persian Mithras-Sol as well as the Palestinian cult of Christ.

Left: The mysterious Roman Mithraic cult centred around the originally Persian god Mithras, here shown slaying a bull.

NEW TOWNS OF THE ROMAN AGE
AD 50–300

The old tribal British settlements or **oppida** *were straggling, often temporary, enclosures of wicker and timber that held fluctuating numbers of people and cattle. Gradually they were replaced by planned, geometrically regular towns that were a visible stamp of Roman organization and power. Nothing like these new towns had been seen in the British landscape before. The new Roman towns were not just places to live, work and trade, but symbols of the imperial ideals of unity and stability. They defined Britain's new role as a province within a vast, all-encompassing Empire.*

PUBLIC GRANDEUR

As in towns and cities throughout the Empire, at the centre of Romano-British towns lay the forum. This served as a meeting space for the inhabitants and as a setting for public ceremonies. Here were erected the statues and the Latin inscriptions to the Emperor and more local dignitaries that publicly demonstrated the settlement's loyalty to the idea of Rome. The town basilica, where council meetings and law courts were held and the civic archives and treasury were located, usually took up one side of the forum. These long rectangular halls dominated the urban scene, no more so than in London, which boasted an enormous basilica almost 152 m (500 ft) long and over 24 m (80 ft) high. At the centre of the larger towns stood a *macellum* or dedicated market hall: the Roman mall at St Albans consisted of two facing rows of nine shop units. By AD 150, the civic centre of many Romano-British towns would have been instantly recognizable to the Roman traveller.

PLAYING GAMES

The Roman taste for bloody gladiatorial combat was catered for in most larger British towns. Amphitheatres existed at civilian

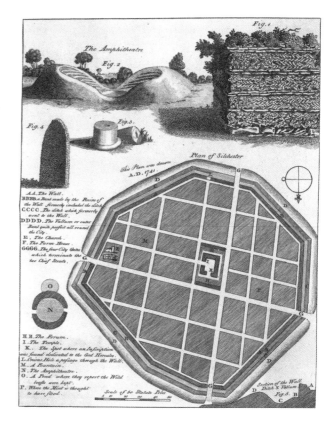

Above: A plan of the Roman town of Silchester shows the forum at the centre and the amphitheatre outside the circuit of the town wall.

TIMELINE	
c. AD 45	*Colchester develops from Celtic to Roman settlement*
c. 50	*Verulamium (St Albans) granted the rank of* municipium
71	*Roman York or Eboracum founded*
79	*Fortress and town of Deva Victris (Chester) founded*
c. 120	*Londinium reaches peak population of 60,000 inhabitants*
155	*Verulamium destroyed by fire but quickly rebuilt*
c. 380	*Final brief period of growth in Roman towns*
c. 450	*Evidence of extensive 'Germanization' of Roman settlements.*

TOWN TYPES

There were four main classes of town in Roman Britain:

- *colonia* – settled by retired veterans who provided a military reserve and acted as a model of Romanization to the surrounding British population e.g. Lincoln
- *civitas capital* – important self-governing towns which acted as capitals for the surrounding region e.g. Dorchester
- *municipium* – a town elevated to the rank of honorary *colonia* whose inhabitants enjoyed the legal status of Roman citizenship e.g. St Albans
- *vicus* – a temporary settlement that grew up close to a Roman army fort to cater for the needs of the troops, often developing into a permanent town e.g. Alauna (now Maryport).

settlements such as Silchester and Dorchester as well as at military locations such as Caerleon and York. However, unlike the impressive stadia of the Mediterranean world, Romano-British amphitheatres were usually raised earthen banks, revetted with timber and stone, around a sunken area. Mosaics of exotic beasts such as tigers at Woodchester Villa suggest that the usual slaughter took place in these British arenas. The Silchester amphitheatre could accommodate about 2,500 spectators, probably around half of the town's population.

The spread of Latin amongst the British elite meant that they could follow and enjoy classical drama. By AD 60, Colchester already had a theatre for literary and dramatic spectacles. Theatres were often built close to significant temples, as at St Albans, for they also provided a suitably impressive setting for religious and public ceremonies. A hated symbol of Roman cultural influence, Colchester's theatre was burned down by Boudicca's warband in the Iceni revolt. No evidence has yet been found of a permanent circus for chariot-racing in Britain, but several mosaics tell us that the Romano-British certainly knew about this most exciting of Roman sports.

KEEPING CLEAN AND HEALTHY

The Roman obsession with cleanliness had a significant impact on the urban landscape of Roman Britain. Bathing was an essential social and fitness activity for the members of the Roman establishment and so large bathing structures were quickly built at military and administrative centres such as Exeter and York. Gradually, substantial bathing complexes also arose in civilian towns. The impressive bath-house remains of the Old Work at Wroxeter and the Jewry Wall at Leicester indicate the massive investment that went into providing these vital civic facilities. The monumental spa at Bath or Aqua Sulis even became a centre of pilgrimage because of the reputed healing powers of its water.

Since baths needed high, vaulted roofs of brick and plaster rather than timber which succumbed to the effects of moisture and heat, they may have been the largest buildings in a number of British towns. The British climate was unsuitable, however, for the open-air exercise yards or *palaestrae* found at baths in the Mediterranean world. In Britain, these developed instead into long covered exercise halls. Fresh water for the baths was usually supplied by a network of open stone channels and conduits cut into the landscape. At York, an underground grid of masonry sewers disposed of the dirty water.

Left: The bath-house was a focal point for social and physical activity in Roman Britain. Many bath-houses, such as those at Leicester and Bath, have survived to the present day.

THREATS TO THE ROMAN PEACE
AD 180–300

For over 350 years, much of Britain prospered from the pax romana.
Under energetic emperors such as Trajan, Hadrian and Marcus Aurelius,
Britain shared in the security of the Empire. After AD 180 however, a
number of events and crises periodically reminded the Romano-British
that their way of life and their very safety were increasingly under threat.

THE THREAT FROM THE NORTH

In the late 2nd century, the tribes of Caledonia began to coalesce into
stronger, more powerful units. In AD 180, the Roman strategy of bribing
their northern neighbours with subsidies failed disastrously. Taking
advantage of the weakness that followed the death of Marcus Aurelius,
the Caledonians, as described by Cassius Dio, 'crossed the wall which
divided them from the Roman legions and cut down a Roman general and
his troops'. The legionary camp at Trimontium near Melrose, the key to
holding southern Scotland, was abandoned soon after. In 207 the 'barbarians
again rebelled, over-running and destroying the land, and taking much
booty'. Emperor Septimius Severus and his sons Caracalla and Geta
took charge of the response themselves, gathering an impressive
force of 20,000 troops at York the following year. Despite penetrating
into the unknown lands to the far north of the Tay in 209–10,
Severus ultimately failed to bring the tribes to a final battle. Southern
Scotland was lost to Rome. For the rest of the Roman period, the
frontier lay along Hadrian's line from the Tyne to Solway with only a
few outposts in southern Scotland to act as listening posts.

Above: After the strong government of
Marcus Aurelius, Britain shared in the
turmoil and misery that descended upon the
Empire in the middle of the 3rd century.

THE THREAT FROM THE LEGIONS

A minimum of three legions were needed to protect the Romanized
parts of Britain, and a force of that size was a powerful tool in the
hands of an ambitious governor. Clodius Albinus used his command of the
legions in Britain in an unsuccessful bid to win the imperial purple in AD
194–96. To dilute this temptation, Severus split Britain into two separate
provinces in 210, thereby reducing the ability of the army to raise up
potential Emperors. This strategy brought several decades of stability until
Britain was drawn into the great crisis of the mid 3rd century.

In the 250s, the Roman Empire split apart under the simultaneous
pressures of civil war, Gothic invasion, hyperinflation and war with Persia.
With Gaul and Hispania, Britain became part of the independent Gallic
Empire set up by Postumus, commander of the Rhine legions, in 260. With
its own capital and senate at Trier in modern Germany, the Gallic Empire
experienced the short reigns of five Emperors before Aurelian successfully

Above: The Emperor Septimius Severus undertook to defeat the troublesome tribes beyond Hadrian's Wall. He failed in his quest and in 211 he fell ill and died at York.

reunited these breakaway provinces with the rest of the Roman world in 274.

THE THREAT FROM THE SEA

From around 280 onwards, Germanic sea raiders such as the Angles, Saxons and Jutes began to harass sea traffic in the Channel and to raid the east coast of Britannia. The Irish were also a growing menace, prompting the building of forts at Holyhead and Hen Waliau near Caernarvon. To meet the Saxon threat, Aurelian planned a chain of ten large forts along the south-eastern coast from Portchester in Hampshire to Brancaster in Norfolk. The separatist 'Emperor' Carausius completed the plan in the 290s, installing garrisons of heavy cavalry that could act as a mobile rapid reaction force. With walls up to 9 m (30 ft) high and 4.5 m (15 ft) thick, the massive fortifications of the 'Saxon Shore' defended the key river estuaries. Nevertheless, throughout the late 3rd century, many towns constructed walls as a sense of unease and insecurity swept across Roman Britain.

CARAUSIUS, EMPEROR OF BRITAIN

An able soldier of humble birth, Carausius rose to the post of commander of the *Classis Britannica* or Fleet of Britain based in Boulogne. Ordered to suppress the Franks and Saxons along the northern coast of Gaul, he was accused of keeping treasure rescued from the barbarians, and even of delaying action until they were returning from Britannia laden with booty. Sentenced to death by Maximian in 286, he sailed to Britain and took the title of Emperor. He maintained control of the British provinces and northern Gaul, defeating forces sent against him in 288 and building alliances with the Franks of the Rhine delta. His short-lived British Empire disintegrated when he was assassinated in 293. His murderer and successor Allectus fell in battle near Silchester in 296. The victor Constantius divided Britain into four, even weaker, provinces and separated the civil and military systems of command on the island. Making York his imperial headquarters, he reformed the army and strengthened the defences against the threat from the Welsh, the Brigantes and the Picts of the north.

TIMELINE

AD 180	*Beginning of serious raids into northern Britannia*
208–10	*Emperor Severus' expedition into northern Britain*
210	*Britannia divided into two imperial provinces*
250–74	*Imperial crisis due to civil war and Gothic invasion*
260–74	*Britannia part of the breakaway Gallic Empire*
c. 280	*Escalation of raids by Germanic Saxons*
286–93	*Brief 'Empire of Britain' under Carausius*
c. 290	*'Saxon shore' fortifications completed on south and eastern coasts*
c. 300	*Most Roman towns fortified by this date*
306	*Britannia divided into four imperial provinces*
c. 360	*Suburbs of many Roman towns such as Exeter abandoned.*

THE CULT OF CHRIST IN ROMAN BRITAIN
C. AD 200–400

Christians first worshipped in numbers in Britain in the late 2nd century. An outlawed and secretive cult, the Christian faith made unspectacular progress in winning converts in the following decades. Christianity long remained a niche cult, with small communities of believers scattered throughout the country in specific social circles. Nevertheless an existing church organization quickly began to emerge into the light once the faith was given official status as a religio legitima *in AD 260.*

Above: The distinctive Chi-Rho monogram, made up of the first two letters of the word Christ in Greek, was engraved on many artefacts of 3rd-century Britain.

CRYPTIC CLUES

As Christianity was for a long time a forbidden and often persecuted faith, it is not surprising that evidence of early believers is limited and often mysterious. The earliest British Christian inscription is probably the late 2nd-century word square cut into a fragment of an amphora found in Manchester. Once re-arranged, the letters of this palindromic grid are thought to spell *paternoster* and repeated pairs of *alpha* and *omega*. Fifteen of the twenty-seven objects discovered in a treasure hoard at Water Newton near Peterborough bear the Chi-Rho monogram formed by the first two letters of Christ's name in Greek. Mosaics of the pagan Orpheus with his flock found in richer homes may also have been secret allusions to the Good Shepherd.

THE VILLA CHRISTIANS

Christianity probably reached Britain through the larger ports, especially London. It was probably a relatively humble brethren that scratched the Chi-Rho symbols found on many everyday items such as pewter plates and goblets from all regions of 3rd-century Britain. However the most spectacular Christian remains from this period reveal that the faith had penetrated to the highest levels of Romano-British society. The grand 4th-century villa at Lullingstone in Kent contained a private Christian chapel, richly decorated with images which included three *orantes* or believers with arms outstretched in prayer. Similarly rich expressions of faith decorate the villas of Frampton and Hinton St Mary in Dorset. These images prove that by the early 4th century, Christianity had penetrated into rural as well as urban areas and was a faith for rich as well as poor.

A CHRISTIAN LAND?

Although many small objects with Christian decoration have been found in Romano-British sites, no buildings have been conclusively identified as Christian churches. A small structure in Silchester and another at the port of

THE FIRST BRITISH SAINTS

The first Christian martyr in Britain was probably Alban of Verulamium, a pagan soldier executed for giving shelter to a fugitive believer at a time of official persecution. The difficulties of tracing the early history of the faith in Britain are shown by the fact that dates as far apart as 209 and 304 have been suggested for Alban's death. The Welsh martyrs Aaron and Julius were probably put to death at Caerleon in the mid 2nd century but little else is known about them. St Ninian, the apostle of the southern Picts, is only a slightly more tangible character. Early writers believed that he was a Briton who had trained in Rome and Gaul before leading a mission north to Pictland and building a white church, the Candida Casa, in Galloway in 397.

Richborough seem to have been used for worship by the early Christians, but this is hard to prove. The number of Christians in Roman Britain is also difficult to calculate. However, the majority of the 5,000 burials in the late Roman cemetery at Poundbury in Dorset were laid out in a Christian manner, facing east to west and without grave goods, suggesting a large community of believers here from around 275 onwards. Not only was the flock growing, but a church administration was also developing to minister to their needs. Bishops from the dioceses of London, York and Colchester travelled to the Church Synod held in Arles in 314. British bishops also participated in the Council of Nicea in Asia Minor, called by Constantine the Great in 325 to deal with the Arian heresy.

PAGAN SURVIVORS

Once Christianity became the favoured religion of the Empire after 313, Church leaders were energetic in suppressing other beliefs. All five Mithraic temples found in Britain, at Caernarvon, Carrawburgh, Housesteads, Rudchester and London, show signs of their desecration by Christians. Nevertheless, the evidence of coin offerings to the gods suggests that more than twenty pagan temples, mostly in the south-west, continued in business well into the later decades of the 4th century. The Jupiter column at Cirencester was restored in 360 during the reign of Julian the Apostate, while a pagan temple with accommodation for its priests was still operating within Maiden Castle in Dorset around 400. The survival of paganism into the early 5th century was probably due to the insular nature of Roman Britain, far from the centre of power and the imperial drive to eradicate all traces of the old gods.

Right: The remains of a 3rd-century temple of the Mithras cult, known as a *Mithraeum*, at Carrawburgh at the most northern point of Hadrian's Wall.

THE BARBARIAN ONSLAUGHT
AD 367

In the years after AD 300, life in Roman Britain was still relatively secure and prosperous. Although the towns had raised strong walls, in most of the province the threat from raiders, or from rival military factions intent on plunder, was still slight. The army garrisons in Britain had been repeatedly weakened as units were transferred to other trouble-spots in the Empire or led away to support a claimant for the imperial purple. Despite this, the Roman forces were usually strong enough to defend Britannia, as long as its enemies never acted together…

THE RISE OF THE PICTS

In the 4th century the unified tribes of Caledonia, now known as Pictii by the Romans, presented a serious threat to Roman Britain. Several emperors tried to deal with the troublesome Picts. Constantius Chlorus campaigned throughout the length of Pictland in 305. His son Constantine also marched northwards in 312 and his son Constans followed suit in 342. Despite the best efforts of the Constantine dynasty, a Roman commentator complained in 360 that 'the Picts disrupted the agreed peace, raiding and destroying many places near the frontier'. Like earlier emperors, Magnus Maximus thought that he had finally defeated the Picts in 382, but little more than a decade later the Roman general Stilicho had to divert resources northwards to meet this resilient and incessant foe.

THE BARBARIAN CONSPIRACY

In 367, Roman Britain found itself under attack from all directions. The Picts stormed southwards in great numbers, while waves of Scotii from Ireland crossed the Irish Sea to harry the western marches. Along the south and eastern coasts, large bands of Saxons and Franks overwhelmed the Roman defences. Saxon attacks in Gaul meant that no help could be sent across the Channel. The Roman forces in Britain were unable to cope with these concerted attacks. Even when understrength, the garrison on Hadrian's Wall had usually managed to cope. In 367 however, the Wall was seriously breached, or perhaps simply by-passed by tribes that had now mastered the skills of coastal sea-faring. Nectaridus, the *comes* or count in charge of the Saxon Shore, was defeated and killed. Fullofaudes, the *Dux Britanniarum*

Above: The tribes of Caledonia, now known collectively as the Picts, began to make more incursions into Roman territory, pushing further and further southwards.

THE ATTACOTTI

One of the most mysterious of the British peoples, the Attacotti contributed to the mayhem of 367. They probably originated from western and northern Ireland or from the Scottish Hebrides. St Jerome met some of the Attacotti in Trier some years later and noted 'their delight in the taste of human flesh'. In addition to cannibalism, Jerome was appalled by their practice of polyandry, 'promiscuously holding their wives in common'. Although a belligerent people and initially much feared by the Romans, even the Attacotti were absorbed over time into the Roman world. Three regiments bearing their name are recorded in the army registers of the late 390s serving in Gaul, Italy and Illyricum.

or senior military commander in the north, was besieged and probably captured near York. Roman Britain was temporarily vanquished. Roman writers believed that the province had been the victim of 'a barbarian conspiracy' but the simultaneous attacks of 367 may simply have been the accidental climax of a decade of ever bolder acts by peoples who could see their enemy visibly weakening over time.

A YEAR OF CHAOS

In the year of pillage and plunder that followed, the social order of Roman Britain collapsed. Bands of slaves (and the virtually enslaved estate workers known as *coloni*) took their long-awaited revenge. Companies of army deserters also exploited the situation, rampaging through the countryside in search of cattle, treasure and slaves. Poorly defended settlements in the countryside probably suffered most. The attack upon Brislington villa near Bristol is typical of many. The villa buildings were torched and looted, probably by Scotii pirates, and the inhabitants were slaughtered and thrown down the well.

Below: In 367 Hadrian's Wall was seriously breached. Attacks by the Saxons and Franks in the south led to a breakdown of order across Roman Britain.

THE THEODOSIAN RESTORATION

In 367 it seemed as if the Roman world in Britannia had ended. However by the end of 370, Count Theodosius had restored order throughout the province, recalled the deserters to the colours and made peace with the 'buffer' tribes of southern Caledonia. A line of coastal towers and beacons were built in the north to watch over the mouths of the Tyne, Tees and Humber. Hadrian's Wall was repaired but downgraded. Instead Theodosius embarked upon a busy programme of fort building in all parts of southern Britain to house the mobile forces that were needed to meet an agile enemy. Towns were garrisoned and their walls were stiffened with towers to house ballistae and other war machines. His effective military reforms allowed the towns of Roman Britain to defend themselves well into the 5th century.

THE FALL OF ROMAN BRITAIN
370–450

The end of Roman Britain was not the result of one event but the culmination of several processes at work over decades. Over time, the army and the imperial administration were scaled down and the links with the wider economy of the Empire were let slip one by one. Eventually, the population of Britain found itself alone and isolated.

THE FATAL WEAKENING

Thanks to the military reforms of the 370s, Roman Britain enjoyed several more decades of stability. In 383, Magnus Maximus took much of the British garrison with him to Gaul to support his bid for imperial power. In addition, he was accompanied by a force made up of British volunteers. Few of these men ever returned to Britain. Removing the 20th Legion from Chester and Caernarvon left much of western Britain fatally exposed to raids from Ireland. By the late 390s, the Irish Scotii had occupied the Lleyn Peninsula. Another Irish people, the Deisi, were busy along much of the south coast of Wales from Pembrokeshire to the Gower. Significantly, these raiders became settlers. There were now too few legionaries left in Britannia to turf them out.

THE DECADE OF DISASTER

In the first decade of the 5th century, waves of barbarian attacks threatened to bring the Roman Empire in western Europe to its knees. Whole nations of Visigoths, Vandals, Alans and Sueves pressed upon its depleted frontier forces. In 401, Rome's general Stilicho, himself a barbarian, was forced to transfer even more men from Britain to thwart the Visigothic King Alaric who had crossed into Italy. The remnants of the Roman army in Britain shipped out of the island in 407 under the command of Constantine III, who had to choose between defending Britain or rescuing the far more important provinces of Gaul and Spain. The year 410 is traditionally held to mark the end of Roman Britain. There was, however, no sudden withdrawal of legions on that date. Roman strength in Britain had been seeping away for years. Rather, 410 marks the year that barbarian invaders knew that they could assault southern Britain with total impunity.

Above: Alaric, king of the Visigoth tribe who swept through Europe in the 4th century. Roman legions were forced to leave Britain to try and maintain control on the Continent.

THE ROMAN LEGACY

Three and a half centuries of Roman civilization left a lasting mark on the British landscape. Grass grew up through the roads the legions had built but they continued to be used and to form a network of routes that has survived to the present day. Some Roman settlements faded away. Wroxeter never recovered from its burning at the hands of Irish raiders, but most Roman towns continued in use as settlements even though they slowly changed in character. On top of this infrastructure, the Romans bequeathed something more. The limits of Roman power in the north and the west reinforced the natural constraints of geography. They had realized that highland and lowland Britain were different places, enshrining this in their separation of Caledonia from Britannia. The Roman failure to conquer all of the island ensured that there would be more than one future centre of power on the British mainland.

Above: The distinctive Roman roads are still visible in many locations across Britain, cutting across the landscape in long straight lines.

ECONOMIC DECLINE

The fall of Roman Britain was as much an economic as a military event. There are some signs that the Romano-British economy recovered after the disaster of 367. As wealthy villa owners moved into the more secure towns, they brought their purchasing power with them, sparking a temporary boom. New houses were built at St Albans and some other larger towns in the late 4th century. Garrisons of paid soldiers, although increasingly barbarian auxiliaries rather than citizen legionaries, also had cash to spend in the urban markets.

This economic boom ended abruptly in 402. After that date, no imperial coinage could be spared for distant Britannia. Money become scarce and the demand for luxury goods dried up. The ships carrying quality produce from Europe arrived less frequently and the quality of British goods such as pottery deteriorated badly. Over time, the need and the skills to make mosaics or window-glass faded away. Romanized homes were expensive to maintain. By the 450s, Germanic settlements of thatched timber huts behind palisades had spring up in and around the crumbling towns of the bygone Roman age. The British elites who sat on the urban councils tried to continue exercising authority well into the 5th century. A Romanized life continued for some decades, but the public baths and temples gradually lost their meaning and fell into disrepair and disuse. Finally, outbreaks of plague and years of famine around 450 did as much as any barbarian warrior to draw a line between Britain's Roman past and its uncertain future.

TIMELINE

367	*Invasion of Britannia by Picts, Scots and Saxons*
369	*Order in Britannia restored by Theodosius*
383	*Weakening of British legions by Magnus Maximus*
c. 400	*Hadrian's Wall finally abandoned*
401	*Main army units transferred to Italian campaign*
402	*Economic links to the rest of the Empire weakened*
407	*Remaining Roman legions in Britain deployed to Gaul*
440s	*Evidence of Germanization of former Roman settlements.*

GERMANIC INVADERS
450–500

Germans were no strangers to early Britain. Units of Germanic troops had long served in the legions, often helping to protect the Roman province from their Saxon kinsfolk. However in the 5th century, Germanic peoples, led by a warrior elite, settled in lowland Britain in larger numbers than before. Over time, these settlers forged new kingdoms and a new English culture.

The Angles, Saxons and Jutes belonged to the great pool of German tribes that had been pressing upon the Roman world for centuries. Their homelands lay along the coasts of Frisia and north-west Germany, stretching northwards into Schleswig-Holstein and Jutland. The small peninsula between Kiel and Flensburg, still known as Angeln, has the best claim to be the ancestral home of the people that would give their name to much of southern Britain. Warriors from this region had been raiding the coasts of Gaul for a long time. However, the penetration of the powerful Franks into northern Gaul after 420 probably blocked off that avenue of potential profit. After 450, these northern tribes increasingly looked across the North Sea for plunder and new land.

Above: The British chieftain Guthigern receiving Saxon mercenaries as allies, a decision that would eventually to lead to his downfall.

THE SAXON ADVENT

The years after the end of Roman administration are confused and difficult to interpret, as their old nickname 'Dark Ages' suggests. Very few

THE RUIN OF BRITAIN

Gildas was a priest rather than a historian and his aim in *The Ruin of Britain* was to use the German invasions in a moral tale rather than to write accurate history. In Gildas' eyes, the error of Gurthigern and his council was to trust in pagan allies rather than in the Christian God. For this, and for their other sins, the wicked British had to be punished. Not surprisingly, Gildas' description of the clash between German and Briton was truly apocalyptic. 'High towers tumbled into the middle of the streets. Stones of high walls, holy altars, fragments of corpses, covered with bright clots of congealed blood – all crushed together as if in a press and left unburied except in the ruins of houses, or in the ravening bellies of wild beasts and birds.' Gildas' tale of British woe was embellished by later writers. Their belief that the native British were suddenly and violently replaced by waves of migrants survived into modern times, and has only been challenged in recent decades by the more complex story revealed by archaeology and science.

TIMELINE

440s	*First Germanic settlements in southern Britain*
449	*Traditional date for the Saxon advent*
457	*Saxon victory over the British at Crayford, Kent*
540	*Gildas writes* The Ruin of Britain.

contemporary written sources survive and the archaeological record for the period is complicated. Earlier historians were largely forced to rely on the monk Gildas whose dramatic history *The Ruin of Britain* was probably written around AD 540, approximately a hundred years after the events it attempted to describe. Gildas told of a British chieftain, known as Gurthigern or Vortigern, who ruled the Britons of south-eastern England. Pictish raids in the 440s forced Gurthigern to resurrect the old Roman policy of hiring *foederati* or mercenary allies from amongst the 'fierce and impious Saxons, a race hateful both to God and men'. The first three *cyul* or keels filled with Germanic warriors probably landed in 449 and were soon followed by many others. Later legends told of the Jutish warlords, Hengist and Horsa, quarrelling with Gurthigern over pay and supplies and inviting their kinsfolk to join them in the conquest of the weak and disorganized British. Defeated by the Jutes near Crayford, the Britons abandoned Kent to the invaders in 457. As Angles and Saxons greedily poured into southern and eastern Britain, the native British were quickly forced by Germanic hordes to leave the towns and the rich lowlands for more meagre lives in the north and west.

CHANGE AND CONTINUITY

Archaeological evidence suggests that far fewer Anglo-Saxons migrated to Britain than was once imagined. Their enclaves were localized and often existed alongside older British settlements, albeit in a state of tension. Even where the Anglo-Saxon warrior elite held the upper hand, cemetery evidence indicates that the local British survived and only very gradually adopted the customs of the incomers. The relative scarcity of Celtic-British place names in eastern and southern England, once seen as evidence of a mass extermination of the British, probably reflects instead the social and linguistic influence of Anglo-Saxon culture in these areas over the centuries between AD 500 and 1066. Recent genetic studies have also confirmed that the indigenous Britons were not slaughtered and displaced on the scale that Gildas imagined.

BRITISH RESISTANCE
450–600

Native Celtic-Britons long remained the largest element in the population of southern Britain, even in areas such as Kent and Sussex that soon acquired new Anglo-Saxon masters. Under a strong leader, the British were capable of beating the Saxons in battle, winning victory and a generation of stability. Distinctly British communities survived in eastern Britain into the 7th century, but British political rule was increasingly restricted to the north and west.

PLAGUE AND FAMINE

During the 5th century, the four million native British endured several epidemics that weakened the population, adding to the impact of a dislocated economy. Dendroclimatology indicates that the British climate entered a cooler, wetter phase after 440, with shorter growing seasons and reduced fertility in upland farmland. The areas of continuing British power in the higher lands of the north and west were therefore affected disproportionately by the increased difficulty in growing grain. These natural developments probably posed as great a threat to the British as any Saxon sword.

MONS BADONICUS

After the shock of the first territorial losses to the Saxons in the 450s, the British quickly reorganized themselves. The name of Ambrosius Aurelianus has survived as a powerful British leader of the late 5th century who successfully campaigned against the Saxons. Possibly based at Amesbury in Wiltshire, Ambrosius is credited with inflicting a serious defeat upon the South Saxons around AD 500 at the battle of Mons Badonicus, a site traditionally linked to Badon Hill near Bath. This British success seems to have brought

Right: Arthur of the British – whether he existed or not – has entered folklore with the reputation of a wise and just warrior king.

ARTHUR OF THE BRITISH?

Ambrosius Aurelianus is one possible source of inspiration for the later tales of a Dark Age British prince who led his people against the 'barbarian' invaders. Other contenders for the role include Arthnou, a 6th-century warlord who may have built the original fortress of Tintagel, and Artuir of the Scotti who has been linked to the old Roman fort of Camelon near Falkirk. Similar scraps of history and half-remembered myths eventually fed into the imagination of Geoffrey of Monmouth, the 12th-century priest who penned the fullest of the early versions of the Arthurian legend in his fanciful *History of the Kings of Britain*. However, writing around six hundred years after the period in question, Geoffrey was probably as much in the dark as modern scholars who have sought this historical 'holy grail'.

Above: The settlement at Tintagel on the Cornish coast is believed by many to have been the seat of the legendary King Arthur.

several generations of relative peace and stability. There were no major incursions into Celtic-British territory until the 570s and the British were still managing to resist Saxon aggression into the next century. The outcome of Mons Badonicus seems to have encouraged the Anglo-Saxon Wessex elite to treat their British counterparts with much greater respect. The records suggest greater co-operation here between native and invader power-brokers throughout the 6th century.

BRITISH STRONGHOLDS

By the mid 6th century, centres of British power had emerged at Tintagel on the north coast of Cornwall and South Cadbury near Yeovil in Somerset. These fortified settlements were not only military forts, but trading posts with links along the Atlantic coast of Europe to the Mediterranean beyond. Rheged in Cumbria was the probable homeland of King Urien, whose victories over the Saxons are celebrated in the Welsh *Book of Taliesin*. York remained in Celtic hands until 580, while the kingdom of Elmet flourished in Yorkshire until it was subsumed within Northumbria in 616. The men of Gododdin, a kingdom stretching from the rich Lothians down into Northumberland, are remembered in the early Welsh poem that tells of their fateful journey to heroic death in battle at Catterick. The kingdom of Alt Cluth, later Strathclyde, maintained its independence against Pict and Northumbrian alike until well into the 8th century. British culture was also transplanted to Europe by the migration of Britons to the old Gaulish province of Armorica or Brittany in north-west France, and possibly to Galicia in north-western Spain.

BRITISH SURVIVAL

Though traditional historians believed that the Britons were wiped out by the Germanic invaders, modern scholars point to the persistence of the native population in areas ruled by Anglo-Saxons. Some old Roman towns such as Silchester and Verulamium maintained a distinctly British character well into the 6th century. In the early 8th century, the laws of Wessex refer to the British community of *wealas* or Welsh, who continued to enjoy a separate legal status. The 7th-century law codes of Ethelbert of Kent tell a similar story. Nevertheless, with the richest parts of southern Britain in Anglo-Saxon hands, the traditions and lore of the native population were gradually assimilated within a new, emerging English identity.

TIMELINE	
c. 480	*Westward expansion of the Saxons*
c. 500	*Traditional date of the Battle of Badon Hill*
c. 510	*Expansion of Saxons into Hampshire*
c. 550	*Centres of British power concentrated in western counties*
c. 600	*Men of Gododdin fall in the Battle of Catreath.*

AN AGE OF SAINTS
450–700

The Christian faith survived in the British Isles after the Roman departure, despite the fact that the new Anglo-Saxon kings of southern Britain were pagan. In the west, where the British influence was strongest, Christian power centres developed. Celtic missionaries vigorously carried the gospel to the pagan courts of England, but the future of the Church lay within the continental Roman Catholic tradition.

CHRISTIAN SURVIVORS

Christian worship continued in Britain despite the collapse of the Roman state. St Germanus, Bishop of Auxerre, twice visited Britain in 429 and the 440s and found a thriving, if in places heretical, congregation that still tended holy places such as the tomb of St Alban. In the wake of the Germanic invasions, many Christians seemed to have fled to the western shores of Britain for the protection of British authorities who shared their faith. However, the pagan rulers in the south-east seem to have tolerated the beliefs of their native subjects and Christian worship survived in the spaces between Anglo-Saxon settlements.

Below: Missionary saints such as Aidan (shown here being received by Oswald of Northumbria) spread the Christian word amongst the kingdoms of Britain.

MISSIONARY SAINTS

The years between 450 and 650 were marked by efforts from the Christian west of the British and Irish Isles to convert the Anglo-Saxon rulers in the east. The example of the Romano-British missionary Patrick in spreading the faith in Ireland in the later 5th century was crucial. Patrick created the template for later saints to follow by founding monasteries, as at Armagh, to act as centres of Christian example, and by facing down the magic of the Irish druids. He carried the Gospel direct to the decision makers of his day, preaching to the High King of Ireland at Tara in County Meath. Columba, the Dove of the Church, followed Patrick's example, although he travelled in the opposite direction. Born in Donegal, Columba founded his abbey at Iona off the island of Mull around 563. He preached to the northern Picts, defeating their Druids in a trial of magic near Inverness and calming the great serpent that arose from the waters of Loch Ness. From his base in Wales, Dewi Sant or Saint David founded twelve monasteries with links to Devon, Cornwall, Brittany and Ireland. His communities were strictly disciplined, with the monks

PAGAN RULERS

The new Anglo-Saxon kings worshipped the gods of their Germanic and Scandinavian homelands. Later Christian writers paid little attention to these ancient deities and our knowledge of them is very limited as a result. Much has to be extrapolated from earlier Roman writers such as Tacitus who observed the Germans in the 1st century, or from later Norse sources. Only the days of the week, named after the Saxon gods Tiw, Woden, Thunor and Frige, serve as a reminder of this brief period of pagan belief in England.

leading an ascetic, and probably teetotal, life. In the 7th century, missionaries from this western 'Celtic' tradition set out to convert the English pagans. Celtic monks from Lindisfarne such as Aidan and Cuthbert worked amongst the Northumbrians, while Chad preached to the Mercians of central England.

THE ROMAN TRADITION

In 597, the monk Augustine landed with forty companions at the Isle of Thanet, charged by Pope Gregory with converting the pagans and bringing the British Isles within the jurisdiction of the Roman church. Augustine succeeded in his first duty. Ethelbert of Kent converted to Christianity in 601, although his Frankish Christian wife Ethelburga probably had as much influence in this decision as any missionary. Before his death in 604, Augustine also founded two bishoprics at London and Rochester. However, his mission to convert the keenly independent Christians of western Britain was unsuccessful. They preferred to maintain their own 'Celtic' traditions in liturgy and church government rather than accept the orthodoxy of the Roman Catholic Church.

THE WHITBY DECISION

The differences between the Celtic and Catholic churches came to a head over the issue of calculating the date of Easter. This most important Christian feast was observed on different days by the two denominations. In Northumbria, King Oswiu celebrated the Celtic Easter, while his southern wife marked the Catholic date. The result at Oswiu's court was confusion, as one faction fasted for Lent, while another feasted to celebrate the rebirth of their saviour. In 664, after a synod or meeting of church leaders at St Hilda's Abbey in Whitby, Oswiu settled on the Roman date. Although he venerated St Columba of Iona, the King feared being turned away from paradise by St Peter. In this and other church matters, the Roman Church was now the ultimate source of authority in much of England. The influence of the Celtic Church tradition was increasingly limited to its homelands in the west, the north and Ireland.

Right: The Synod of Whitby, when the debate surrounding the date of Easter was finally settled, was held at Saint Hilda's Abbey in modern Yorkshire.

TIMELINE

432	Traditional date of Patrick's first ministry in Ireland
560s	Dewi Sant (Saint David) establishing monasteries in Wales and Cornwall
563	Arrival of Columba in western Scotland
597	Arrival of Augustine in England with 40 monks
635	Aidan begins his mission to the Northumbrians.

NEW KINGDOMS
500–800

In the first two centuries of the early Middle Ages, local kingdoms developed in all parts of the British and Irish isles. Although some were pagan and some Christian, all were led by a warrior elite. The fortunes of these petty kingdoms varied as battles and territory were won and lost. However by 800, power was becoming centralized into a smaller number of hands.

THE HEPTARCHY OF ENGLAND

The 6th and 7th centuries saw land ownership and influence ebb and flow dramatically as a succession of petty kings and warlords throughout England won and lost power. Later medieval historians tidied up the confusion of early Anglo-Saxon England into a neat pattern of seven petty kingdoms, each with its own distinct regional identity. By general agreement, membership of this heptarchy, or rule of seven kings, was conferred upon Kent, Essex, Sussex, Wessex, East Anglia, Mercia and Northumbria. Recent research has revealed a much more fluid pattern of power and identity during the first three centuries of the Anglo-Saxon period. Essex and Sussex ranked far below the powerful realms of Northumbria, Mercia and later Wessex. Sub-kingdoms such as Lindsey, which flourished between the Humber and the Wash, had moments of glory before coming under the influence of larger neighbours, in this case Northumbria. The kings of the Hwicce controlled a vast swathe of Worcestershire, Gloucestershire and Warwickshire between 670 and 780, but failed to be remembered in the neat map of England drawn up by monkish historians five hundred years later. Other long forgotten tribes of England include the Gewissae or West Saxons and the Wihtware who gave their name to the Isle of Wight.

Above: Maps of England in the Early Middle Ages have traditionally shown a heptarchy of seven kingdoms, each ruled by its own king.

THE BRITISH KINGDOMS OF WALES

The geography of Wales helped the natives there to resist invasion in much the same way as it had impeded the legions of Rome centuries earlier. In the 6th century, the old local elites had taken the reins of power in a proliferation of new states that included Gwent, Dyfed, Powys and Gwynedd. These Brythonic or British states could call upon their allies in the north, such as the kingdoms of Cumbria and Strathclyde, with whom they shared common cultural and linguistic roots. In the 630s, the kingdom of Gwynedd scored important successes against the Mercians at Exeter and the Northumbrians at Hatfield Chase in Yorkshire. These victories helped to postpone Anglo-Saxon expansion for a century. Over time, however, the Welsh were forced back by Anglo-Saxon numbers and lost their more fertile lowlands. The economy and history of the Welsh would henceforth be a largely upland one.

Below: The natural fortress of Dumbarton Rock formed the strategic and military centre of the kingdom of Strathclyde.

KINGDOMS IN THE NORTH

The situation in 6th and 7th-century Scotland was just as fragmented. In the south, the kingdom of Rheged stretched around the Solway Firth from Dumfries down into Cumbria. By the 6th century, the ancient Lothian tribes of the Votadini had evolved into the British kingdom of Gododdin. In west central Scotland, the British kingdom of Strathclyde based its security upon the impregnable fortress of Dumbarton Rock that rose out from the river Clyde and took its wealth from the rich farmlands of Ayrshire and South Lanarkshire.

Much of northern Scotland beyond the Tay continued to be Pictish. In the far west however, a new element came into view after the year 500. The people of Dal Riata in Argyll were Gaels, who shared many cultural links with their cousins in Antrim, a short sea passage away. Tradition long held that the Dal Riata, later known as the Scotti, migrated from Ireland to Kintyre under their king Fergus. Modern archaeology has found no evidence to support this legendary migration, but the people who lived in the southern Hebrides, a world of small islands and seaways, enjoyed many contacts with the Irish.

FERGUS MOR MAC EARCA

Like most Dark Age warlords, virtually nothing is known about this early king of the Scotti. Fergus, son of Erc, appears in early king lists and was recorded as 'holding part of Britain' in 501 by the Irish writer of the *Annals of Tigernach*. Fergus only became significant in the medieval and Renaissance periods when later writers looked to emphasize the antiquity of the Scottish Crown. They traced the line of Scottish monarchs back to Fergus, whose writ probably ran little beyond the rock fortress of Dunadd in Argyll that served as the first capital of the Scots. With the union of the Scottish and English crowns in 1603, however, Fergus became the earliest identifiable historical ancestor of the British monarchy.

NORTHUMBRIAN GLORY
600–730

The kingdom of Northumbria burst upon British history in the early 7th century. The Northumbrians, an energetic people of German descent, dominated northern Britain between the Humber and the Forth. Along with military and economic power came a sudden artistic and spiritual flowering. The Northumbrian candle burned intensely, but it soon dimmed, and by 700 its great age was already ending. Yet this northern kingdom left an important legacy for the peoples of Scotland and England.

Below: The monastery at Lindisfarne was one of the great centres of Christian learning. The monks founded the first known school in the region, where reading, writing and Latin were taught.

AETHELFRITH – FOUNDING FATHER

Around 500, settlers from Angeln, possibly collaborating with Germanic remnants of the Roman legions, founded two small kingdoms on the eastern coast of Britain. Bernicia lay between the Tweed and the Tyne. Its southern neighbour of Deira stretched from the Tees to the Humber and annexed the British kingdom of Ebrauc or York in the 580s. Enter Aethelfrith, who took Bernicia in 592 and added Deira to his lands in 604, becoming the founder king of Northumbria.

In his *Ecclesiastical History of the English People*, Bede described Aethelfrith as the first great king of the English, who 'harassed the British and conquered more British lands, expelling them and settling his own people, than any other king of the English.' In 603, Aethelfrith successfully repulsed an invading Scotto-Irish army and laid the foundation for the later annexation of the lands between the Tweed and the Forth. His victory over the army of Powys at Chester in 616 was a mortal blow for the loose confederation of old Brythonic kingdoms. Although Aethelfrith himself died soon after, his successors dealt with further threats from the Welsh and the Mercians, quickly consolidating Northumbria's position as the leading power in northern Britain.

NORTHERN EXPANSION AND DECLINE

After defeating Cadwallon of Gwynedd in the 630s, the Northumbrians looked north to the farmlands of southern Scotland. Oswald (r. 634–642) absorbed the eastern kingdom of Gododdin as far as the Firth of Forth and

TIMELINE

604	*Union of Bernicia and Deira*
616	*Aethelfrith defeats the Welsh and their allies*
638	*Oswald captures Din Eidyn*
655	*Oswiu defeats the Mercians*
664	*Synod of Whitby endorses Roman church traditions*
685	*Northumbrian elite eliminated at Nechtansmere*
715	*Production of the Lindisfarne Gospels*
731	*Bede writes his* Ecclesiastical History of the English People.

made inroads into the western British kingdoms of Rheged and Strathclyde. By the year of his death, Oswald's kingdom encompassed much of southern Scotland as well as most of northern England. Only the central English kingdom of Mercia still posed a threat. Oswald died in battle at the hands of the Mercians but his successor Oswiu won control of Mercia in the 650s. For a few brief decades, the Northumbrians were the masters of most of Britain.

THE BATTLE OF NECHTANSMERE, 685

Northumbria's fall was almost as quick as its rise. The Mercians successfully rebelled against Northumbrian rule in the 650s. Plague seems to have weakened the northern lands in 664. However, the most damaging blow to Northumbrian power was largely self-inflicted. In 685, King Ecgfrith moved against the northern Picts who lived beyond the Firth of Forth. Ecgfrith's greed for slaves and plunder was said to have made him deaf to his more cautious advisers. The Picts lured the Northumbrian host ever northwards, then defeated them at the battle of Nechtansmere, at a site traditionally believed to be in the Pictish heartlands of Angus. Ecgfrith and his warrior elite were eliminated and their destruction is commemorated on the great carved stone of Aberlemno. Pictish success at Nechtansmere helped to ensure that the far north of Britain would not be easily subdued or absorbed by southern forces. Northumbrian military power was crushed and never recovered.

GOLDEN NORTHUMBRIA

Northumbria's true legacy lay in the realm of culture and the arts. A Christian kingdom after 627, it was initially influenced by Celtic missionaries from Ireland and the north. Among these was St Aidan from Iona, who built his monastery on Lindisfarne to be near the royal fortress of Bamburgh. Although Roman forms of church government prevailed at the Synod of Whitby in 664, Celtic influence can be seen in the Lindisfarne Gospels, an illuminated manuscript produced around 715 that fused Celtic and Anglo-Saxon traditions. Nor was Lindisfarne the only powerhouse of the Northumbrian intellect. The monastery at Monkwearmouth was famed throughout Europe for its collection of books, while at nearby Jarrow, Northumbria gave England its first historian in the shape of Bede, who finished his *Ecclesiastical History of the English People* there in the 730s. The spiritual intensity of Northumbrian life is best represented by the ascetic St Cuthbert, a healer and teacher in his youth, who later chose the austere life of a recluse on the Farne Islands.

Below: A page of the magnificent Lindisfarne Gospels, illuminated manuscripts that combine the Celtic and Anglo-Saxon traditions.

DARK AGE WALES
500–878

In the 6th and 7th centuries, the Brythonic peoples of the north and west were detached from each other as a result of Anglo-Saxon penetration into their lands. In Wales, a sense of identity developed – thanks to the bonds of language, localized Christian traditions and a feeling of separateness from their neighbours – that accelerated after the construction of Offa's Dyke in the late 8th century.

THE WESTWARD RETREAT

In the 6th century, there were strong links between the peoples of Wales and their Brythonic cousins in other parts of Britain. The poet Taliesin served as bard to princes in Wales and at the Cumbrian court of Rheged. In the early 7th century, a Welsh speaker in southern Scotland, possibly at Din Eidyn or Edinburgh, may have written the epic *Y Gododdin*. There were also economic and military links between Wales proper and the north Welsh lands, as well as with the Cornish kingdom of Dumnonia. These bonds weakened as Anglo-Saxon influence pushed ever westward. Saxon victory at Deorham in Gloucestershire in 577 drove a wedge between the Welsh and the Cornish when Cirencester, Gloucester and Bath were lost. Contact with Cumbria was more difficult after the battle of Chester in 616, where the Northumbrians defeated a Welsh confederacy. The 'Welsh' culture that had spanned much of western Britain was increasingly confined to the territory that became Wales.

OFFA'S DYKE (CLAWDD OFFA)

Built by Offa of Mercia at some point after 785, this earthwork barrier marked the border between Powys and Anglo-Saxon England. In places over 25 m wide and 8 m high, from ditch bottom

to bank top, the dyke was probably designed to deter and hamper attacks on the low-lying Mercian farmlands that had once been Welsh. Although it was an impractical fortification and soon abandoned, Offa's Dyke came to symbolize the clear distinction between the cultures of Celtic and Saxon Britain.

Left: The ditch and earthern banks that formed the barrier of Offa's Dyke are still clearly visible in places today.

WELSH KINGDOMS

Geography played an important part in the political development of Wales. The mountains and river valleys that cut up the land were also a barrier to creating a single power structure. As a result, early medieval Wales was divided into a number of independent principalities. The most powerful of these was Gwynedd in the north-west, based in the same areas of Ynys Mon and Snowdonia that had once held out against the Romans. Under its

TIMELINE

577	*Defeat at Deorham separates British of Cornwall and Wales*
616	*Welsh and Cumbrians separated after defeat at Chester*
785	*Offa's Dyke creates border between Powys and Mercia*
850	*Rhodri Mawr rules over much of Wales*
942	*Hywel Dda adds Gwynedd to his kingdoms.*

Christian king Cadwallon, the army of Gwynedd was strong enough to invade Northumbria and defeat Edwin at Hatfield Chase near Doncaster in 633. Significantly however, Cadwallon allied himself with the pagan Saxon Penda of Mercia rather than with the distant British kingdoms with whom contact continued to diminish.

The principality of Powys in central Wales had the misfortune to lack a defensible border to the east. In the 7th century, kings of Powys fell in battle against the Northumbrians. In the 8th century, Powys had to face the well-organized Mercians. By the 820s, this middle Welsh kingdom seems to have been exhausted by decades of warfare and much of its eastern territory was annexed by Cenwulf of Mercia.

LANGUAGE AND IDENTITY

The 7th and 8th centuries saw the development of a greater sense of Welsh identity. The earliest known inscription in Welsh on the Towyn stone in Gwynedd was probably carved between 650 and 750. Welsh began to replace Latin as the language of business and law. More importantly, the Welsh increasingly referred to themselves as *Cymry* or fellow countrymen, using their own word to define themselves in preference to the pejorative Saxon term *wealas*. At the heart of Welsh identity were the localized Christian traditions that owed more to Celtic tradition than Roman administrative patterns. As in Ireland, hermitages and monasteries were the key places of spiritual power, while the saints that the Welsh revered, such as Asaph, Canna and Tydfil, often had specific local roots.

Below: The construction of Offa's Dyke was supervised by King Offa of Mercia, who wished to protect the low lying farmlands to the west of his kingdom.

RHODRI MAWR

Rhodri Mawr, the Great, has a good claim to be called the first high king of all Wales. Rhodri inherited Gwynedd in 844, but the kingships of Powys and of Seisyllwg in southern Wales later fell into his lap thanks to dynastic accident and marriage. This made him ruler of much of Wales. His son Cadell ap Rhodri added the lands of Dyfed to the kingdom. However, Welsh inheritance customs worked against the creation of a single state and Rhodri's grandson, Hywel Dda, only took possession of the small western kingdom of Ceredigion. A skilful and patient ruler, Hywel the Good eventually ruled most of Wales, codifying Welsh law and minting his own coinage. However, on his death in 950, his lands were shared out amongst three separate heirs.

THE PICTS AND SCOTS OF ALBA
500–950

After 500, Scots, Picts, Angles and Britons vied for the lands that would become Scotland. Pictish kings ruled most of the territory north of the Tay. The Gaels, who came to be known as Scotti, held the western lands. The British kingdom of Strathclyde survived into the 11th century despite suffering numerous defeats at the Viking and English hands. Northumbrian influence in eastern Scotland peaked in the 7th century, but 'Scottish' rulers faced a long struggle to win back the lands south of the Forth.

Below: Frequent Viking attacks on the Atlantic coast forced the people of Dal Riata to migrate inland, clashing with the Picts.

THE PICTS

The Picts were the descendants of the northern tribes that had resisted the Roman invasion of Caledonia. By AD 600, Pictish kings ruled a large part of the land beyond the Clyde and Forth valleys. Most importantly, they held the fertile northeast shoulder that could support a large, belligerent population. Although warlike, the Picts were successful farmers and skilled craftsmen who used a written script known as *Ogam.* Originally pagan, the Picts were won over to Christianity in the 6th and 7th centuries. The impressive Pictish fortress at Burghead in Morayshire was protected on three sides by the sea and by a complex series of ditches and ramparts on the fourth. The large underground water-chamber at Burghead may have been a reservoir, though some writers have connected it to Pictish religious customs and their penchant for drowning prisoners.

THE KINGDOM OF ALBA

In 750, the Picts ruled most of Scotland. A hundred years later their kingdoms had vanished. Traditionally, the Norse have been blamed for this relatively sudden disappearance. By the early 9th century, the Norse occupied large parts of northern Scotland that had once been Pictish, such as Caithness and Sutherland. The Picts had also to contend with pressure from the Gaels or Scots of Dal Riata, who were themselves pushing eastwards in response to Viking attacks on the Atlantic seaboard. Traditional historians believed that the Pictish royal line was exhausted by successive military defeats in the 830s. Choosing his moment well, the King of the Scots Kenneth MacAlpin marched into Pictland and forced the leaderless Picts to accept him as their ruler in 843. The new

TIMELINE	
c. 500	*Dal Riata, kingdom of the Scots, develops in Argyll*
c. 600	*Much of northern Scotland under Pictish control*
685	*Picts defeat Northumbria at the Battle of Nechtansmere*
830s	*Norse control large parts of Pictland*
843	*Union of the Picts and Scots under Kenneth MacAlpin.*

PAINTED PEOPLE?

We do not know what the Picts called themselves. The word *Picti* first appears in a 3rd-century Latin poem and early historians believed that it stood for 'painted people'. They assumed that the Romans were referring to a Caledonian habit of tattooing or body-painting. Modern scholars have instead suggested that the name comes from an ancient Celtic word, *pett* or *pit,* meaning a piece of land. Pit survives as a common prefix for place names in the old Pictish heartlands of Angus, Aberdeenshire and Fife. Anglo-Saxon and Norse chroniclers called the tribes of northern Scotland the *Pehtas* or *Pettar,* while the Viking seaway between Scotland and the Orkneys was known as *Pettlandsfjord*. Perhaps these ancient words are an echo of the name that the Picts used for themselves.

Above: The Pictish people have been variously portrayed down the ages. Here they are shown as elaborately painted, headhunting warriors.

unified kingdom was known in Gaelic as Alba, though in time its Latin name of Scotia became more common.

However, recent scholars have tended to stress the similarities rather than the differences between the Picts and the Scots. The two groups shared many traits and had common enemies. Pictish and Scottish ruling families frequently intermarried and the archaeological evidence suggests that they traded successfully. Kenneth MacAlpin had blood ties to both peoples and was the ideal leader for their common struggle against the Norse. The union of 843 may therefore have been one of mutual advantage. Nevertheless, the languages and traditions of the Picts seem to have died out relatively quickly, possibly because the MacAlpin ruling elite spoke Gaelic, which became the power language of the new kingdom. There is also evidence that some 're-branding' took place after the union of 843, with churches in Pictland being given new saints that fitted more comfortably with Alban ideology.

CONSTANTINE II

Perhaps the wiliest of the Alban kings, Causantin or Constantine II, ruled from 903 to 943. The length of his reign alone suggests that he was an able ruler. Despite setbacks, such as losing to the English at Brunanburh in 937, Constantine steered a careful course between the Norse threat from the west and the English threat from the south. Early in his reign he inflicted a serious defeat upon the Norse, clearing them out of fertile Strathearn. Later, he allied himself with Viking rulers in York and Dublin, as a counterpoise to the growing power of the English. This successful diplomacy helped him to push the southern border of Alba down into the long-lost Lothians.

DARK AGE CULTURE
500–1000

Earlier historians originally used the term 'Dark Ages' to describe the centuries after the end of Roman rule, a period that they believed was unremittingly brutal and primitive. Modern scholars believe that a bright, vital and complex culture developed in these islands after 500, but we can only glimpse it, for the surviving sources are few and fragmented.

THE LIGHT OF FAITH AND LEARNING

The Christian Church dominates our understanding of early medieval culture. With its abbeys, schools and dedicated manpower, it had the mechanism to spread and preserve its traditions and writings. In the 6th and 7th centuries, the Celtic and Irish influence was paramount and the great abbeys and schools at Iona (563), Lindisfarne (635) and Monkwearmouth-Jarrow (674) were as much powerhouses of learning as of missionary activity. Their synthesis of native and Christian religious and artistic traditions reached its highpoint in the illuminated Gospels begun at Iona, but transferred for safety in the Viking age to the Columban foundation at Kells in County Meath. Christians from the Roman mission to England were also quick to establish schools, notably at Canterbury in 598 and at St Peter's in York in 664. The monastic contribution to historical scholarship was especially important. Much of what we know about Britain in this period flowed from the pens of monks such as Gildas, Bede and Nennius, author of the 9th-century *Historia Brittonum*. Other arts flourished in these citadels of learning. The earliest known English poet, Caedmon, wrote his vernacular songs and verse at Whitby Abbey in the later 7th century.

Above: Bede, a Northumbrian monk, is best known for his *Ecclesiastical History of the English People*, still a vital resource for Dark Age historians.

COURTS AND CULTURE

The other great source of patronage for the arts and learning were the royal courts of the period. Dark Age rulers were just as aware of the political power and propaganda value of the arts as any Roman emperor. Thus Edwin and Oswald of Northumbria replaced the first wooden minster at York with a stone

BEOWULF

The Old English epic poem *Beowulf*, of the 8th century, takes us into the imaginative world of Saxon warriors such as Raedwald of the East Anglians. The hero Beowulf overcomes the monster Grendel to win fame, honour and eventually the kingship of the Geats, a Scandinavian people. In old age, Beowulf picks up his sword again to fight a great dragon, but is slain in the moment of victory. His people lay out their beloved chieftain on a great ship 'covered in many treasures and ornaments from far off lands, a vessel fitted out with weapons of war and a host of treasures to travel far with him into the power of the flood'. The 8th-century poet paints the very scene that was eventually brought to light by the archaeology of Sutton Hoo.

TIMELINE

563	*Foundation of the Columban abbey on the island of Iona*
598	*Establishment of the school at Canterbury by Augustine*
625	*Likely date of the Sutton Hoo burial ship*
674	*Twin monasteries of Monkwearmouth and Jarrow founded in Northumbria*
675	*Likely date of the poet Caedmon's taking of holy orders*
682–735	*Bede teaching and writing at the Jarrow monastery*
750–800	*Traditional date of the epic poem* Beowulf
c. 800	*Illuminated* Book of Kells *created, probably at Iona Abbey*
880s	*Alfred of Wessex lays down his* Book of Dooms *or judgements*
940s	*Hywel Dda codifies Welsh law.*

structure in the 630s, to demonstrate both their piety and the impressive resources at their disposal. Athelstan's interest in relics was both antiquarian and practical. By acquiring the swords of the great Christian emperors Constantine and Charlemagne, he bolstered his own claim to rule not just the English, but all the peoples of Britain. Alfred of Wessex is rightly remembered as a champion of learning who established abbeys and schools, invited scholars from other lands to his court, and successfully put himself back through school as an adult. However, his motives were not merely altruistic. Thanks to the imported Welsh cleric and biographer Asser, Alfred's place in history was secured. We know far more about Alfred and his achievements than any other Dark Age prince. Alfred's *Book of Dooms* or laws not only made sense of the separate legal customs of his Mercian, Kentish and Wessex subjects, but reinforced his position as overlord of southern Britain. In the same way, Hywel Dda's *Law Code* established his pre-eminence amongst the Welsh princes in the 940s.

Right: The iron and gilt bronze helmet found at the Sutton Hoo burial ship in Suffolk shows the influence of Germanic and Scandinavian cultures on contemporary design.

WARRIOR CULTURE

The 7th-century burial ship discovered at Sutton Hoo in Suffolk gives us our best glimpse of the material culture of the Dark Ages. The fabulous treasure, laid out along the 28 m-long ship, demonstrates the skill of Saxon artistry as well as the wealth of resources that an overlord such as Raedwald of the East Anglians could command. The Saxon decorative arts drew deeply from the rich well of Germanic and Scandinavian mythology. The helmet and shield found at Sutton Hoo are close in style to those found in the Vendel lands of southern Sweden. Other finds demonstrate the lingering power of the Roman dream. The silver and gold trappings of kingship found in the grave echo the costumes of late Roman potentates. Spoons engraved with the names Saulos and Paulos and silver bowls marked with the cross hint at wider links to the Christian lands of southern Europe.

VIKING DAWN
790–980

Danish warships were first mentioned in the **Anglo-Saxon Chronicle** *in 787. Within a few years, the British and Irish Isles were bearing the brunt of 'the fury of the Northmen' as the Vikings burst out of their Scandinavian homelands to plunder throughout Europe. As they occupied land and settled, these new invaders had a profound impact on the peoples and kingdoms of Britain.*

Above: The forces of King Alfred of Wessex put up a fierce resistance to Danish invaders at Swanage Bay in 877.

EARLY RAIDERS

Danish pirates sacked the Northumbrian monasteries of Lindisfarne and Jarrow in 793 and 794. The abbey on Iona suffered the same fate the following year. By the 830s, the Norse were settling in the Shetlands and Orkneys and along the north and western coasts of Scotland. Here the Northmen found a familiar geography; a fragmented, sheltered coastline with sea lochs running deep inland. The rivers and loughs of Ireland also gave them access to that island's interior, even if their longships had to be portered in places.

By the 840s, Viking forces were overwintering in coastal bases that developed into trading and manufacturing centres. The chain from Dublin to Wexford, Waterford, Cork and Limerick tied up the Irish coast. From here the Norse could dominate the Irish Sea and harry the coasts of Wales and western England. In 850, Danish warbands took up winter quarters at the Isle of Thanet in north-east Kent, just as their Germanic cousins had done four centuries before. Further along the coast, the Isle of Sheppey provided the Danes with a second base in 854. The summer raiders now had the potential to conquer and settle.

THE GREAT HEATHEN ARMY

The Danish horde that arrived in England in 865 was larger than any previous Viking army to land on these shores. The 'Great Heathen Army' was also an experienced force, having campaigned in France for years, sacking Rouen in 850 and rowing up the Seine to besiege Paris. Anglo-Saxon chroniclers fearfully described this invasion force in terms that emphasized its godlessness as much as its size. Having picked northern France clean, it sailed for England and by 870, it had subdued the local kings of East Anglia and Northumbria.

TIMELINE	
840s	*Norse penetration deep into Ireland and western Scotland*
850s	*Danish invasion of southern England*
865	*Arrival of the Great Heathen Army of Danes*
878	*Flight of Alfred to the Somerset Levels in January*
878	*Alfred defeats the Danes at Edington in May.*

English chronicles record the arrival that summer of a second Scandinavian fleet, carrying reinforcements and a host of settlers. Using York as a base, the Danes now turned their attention to the southern Picts and the Anglo-Saxon kingdoms of Wessex and Mercia. When the Danes marched on the old Mercian capital of Repton in 874, Burgred, the last king of once proud Mercia, fled to a life of contemplation in Rome.

WESSEX AND THE DANELAW

With Mercia lost, the kingdom of Wessex was left to face the Danes alone. The Danes held the upper hand throughout the 870s, almost capturing Alfred, the young king of Wessex, in January 878, and forcing him to take refuge in the impenetrable wetlands of the Somerset Levels. At his secure base at the Isle of Athelney, Alfred was able to reorganize his men while encouraging the local lords of Wiltshire and Somerset to join his cause rather than negotiate with the Danes. In May, Alfred marched out to defeat the Danes at Edington, stopping the Vikings' westwards advance and probably saving Anglo-Saxon England from extinction. The Danish leader Guthrum was forced to accept a Christian baptism and limits to his ambition. The later treaty between Alfred and Guthrum defined the border between Wessex and the lands of the Danes, later known as the Danelaw, which were to lie east and north of a line from London to Chester.

THE VIKING IMPACT

The Viking incursions of the 9th century swept away the old Anglo-Saxon heptarchy. Kingdoms such as East Anglia and Mercia simply disappeared. Wessex emerged as the focus of English resistance and later as the core of a wider royal authority. If place names and surnames are to be trusted, eastern England experienced extensive Scandinavian immigration, although modern scholars have tended to emphasise continuity rather than a sudden change in the population. In the west, the Norse left a deep imprint on Man, in Cumbria, and Ireland. In the north, the jarldom (earldom) of rich and fertile Orkney was an independent Norse power well into the medieval period. In 870, Vikings from Ireland even sacked Dumbarton, the ancient British capital of Strathclyde, and carried its people off to the slave markets of Dublin. Throughout the British and Irish Isles, native peoples and princes were now forced to reorganize and co-operate to meet the Viking threat. Winning back land from the Vikings would keep English, Irish and Scottish kings and armies occupied for decades to follow.

Below: Athough the Vikings' reputation is primarily as a warfaring people, they had a rich culture of mythology and storytelling.

THE WARRIOR KINGS OF ENGLAND
880–980

By destroying most of the old Anglo-Saxon royal houses, the Vikings paved the way for the kings of Wessex to emerge as the leaders of 'English' resistance to the invaders. Wessex was also lucky in having a succession of able and energetic leaders who strengthened their realm and soon had pretensions to rule as kings of all Britain.

Below: Alfred of Wessex, known as 'The Great', held out against Danish incursions into his territory, and expanded his realm across Kent and Mercia.

ALFRED THE GREAT

Victory at Edington in 878 gave Wessex valuable breathing space. Alfred used the resulting period of peace to prepare for future war, putting in place a three-point strategy to protect his kingdom. The Wessex *fyrd* or militia was organized on a rota basis that allowed local leaders to raise troops in an emergency, but left sufficient men behind to rest or concentrate on essential economic tasks. A network of *burhs* or fortified settlements spread out from Alfred's capital of Winchester to almost every strongpoint in Wessex.

A revived and improved fleet provided the outer layer of defence and communication. These measures proved their worth when war with the Danes was renewed in 884, and again in 892 and 896 when Alfred was able to confound Danish attempts to migrate in numbers to southern England. Before his death in 899, Alfred, the only English monarch known as Great, had recaptured London and added the lands of West Mercia and Kent to his realm. Perhaps Alfred's greatest victory lay in aligning the cause of Wessex with a wider burgeoning sense of 'Englishness'.

CHILDREN OF ALFRED

Alfred's well-trained children continued his work. After securing his position against ambitious relatives, Edward took possession of his crown in 900, using the title of King of Angles and Saxons to emphasize the national role that the Wessex kings now played. Edward built important fortresses at key points such as Tamworth and Stafford and pushed the belligerent Northumbrian Danes north of the Humber. Alfred's remarkable daughter Aethelfled survived an attempted kidnap by the Danes and became a notable administrator and strategist. Given the title Lady of the Mercians, Aethelfled ruled from Stafford for eight years, capturing Derby and playing a major part in the English reconquest of Leicester.

BRUNANBURH

In 937, Athelstan's 'imperial' ambitions spurred the formation of an anti-English alliance between the Scots, Britons of Strathclyde, Cumbrians, Irish and Norse. The resulting Battle of Brunanburh was one of the bloodiest in a bloody century and it saw the slaughter of numerous kings, earls and thanes. According to one Irish annalist, 'a multitude of Saxons fell but Athelstan obtained a great victory'. Athelstan died a year or so after the battle, but his success against the alliance ensured that England would survive as a unified state.

Above: Athelstan's army was victorious over the anti-English alliance at Brunanburh, one of the bloodiest battles of the age.

ATHELSTAN

Edward's successor continued the mission of the Wessex dynasty with vigour. Athelstan was a bold and successful soldier who pushed the borders of his realm almost to those of modern England. Within three years of his accession, he had seized York and absorbed Northumbria into his kingdom. In the far west he pushed the independent Cornish back beyond the river Tamar. Athelstan also pressed his father's claim to be overlord of all Britain. Charters and documents from his court frequently referred to him by the Greek term *Basileus* or Sovereign, or by the Latin phrase *rex totius Britanniae,* King of all Britain. Some of the kings of Wales, including Hywel Dda, seem to have found a way of existing with Athelstan despite his imperial pretensions. Other neighbouring rulers were less willing to co-exist with their expansionist neighbour.

THE SECRET OF WESSEX SUCCESS

The fortunes of peoples and kingdoms in this period often rested on the outcome of a single battle. However the administrative skills of the Wessex dynasty did much to ensure that their kingdom would prevail in the longer term against its neighbours. A dependable chain of royal officials in the shires, from ealdorman to shire-reeve and hundredman, ensured that commands were carried out. Service to the king was increasingly rewarded by systematic grants of land and status rather than by sporadic distribution of booty. Systems of law, taxation and military service ensured that Wessex could withstand unexpected shocks. The creation of a Viking kingdom in York and the North Midlands after Athelstan's death in 939 was only a brief setback for the new English state. A little more than a decade later, this loss had been made good with the assassination of Eric Bloodaxe, the last Viking ruler of York, in 954. The Wessex kings had the resources in place to quickly and quietly reabsorb the north.

TIMELINE

886	*Boundaries of the Danelaw established by Alfred and Guthrum*
915	*Alfred's son Edward restores the Danelaw to English rule*
930	*Border between Cornwall and England established along the Tamar*
937	*Althelstan wins the bloody Battle of Brunanburh*
950s	*Kings of Wessex reabsorb much of northern England.*

SCANDINAVIAN ENGLAND
990–1042

By the late 10th century, the challenge from Scandinavia seemed to have been met in all parts of the British and Irish Isles. The Viking threat had spurred political consolidation in England, Scotland and Ireland. However, a new wave of Danish aggression after 980 culminated in the absorption of England within a Danish North Sea empire.

FALSE CALM

By 950, a strong, unified England had emerged from the long struggle against the Viking invader. The Danish settlers in eastern England were by the mid 10th century increasingly Christian and beginning to merge with the existing population. In Scotland, the kings of Alba had also learned to deal with the Viking threat. A warband of seven score Vikings who landed on the shores of Argyll in 986 were summarily rounded up and hanged. Malcolm II efficiently despatched a Danish host at Mortlach in Morayshire in 1010. Conflicts with the Norse now tended to take place on the edges of the Scottish kingdom, rather than pose a threat to its existence. In Ireland, Brian Boru captured the Norse bases of Limerick and Dublin in the 960s, before breaking the power of the Vikings in Ireland in the great slaughter of Clontarf in 1014. However, despite these successes against the Northmen, England fell completely under Scandinavian sway in the early years of the 11th century.

MALDON

In the summer of 991, a Danish army of 4,000 troops met and defeated a smaller English militia on the banks of the River Blackwater at Maldon in Essex. From the Anglo-Saxon poem of the battle, we learn of Byrhtnoth, the heroic ealdorman of Essex, who chose death in battle rather than surrender to the invader. The survival of the poem has perhaps lent too much importance to this conflict, which was only one of many in the period. Large Danish forces had in fact been active along English shores again since the early 980s. However, the lasting significance of the Battle of Maldon lies in the reaction of the English king Aethelred, who sought henceforth to placate the Danes with cash payments raised from taxes known as Danegeld.

DANEGELD

Earlier English kings, including Alfred, had found it prudent on occasion to buy off the Vikings with bullion. After Maldon, Aethelred handed over

Below: King Sweyn of Denmark launched repeated revenge attacks against England after the St Brice's Day massacre of Danish settlers in 1002.

Above: When Danish attacks eventually forced Aethelred to flee, Sweyn's son Cnut the Great became King of England and ruled for nineteen years.

4,500 kg (10,000 lbs) of silver to the Danes 'on account of the great terror that they caused'. Sweyn Forkbeard was persuaded to call off his siege of London in 994 thanks to a similar inducement. The weakness of Aethelred's Danegeld policy, which may have been pressed upon him by his adviser Sigeric, Archbishop of Canterbury, was illustrated by further payments made in 1007 and 1012. The price of peace escalated to 16,000 kg (36,000 lbs), then 22,000 kg (48,000 lbs) of silver. Over sixty million silver pennies were transferred from England to Denmark between 990 and 1016, yet that year's compiler for the *Anglo-Saxon Chronicle* still complained that 'the Danes went about England as they pleased'.

THE ST BRICE'S DAY MASSACRE

In 1002, perhaps driven by a mixture of fear and frustration, Aethelred ordered the murder of all Danes in England. The massacre was planned for St Brice's Day on 13 November, and many members of the Danish elite in England were duly eliminated. However, rather than solving Aethelred's problems, the killings provoked King Sweyn of Denmark to launch prolonged revenge attacks upon England in 1003 and 1013. These ultimately forced Aethelred to flee to Normandy and led to England's subjugation by the Danish Crown. In early 1017, the English nobility recognized Sweyn's son, Cnut the Great, as sole king of all England.

SCANDINAVIAN RULE

In the course of his nineteen-year reign, Cnut also became King of Denmark and Norway, as well as overlord of Schleswig and Pomerania. England was therefore only one part, if an important one, of his empire. After making himself secure and raising a final Danegeld payment of over £82,000, Cnut ruled his English possessions with a relatively light touch. He confirmed the laws of his Anglo-Saxon predecessors and was generous to the Church. His reformed coinage was of equal value in all his realms, greatly helping to promote the recovery of English trade with the Continent after years of turmoil. After Cnut's death in 1035, his sons Harold Harefoot and Harthacnut enjoyed only brief reigns. Scandinavian forces appeared on English shores again in 1066, under Harald Hardrada of Norway, while the Danes attempted to regain their old influence in English affairs in 1069 and 1075. These forays were all unsuccessful. The Viking Age in England was over.

TIMELINE	
991	*Danish victory at Maldon in Essex*
991	*Aethelred buys off the Danes with 4,500 kg (10,000 lbs) of silver*
1002	*St Brice's Day massacre of Danish elite in England*
1013	*Aethelred of England flees to Normandy*
1017	*The Danish Cnut the Great accepted as king in England.*

THE LAST OF THE OLD KINGS
1000–1065

By 1050, England and Alba (increasingly known by the Latin name of Scotia) had taken strides towards becoming unified kingdoms, based around a recognized territory and an embryonic sense of nationhood. Wales too seemed to be cohering politically and finally overcoming the handicaps imposed upon it by geography and tradition.

'KING OF ALL THE BRITONS'

In the mid 11th century, a remarkable warlord united the Welsh-speaking peoples of western Britain under his rule. To his original base in Powys, Gruffydd ap Llywelyn added the kingdom of Gwynedd, as well as border lands won back from the Earl of Mercia at Y Trallwng in 1039. By 1055, after absorbing Gwent and Morgannwg, Gruffydd exercised the powers of a king throughout all Wales from his court at Rhuddlan, and his rights to do so were recognized by Edward the Confessor. However, political unity in Wales still largely depended on the sword of an energetic man, and after Gruffydd's death in 1063, his domain splintered back into its traditional parts.

FROM ALBA TO SCOTLAND

The Gaelic-speaking kings of Alba were more successful at kingdom building. Malcolm II's victory at Carham in 1018 finally secured the lands north of the Tweed and Solway, including the rich Lothian farmlands. Although much of the north and west still owed its allegiance to Norse jarls (chieftains), and the writ of the King of Scots was seldom obeyed in wild and

MACBETH, KING OF SCOTS

Like his Shakespearean character, Macbeth was a successful warrior and a key figure in the government of King Donnchad or Duncan. There are similarities with the end of the play, although the real Macbeth deposed Duncan after defeating him in open battle near Elgin in 1040, not by secret assassination. Macbeth seems to have been a popular king, while his wife Gruoch was a pious woman who endowed monasteries and may have accompanied Macbeth on his pilgrimage to Rome in 1050. Macbeth resisted the massive English invasion of Scotland under Earl Siward of Northumbria in 1054, designed to place a more pliant character on the Scottish throne. He eventually died at Lumphanan in Aberdeenshire from battle wounds in 1057.

Above: Macbeth has been immortalized in Shakespeare's play of the same name. Here the fictional king is shown instructing murderers to assassinate his ally Banquo.

Above: The reign of Edward the Confessor, King of England from 1042–66, saw a gradual loss of royal control to competing factions.

distant Galloway, the kingdom of Scotland had assumed most of its final form by the mid 11th century. The ancient divisions between Pict and Scot seemed to have waned. The system of *mormaers* or regional earls provided stable government in the provinces and the rapid supply of military force in times of crisis. Most significantly, a mere three kings, Malcolm II, Macbeth and Malcolm III, ruled Scotland for a total of eighty-one years during the 11th century. These Alban kings had time to gain experience of government, learn from their mistakes and stamp their mark upon northern Britain.

THE LAST ANGLO-SAXON KINGS

By the 11th century, England was the most powerful state in the British and Irish Isles and was beginning to merit comparison with the wealthier and more populous states on the Continent. A strong king of England could harness the kingdom's resources effectively and use the powerful marcher earls (lords with special powers over the border lands) to good effect against the Welsh, Scots and Vikings. The reign of the penultimate Saxon king began well. Edward the Confessor was a popular king and during his twenty-four years on the throne trade prospered as did other links with Europe. A pious monarch, Edward founded an abbey outside London at Westminster that was to develop into the seat of English government and ceremonial. His main failing as a king was his inability to produce an heir.

Having grown up in Normandy, Edward was shrewd enough to appreciate the administrative and military gifts that the well-organized Normans could offer his realm. Normans soon took positions of power in Church and State under Edward, as they did under his contemporary Malcolm III in Scotland. The Norman influence at Edward's court was however resented by the Saxon and Danish factions amongst the English nobility. In the 1050s, resentment led to riots and insurrection as the Godwin Earls of Wessex contended for control over the childless king. For the last three years of his reign, Edward was effectively the puppet of Harold Godwinson, a vigorous soldier who destroyed Gruffydd's forces in Wales in 1063 and even deposed his own unpopular brother Tostig from the earldom of Northumbria. Upon Edward's death in 1066, Harold was his natural successor. He controlled the key earldoms of England and had proven experience in war and government. Unsurprisingly, the Witanagemot – or ancient convocation of wise and senior men – approved the accession of Godwinson as Harold II in January 1066.

TIMELINE	
1018	*Scottish victory at Carham secures the Tweed-Solway border*
1039	*Expansion of Llywelyn power over Gwynedd*
1040–1057	*Rule of Macbeth of Alba*
1042	*Edward the Confessor becomes King of England*
1058	*Malcolm III, Canmore or Great Chief, becomes King of Scots*
1060	*High point of Gruffydd ap Llywelyn's rule in Wales*
1063	*Harold Godwinson becomes the strongest figure in England*
1065	*Consecration of Westminster Abbey*
1066	*Death of the childless Edward the Confessor on 4 January*
1066	*Godwinson crowned as Harold II on 5 January.*

THE YEAR OF THREE KINGS
1066

Normans held positions of influence in England and Scotland before 1066, but the events in the autumn of that year marked one of the most significant moments in English history. Power was suddenly transferred from the old Anglo-Saxon elite to the new incomers from France. Scotland, Ireland and Wales were also to be affected by the catastrophic events of 1066.

RIVAL CLAIMANTS

Although acclaimed as king by the English nobility and crowned at Westminster within a day of the Confessor's death in early January 1066, Harold II knew that he would have to fight that summer to keep his crown. Attacks could be expected from two directions, Scandinavia and Normandy, where rival factions were soon rehearsing their claims to the English throne and gathering their troops. Duke William of Normandy argued that Edward had promised him the succession when visiting France in 1051. He even said his claim had been accepted by Harold Godwinson in 1064, when the latter had been blown onto the Norman shore by a storm. Harald III of Norway, known as the Hardrada or Stern Ruler, also felt cheated by Harold's accession, basing his claim on a mixture of blood and marriage ties and treaty deals.

Above: A section of the famous Bayeux tapestry depicting the events of 1066. Here, the troops of Harold II are shown patrolling the southern coasts, on the lookout for Norman invaders.

A SEASON OF BATTLES

As the Normans were the stronger threat, Harold patrolled the south coast with his *fyrd* or militia throughout the summer months. However, the huge Norman fleet of 600 ships was penned up in the Baie de la Somme by difficult winds in the Channel and the first invasion force to appear was from Norway, landing in Yorkshire in September. Harald Hardrada, aided by Tostig, the deposed earl and vengeful brother of Harold Godwinson, easily dealt with the Mercian and Northumbrian forces sent to meet

TIMELINE – 1066	
4 Jan	*Death of Edward the Confessor*
5 Jan	*Coronation of Harold II*
August	*Harold II disperses the fyrd*
Early Sept	*Norwegians land and capture York*
20 Sept	*Norwegians defeat the Earls of Mercia and Northumbria*
25 Sept	*Harold defeats Hardrada and Tostig at Stamford Bridge*
28 Sept	*Duke William lands at Pevensey*
13 Oct	*The English army arrives at Senlac Hill*
14 Oct	*Battle of Senlac, later called the Battle of Hastings*
Nov	*William moves northwards to London*
25 Dec	*William I 'the Conqueror' crowned at Westminster.*

them at Fulford. Having stood down his men, Harold was forced to recall his troops and march them northwards at speed. Catching the Scandinavians by surprise, the English won a convincing but costly victory at Stamford Bridge in which Tostig and Hardrada were both slain. Their defeat marked the end of the Viking age in England, but Harold's success was pyrrhic. As he counted his many casualties, news arrived that the sea winds had calmed. Duke William had successfully landed over 7,000 men at Pevensey in Sussex and was now encamped within a prefabricated wooden fortress near Hastings. Harold now had to march his weakened forces almost 400 km (250 miles) southwards to meet the Norman threat.

SENLAC HILL, 14 OCTOBER 1066

The tired and depleted English army faced a larger, fresher foe and so Harold wisely took up a defensive position on Santlache or Senlac Hill to block the road to London. His strategy was to let the Norman cavalry tire themselves out by running uphill against the shieldwall of the English infantry. For much of the day, Norman archery and cavalry were ineffective

against the cautious English. The battle turned on the successful feigned retreats by which the Normans lured the English on to lower, flatter ground where they could easily be run down by the chain-mailed and stirruped Norman cavalry. News of Harold's injury and death later in the day also discouraged many in the *fyrd,* who began to slip away into the densely-forested Weald. Tradition says that Harold's housecarls defended his corpse and the battle standards of Wessex to the last man. The heavily mutilated body of the last 'King of the English' was identified by his tattoos and probably taken to his favourite church at Waltham in Essex to be laid to rest.

Above: This 15th-century illustration depicts the Battle of Hastings as a chivalric affair. In reality it was a bloody massacre in which much of the tired English army was slaughtered or fled the field in terror.

THE MARCH ON LONDON

Duke William rested at Hastings for several weeks after the battle. He may have expected the English to come and submit to their new overlord but he also used the time to prepare his forces for the next phase of the conquest. The march on London was delayed by illness in the Norman ranks, probably dysentery, and William himself fell ill. However, the trickle of southern English landowners offering their submission grew daily as he approached and encircled London. William was crowned King of England at Westminster Abbey on Christmas Day, less than a year after the death of the Confessor.

NORMAN CONQUEST
1066–1072

In the course of just a few weeks England, one of the wealthiest and most organized states in Europe, fell into the lap of a small invading army. Resistance to the Normans was generally restricted to the edges of the kingdom. All the levers of power in Church and State were soon in the secure grip of the Norman elite.

POWER VACUUM

There was a curious lack of resistance to William and his small invasion force. In fact, Anglo-Saxon society had been decapitated in the autumn of 1066. Many of the nobles who might have organized the fight against William were lying dead at Stamford Bridge and Senlac. There was also a faction within Saxon society who openly welcomed the Normans. Wigod, the Saxon lord of Wallingford, not only facilitated William's entry into London, but was quick to align his family with the new regime through marriage. Other Saxon leaders such as Stigand, Archbishop of Canterbury, may have imagined that the English would ride out the Norman storm. Duke William might prove no more permanent than Cnut and his Danes. Such thinking failed to take into account that, throughout Europe, the Normans were systematic kingdom-builders and that William's army consisted of many landless younger men who expected to be rewarded generously for their efforts.

RESISTANCE

Challenges to the Conqueror came from the margins of his new kingdom. The Godwinsons sparked an uprising in Cornwall and there was trouble in the Welsh Marches. From his base on the Isle of Ely, Hereward maintained the Anglo-Danish cause, sacking Peterborough in 1070 before vanishing into the East Anglian fenland. The most serious threat to the Normans came from the north, where the population was largely composed of independent freemen of Scandinavian descent. Northern revolts in 1068 and 1069, culminating in the massacre of the Norman garrisons at York and Durham, were supported by well-equipped Danish and Scottish expeditions. William was forced to act. Throughout the winter of

Left: In 1085, William commissioned a complete land survey of England, known as the *Domesday Book*, to assess the resources and potential of his new kingdom.

NORMAN CASTLES

The Normans were a warrior people of Viking origin and their social order was primarily designed to meet their military needs. The king granted land in return for military service and the provision of trained, armed knights. To keep possession of their lands, Norman lords built castles, first from earthen mounds and stockades, but later with stone keeps. These castles were not merely defensive structures, an insurance against a surly, defeated populace, but centres of power and control. From here the local lord ensured that the castle domain was run as efficiently as possible to feed and equip men and horses for war. After 1086, the *Domesday Book* gave the Crown a shrewd idea of the military potential of every single landholding in the kingdom.

Below: The Norman legacy of castles and keeps, such as this one at Chepstow in Wales, endures to this day.

1069–70, his men brutally harried and scorched the counties of northern England. The population was decimated and dozens of villages destroyed, creating a wasted cordon between the Scottish Border and the richer shires in the south.

THE ABERNETHY STANDOFF

The Scots were not slow to cash in on the troubles further south. Malcolm III sheltered important Anglo-Saxon exiles and sponsored their attempts to re-conquer northern England in 1069. He also led his own troops on a successful expedition into Cumbria and Northumberland. In 1070, Malcolm married into the old English royal family, taking Margaret, sister of the English pretender Edgar Aetheling, as his queen. Four of their children were given the provocatively English names of Edgar, Edmund, Edward and Ethelred, in order to strengthen any future claim to the English throne. In 1072, William marched north and met with Malcolm at Abernethy near Perth. Malcolm found it prudent to acknowledge William's overlordship of his lands in Lothian, which had once belonged to Northumbria. William noted that the Scots, stiffened with their own Flemish and Norman allies, were a prickly foe and resolved to strengthen his northern border with new castles.

NORMANIZATION

In the first years of William's reign, leading Englishmen who were loyal were permitted to keep their lands and titles. After 1070 however, William pursued an active policy of Normanization. Disaffected Saxon lords were stripped of their land, while estates without heir were granted to Normans. Within a generation, a dependable class of Norman landowners who owed their position to the king alone had replaced the old landowning elite. A similar process transformed the Church hierarchy. In 1070 Lanfranc, a noted scholar and Abbot of Caen, was appointed to Canterbury, replacing Stigand who had been deposed. Lanfranc proceeded to promote clerics who shared his continental origins. Native ecclesiastical foundations withered, while new monastic houses with links to Normandy and France were given support. Latin and Norman French were now the languages of government and the Church.

THE KINGDOM BUILDERS
1100–1153

In the early 12th century, both Scotland and England had the good fortune to be ruled by intelligent, energetic kings who were better educated than most medieval monarchs. Henry I and David I were both 'modernizers' who laid sound foundations for their successors.

'BEAUCLERC'

As the fourth son of the Conqueror, Henry was destined for a Church career and had therefore received a more thorough education than most Norman lords, earning him the nickname of 'Beauclerc' (well-learned). He took the crown in August 1100, a mere three days after the mysterious death of his brother William II in a New Forest hunting accident. His surviving brother Robert was conveniently away on crusade. Knowing that most of the barons preferred the belligerent Robert, Henry had to win their support before Robert returned from the Holy Land. He did this by distancing himself from William II's abuses of power and by making a number of concessions to the nobles. In his Coronation Charter of Liberties, Henry accepted that there were limits to royal power and to the king's rights over noble property and church offices. Henry's charter provided a foundation for later challenges to overweening regal power such as the *Magna Carta*.

Above: Henry I 'Beauclerc', the first Norman king to be born in England, cemented his position as sovereign by marrying Edith of Scotland.

SAXON AND NORMAN

Henry was the first Norman king born in England and the first to speak English. During his long reign, the sharp differences between English and Norman society began to abate. By marrying Edith of Scotland, who carried the bloodline of the Saxon kings, Henry merged the old and new dynasties of England. Conscious of the power and ambition of the greater Norman

THE EXCHEQUER

Henry's rule depended on the efficiency and loyalty of his closest ministers. For much of his reign, Roger, Bishop of Salisbury – originally a Caen parish priest who had impressed the King with his zeal – held the key post of Chancellor. Roger created the twice-yearly Exchequer sessions each Easter and Michaelmas at which sheriffs and their revenue officials had to justify their actions and balance their accounts. The earliest of these financial audits were conducted across a long wooden table covered in checked cloth, from which the term 'the Exchequer' derives.

magnates, Henry raised lesser men to positions of authority in the growing royal bureaucracy. Often away visiting his French possessions, he vested power in his justiciar or viceroy who was charged with ensuring that the government of England ticked over smoothly in the absence of the king. Henry also took an interest in the provincial government of his kingdom, sending his own officials to judge local disputes and thereby curb the excesses of local lords and sheriffs.

THE NORMANDY QUESTION

The earliest Norman monarchs valued their French homelands more than their English acquisitions. When Duke William divided his lands amongst his sons, the eldest Robert received the prize cherry of Normandy. Robert's attempted invasion of England in 1101 and his poor government of Normandy gave Henry ample justification for intervention in the duchy. In 1106, Henry decisively routed Robert's forces, and Robert spent the remaining 28 years of his life as Henry's prisoner. However, by reuniting the Norman inheritance with his own name and lineage, Henry had linked the English Crown to France. Royal ambitions across the Channel henceforth distracted Henry's successors for the next four centuries.

DAVID THE GREAT

Like Henry, David I was a well-educated younger son who came to the throne after the relatively early deaths of his brothers. As Earl of Huntingdon and as a vassal of his brother-in-law Henry I, David already held lands in England. He was in many ways the first fully Normanized king of Scotland and continued the modernizing work of his parents Malcolm Canmore and St Margaret. David granted burgh charters and privileges to the largest settlements in his kingdom, minted silver coinage and encouraged fairs to attract English and European merchants to his realm. Like Henry, he used royal officials and the grant of land under feudal terms to increase the power of the Scottish Crown. He used Norman and Flemish troops to police the rebellious elements, Gaels and Galwegians, on the edges of his kingdom. The revolt of the independent Moraymen in 1130 was brutally suppressed and the lands of Moray were given to castle-building knights like Freskin de Moravia. For his great generosity to the Church, David was later dubbed 'a sair sanct for the Croun' by those who feared he had impoverished his heirs. During Henry's reign, the border between the two kingdoms was quiet. It was not until after Henry's death in 1135 that David set himself to extending the Scottish realm southwards, gaining Northumberland and the promise of Cumberland and Westmorland. He died at Carlisle in 1153, in the hard-won castle that was his favourite and most southern possession.

Below: Robert Duke of Normandy, having been defeated by his younger brother Henry, spent the remainder of his years incarcerated at Devizes castle (below) and at Cardiff.

TIMELINE	
1100	*Henry I crowned at Westminster three days after death of William II*
1100	*Henry marries Edith of Scotland who represents the Saxon bloodline*
1106	*Henry defeats his brother Robert at Tinchebrai in Normandy*
1124	*David I becomes King of Scots*
1139	*David acquires the county of Northumberland for Scotland*
1153	*David buried at Dunfermline Abbey.*

ENGLAND AND FRANCE
1154–1420

By repossessing Normandy, Henry I diverted the attention of his successors towards the Continent. At the peak of English power in France, the king of England overshadowed his French counterpart, but eventually the richest territories slipped from English hands. The cost of military expeditions also had important domestic consequences.

THE ANGEVIN 'EMPIRE'

Born and raised in France, Henry II was very much a French prince. He acquired Normandy and rich Anjou in the lower Loire valley in 1151, and a year later married the most eligible heiress in Europe. As dowry, Eleanor of Aquitaine brought her lands of that name, as well as Touraine, Gascony, Maine and Poitou. Some shrewd diplomacy later brought Brittany into this spectacular property portfolio, which outshone that of the king of France, Henry's titular overlord. In 1154, Henry succeeded to the English throne on the death of Stephen. Eastern Ireland was added in 1171. To manage his vast estate that stretched from the Solway Firth to the Pyrenees, Henry was almost always on the move, and spent only thirteen years of his 35-year reign in England.

Below: Henry II, by marrying Eleanor of Aquitaine, became the owner of lands throughout France. When he acceded to the English throne, he ruled an 'Empire' stretching from the Scottish to the Spanish borders.

THE LOSS OF NORMANDY

Henry's sons failed to maintain their impressive inheritance. Richard the Lionheart spent the first half of his reign on crusade and the second half struggling to regain lands appropriated by the French king in his absence. His brother John met with greater disaster. In March 1204 French troops captured the fortress of Chateau Gaillard that Richard had built to protect Normandy. Within the year, Normandy, Anjou and much else had been lost. John's hopes of recouping this disastrous situation were dashed by the defeat of his allies at Bouvines in 1214. Expensive expeditions to France by Henry III in the 1230s and 1240s simply

TIMELINE	
1154	*Henry II adds England to his continental possessions*
1259	*English possessions in France reduced to Gascony and Aquitaine*
1360	*Treaty of Bretigny marks the English highpoint in the 100 Years War*
1415–20	*Henry V recaptures lands in Normandy after Agincourt*
1422–53	*English lands in France lost during the minority of Henry VI.*

Above: Richard I 'the Lionheart' is best known for his exploits on Crusade. A true medieval warrior king, he led his knights in battle in the Holy Land.

Above: The young warrior king Henry V won an historic victory at Agincourt, thanks to his archers who comprised the bulk of his force.

emptied the royal treasury and bred resentment at home. After the Treaty of Paris of 1259, all that remained of the Angevin Empire was Gascony and a fragment of Aquitaine.

THE HUNDRED YEARS WAR

Despite these catastrophic territorial losses, English kings continued to trumpet their claim to the French throne. Franco-Scottish plotting and a legal dispute over Aquitaine gave Edward III an excuse for war in 1337. The war began well for Edward. The French invasion fleet was destroyed off Sluis in northern Flanders in 1340. Welsh longbowmen proved too deadly for French cavalry at Crecy in 1346 and at Poitiers ten years later. By the time of the 1360 Treaty of Bretigny, Edward seemed to have recovered many of the jewels in the old Angevin crown. Edward promised to renounce his claim to the French throne but was confirmed in his lordships of Aquitaine and Calais. However, before the treaty could be ratified, war had broken out again and this time the wheel of fortune turned against the English cause. After a lifetime of campaigning, Edward was forced to sue for peace at Bruges in 1375, master of little more than three coastal enclaves around the ports of Bordeaux, Calais and Bayonne.

AGINCOURT

In 1415, the young warrior king Henry V resolved to win back the lands in France that had belonged to his ancestors. Forced to fight at Agincourt, en route to Calais, skilled longbowmen again won the day for an English king. By 1419, with the French riven by civil war, Henry had retaken much of Normandy and made a powerful ally in the Duke of Burgundy. In 1420, Henry was betrothed to the French king's daughter and recognized as his heir. On the brink of uniting the two kingdoms, Henry fell ill with dysentery and died. His gains were frittered away during the long minority of his infant son. By 1453, apart from Calais and the Channel Isles, France was lost.

THE PRICE OF WAR

There was a price to be paid at home for adventures overseas. John's failures in France were a key factor in the alienation of the nobility that led to their rebellion in 1215. He was forced to accept the limits to his power set down in *Magna Carta*. Later kings found it necessary to call frequent councils to ensure baronial co-operation. Rising taxes to pay for war in France led to open criticism of Henry III in the 1240s and of Edward III a century later. Indeed, when it elected its first Speaker in 1376, the Commons first found its voice criticizing the cost of war. French adventures also gave the Scots, Welsh and Irish valuable periods of respite and opportunities to recover lost ground.

MEDIEVAL IRELAND
1171–1400

In the 12th and 13th centuries, Ireland seemed on course to become a centralized kingdom on the Norman model, under the English Crown. Two key events in the 14th century, the Scottish invasion and the plague, helped to galvanize Irish resistance and led to the native recovery of the island.

THE TUATHS

In 1100, Ireland was divided into a patchwork of over eighty tuaths or petty kingdoms and a smaller number of regional overlordships. The rulers of these lands were often Gall-Gaels or 'foreign Gaels'. They were of mixed Norse and Irish ancestry, reflecting the gradual absorption of the Scandinavian warrior elite within Irish society throughout the 10th and 11th centuries. According to ancient Gaelic custom, the freemen of the tuaths elected their kings. However, the arrival of a large Anglo-Norman military presence in the 1160s threatened traditional Hibernian forms of society and government.

STRONGBOW

Disputes between local Irish potentates provided an opening for the Anglo-Normans. In 1166, Diarmit, King of Leinster, was forced into exile by his rivals and asked the English King Henry II for support. Three years later, an Anglo-Norman army of around 600 knights amassed by Richard de Clare, Earl of Pembroke, landed at Bannow Bay in County Wexford, ostensibly to support Diarmit's cause. The force included a detachment of Welsh archers – which probably explains de Clare's nickname of Strongbow. Wexford, Waterford and the old Norse kingdom of Dublin had all fallen to Diarmit and de Clare by 1171. At this point Henry stepped in to squash any thoughts de Clare might have had about creating an independent Norman kingdom of Ireland.

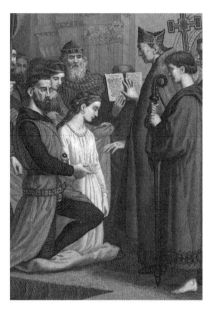

Above: The marriage of Aoife, daughter of Diarmit, to Richard de Clare 'Strongbow' in 1170 cemented the alliance of the two men.

LORD OF IRELAND

At the head of over 4,000 troops, Henry sailed to Ireland to enforce his sovereignty. In 1171, when he landed at Waterford, he became the first English king to step on Irish soil. Here he received the submission of many of the petty kings of eastern Ireland, reminded the Anglo-Norman knights and barons of their place, and formally bestowed the lands of Leinster upon de Clare. However, the title of *Dominus Hiberniae,* Lord of Ireland, was reserved for his younger son John, the later king of England. John twice visited his Irish possessions and did much to consolidate Anglo-Norman control there.

ANGLO-NORMAN IRELAND

The Norman conquest of Ireland was rapid for several reasons. The local Irish elites were divided and lacked the military organization of the Norman incomers. As in their other possessions, the Normans created an infrastructure of power based on castles like that at Carrickfergus. Roads and bridges, such as the crossing over the Shannon at Athlone, facilitated trade as well as Norman expansion westwards into Roscommon and Galway. A silver coinage was introduced in the 1180s and a royal bureaucracy in Dublin upheld the law. The Church in Ireland was also bound to adhere to English administrative patterns. By the 1280s, much of Ireland was held by families that either supported or acquiesced with the Anglo-Norman writ. Native Irish control was limited to the south-west and the lands of the Ui Neill in the north.

Above: Built in 1177, the castle at Carrickfergus was key in maintaining Anglo-Norman control over the island of Hibernia.

THE BRUCE INVASION

Irish resistance to the Anglo-Norman invaders increased after 1280 but was helped by the temporary interference of the Scots in Irish affairs. From 1315 to 1318, Edward Bruce, brother of King Robert, led a powerful army against the centres of English power in Ireland. For the Scots, this was a brief episode in their long struggle to force Edward II to the negotiating table. Many Irish lords initially sided with the Scots, and the three-year campaign did much to loosen the Anglo-Norman grip on Ireland. Key Anglo-Norman settlements in central Ireland were destroyed – the English frontier post of Athlone was so severely damaged in 1315 that it disappeared from the medieval record.

BEYOND THE PALE

After the chaos of the Bruce intervention, the English Crown struggled to retain its former dominance in Ireland. The Black Death seems to have also weakened English settlers in the towns more than the dispersed Gaelic population in the countryside. By 1400, several royal fortresses had either been lost or were now held by Anglo-Irish lords who pursued their own interests, assimilated with the native Gaelic population and adopted the Irish language and customs. Laws to preserve the distinct 'Englishness' of the ruling elite such as the 1367 Statutes of Kilkenny were ignored. By 1400, effective English control was limited to the Pale, the heavily fortified lands around Dublin. Beyond the Pale, Gaelic lords ruled Ireland. They were little troubled by the royal officials in Dublin nor by futile military expeditions from England, such as that led by Richard II in 1399.

TIMELINE

1169	*Arrival of the Earl of Pembroke's forces at Bannow Bay*
1170	*Pembroke ends the old 'Norse' kingdom of Dublin*
1171	*Henry II lands at Waterford*
1180–1280	*Normanization of the eastern counties*
1350–1400	*Rise of Gaelic and Anglo-Irish lords*
1377	*Statutes of Kilkenny to prevent the Gaelicization of the elite.*

MEDIEVAL WALES
1066–1350

The overwhelming resources that the English enjoyed meant that they usually held the initiative in Welsh affairs. After two centuries of struggle, the Welsh lost their political independence in the 1280s, but their language and sense of separate nationhood were secured.

THE MARCHER LORDS

Duke William made no attempt to invade Wales and was initially happy to work with amenable Welsh princes like Rhys ap Tewdwr who he met in 1081. The longer term Norman policy towards Wales lay in the establishment of the marcher or border lordships. Here, a strong man like Roger the Great, Earl of Shrewsbury, could rule almost independently of the English Crown. Marcher lords had a privileged status, with rights that were elsewhere reserved for the king. They could encharter towns, build castles and wage war without royal permission. Although the marchers avoided direct confrontation with Welsh princes who had an understanding with the English Crown, the military resources at their disposal ensured that the land under independent Welsh control was almost always under pressure in the 11th and 12th centuries. As in Ireland, Norman penetration into Wales was underpinned by the extensive construction of *mottes* (fortifications) and new towns, often manned by Flemish settlers as in Pembrokeshire.

TIMELINE	
1070s	Roger the Great becomes marcher Earl of Shrewsbury
1109	Henry I extends English influence deep into Wales
1129	Cistercian abbey founded at Neath in Glamorgan
1260	Llywelyn recognized as Prince of Wales in Treaty of Montgomery
1282	Death of Llywelyn, the last independent Welsh prince
1280s	Edward I conquers northern Wales.

THE ABSORPTION OF THE WELSH CHURCH

The wider cultural influence of the Normans can be seen in the fate of the traditional Welsh patterns of church administration. Welsh prelates had gradually accustomed themselves to Roman usages in the 8th and 9th centuries, but Welsh church leaders had retained a high degree of local autonomy. That independence was to end as the Normans stamped their cultural authority upon southern Britain. After 1100, Welsh ecclesiastical

Below: French monks were invited to found Cistercian abbeys, such as that at Margam in West Glamorgan, which became local centres of commerce and learning.

THE CULTURAL FLOWERING

The loss of political independence in the 1280s posed a serious threat to the Welsh language, which might have been swept away by the power language of Anglo-French. In fact, the succeeding decades witnessed a flowering of Welsh literature that reached its zenith in the work of Dafydd ap Gwilym, (1315–1350) one of the great poets of medieval Europe. The success of Welsh as an intellectual medium at this time reflected the complex interplay of identities in Wales, a feature of life in much of medieval Britain. As in Ireland, Anglo-Norman lords assimiliated with, and ultimately sponsored, the local culture. Contact with the Norman world also exposed Welsh poets to rich continental influences, such as the Provençal songs that echo in Dafydd's amorous and pastoral works.

foundations were gathered under the control of bishops who looked to Canterbury for leadership. However, Wales benefited from the expansion of the Cistercian order in the early 12th century, whose monks set up houses throughout Europe to exploit local farming and commercial skills. Norman and Welsh lords recognized the economic and spiritual value of these energetic and practical men, inviting them to found abbeys at Neath, Margam and at Strata Florida near Tregaron.

LLYWELYN THE LAST

Powerful kings who took a keen interest in Welsh affairs, such as Henry I in the 12th century, could expect to enforce their wishes. Henry took important Welsh centres such as Carmarthen in 1109 and extracted temporary obeisance from the northern Welsh in 1121. Like the Scots however, Welsh princes were quick to spot moments of English weakness. Numerous strongholds were liberated whilst the English were distracted by civil war in the 1140s. Llywelyn the Great razed several English castles and settlements and even dared to win back Gwent in the 1230s. Llywelyn ap Gruffydd 'the Last' continued his work, winning back much territory lost to the marcher lords. Llywelyn skilfully exploited English divisions in the 1260s to extract the title of Prince of Wales in the Treaty of Montgomery, a recognition by the English Crown that its writ did not run far in Wales.

A CONQUERED PEOPLE

This highpoint in Welsh fortunes was short-lived. In the 1270s and 1280s Gwynedd, the heartland of Welsh resistance to Roman, Saxon and Norman alike, was invaded and pinned down by the greatest chain of castles in

Right: The head of Llwelyn ap Gruffydd, known as 'Our Last Leader' by the Welsh, is said to have been paraded through the streets of London after his defeat in 1282.

medieval Europe. Unlike the Scots, with their great northern hinterland, there was nowhere now where the Welsh could retreat and regroup but the high wilds of Snowdonia. Later Welsh revolts by Madog in 1295 and Llywelyn Bren in 1316 were put down with ease. Wales was now essentially under the rule of the English Crown. English criminal law was introduced and English forms of shire administration were imposed. Nevertheless, Welsh identity was secure. Gerald of Wales had already described the elements of Welsh *cymry*, the shared culture, language and sense of nationhood that bound the Welsh together.

MEDIEVAL SCOTLAND
1100–1450

Throughout the Middle Ages, there were several political entities in Scotland, for the King of Scots had little power beyond the central and eastern lowlands. In the west and north, Gaelic and Norse cultures each produced their own civilization and a different identity.

NORMANIZED SCOTLAND

A French visitor to the kingdom of the Scots in 1250 would have felt very much at home. Knightly families, with names such as Bruce, Menzies, Hay, and Stewart that betrayed their recent Anglo-Norman origins, held much of the better land. Royal sheriffs enforced the king's laws. Trade was regulated by royal charter and stimulated by silver coinage. The king and his elite used Latin, French and increasingly some 'Inglis'. Familiar ecclesiastical orders such as the Benedictines and Cistercians were at work improving the souls and the landscapes of Scotland. This Scotland had been thoroughly Normanized, a fact that probably accounted for its survival in the face of sustained pressure from its larger southern neighbour.

TRADING SUCCESS

Normanization made the Scottish kingdom very productive. Ports such as Berwick, Aberdeen and Dundee enjoyed a thriving export trade to Europe in timber, fish, leather hides and wool. Coals from Fife and the Lothians were also sent to London. In the 1370s, over two million fleeces were exported each year. Companies of German and Flemish wool merchants lived in their own 'national' halls within the walled seaport of Berwick, which annually contributed the vast sum of over £2,000 in customs duties to the Scottish treasury. Across the North Sea, staples or ports with a special relationship with the Scottish Crown such as Bruges, and later Middelburg, prospered from their monopoly trade in Scottish commodities. By 1400, Scots merchants were a common sight in the Hansa cities of northern Europe and in the market towns of Scotland's French ally. Scholars such as Duns Scotus and Michael Scotus were equally common in the colleges of France, Italy and the Low Countries. The relative economic success of the Scottish kingdom, despite its limited resources, was due to the willingness of its rulers to adopt new ideas from abroad and welcome settlers with new ideas.

Above: Jedburgh Abbey near the Scottish borders was occupied by Edward I and his troops during the invasion of 1296.

GAELIC SCOTLAND

Another Scotland existed above the Highland line and in the islands of the north and west. Gaelic and Norn were spoken here, rather than Inglis and Scots. Over time the Celtic and Norse elements in the Highland population had mingled to produce a rich Gaelic civilization that cherished music, poetry and storytelling. The arts of war were also valued, and as the medieval Gaelic Highlands were populous, this posed a problem for their Scottish neighbours. The King of Scotland in far-off Dunfermline held little sway here. Power here lay in the hands of the great chiefs, such as the charismatic Somerled, who led his impressive force of Gaelic, Norse and Irish warriors deep in to the Clyde valley in 1154. The Scottish King William the Lion struggled for years to subdue the men of Ross, Caithness and Sutherland. More skilful monarchs, such as Alexander II and Robert I, realized that an honoured place had to be found at their courts for the influential Gaelic princes as well as for the Norman lords who held the Lowlands.

Below: William I of Scotland, known as William the Lion, spent his long reign in perpetual struggle with the chieftains of the north.

THE LORDS OF THE ISLES

The long wars between Scotland and England from 1296 to 1357 gave Highland chieftains an opportunity to build up their power. Chiefs such as the MacDonalds who backed the victorious House of Bruce were rewarded with lands and influence. By 1400, the MacDonald Lord of the Isles controlled almost all of western Scotland. Thanks to their strong army and fleet of swift birlinns (galleys), the MacDonalds were almost as powerful as the King of Scots. A MacDonald army that was set on sacking the rich burgh of Aberdeen was only stopped with great difficulty at the bloody battle of Harlaw in 1411. In 1462, John MacDonald even entered into an alliance with Edward IV of England and plotted with him to divide the lowland kingdom of Scotland in two.

THE END OF NORSE SCOTLAND

Until the 1260s, much of western Scotland still owed allegiance to the king of Norway in Bergen and the Bishop of Trondheim. After the failure of Haakon IV's expedition at Largs in 1263, Norway abandoned the Hebrides, selling them to Scotland three years later for 4,000 merks and an annual quit-rent of 100 merks. The impecunious Christian of Denmark pawned the rights to Orkney and Shetland in 1468–69. This signalled the end of the Scandinavian age in Scotland, although the Norse dialect of Norn was still spoken in the north into the 1700s.

TIMELINE	
1154	*Lowland Scotland invaded by Somerled's Gaelic army*
1170s	*William the Lion campaigns in the northern counties*
1249–86	*'Golden Age' under Alexander III*
1266	*Magnus VI cedes the Hebrides and Isle of Man to Scotland*
1295–1356	*Scotland invaded by Edward I, II and III*
1462	*Lord of the Isles plots with Edward IV to divide Scotland*
1468–9	*Scottish Crown acquires Orkney and Shetland from Denmark.*

THE PLANTAGENET DREAM OF EMPIRE
1277–1357

Early Norman kings looked on their lands as their personal possessions. In the late 13th century however, Edward I tried to realize the Saxon Athelstan's dream of a unified empire throughout Britain. The Plantagenet king launched himself against Scotland and Wales with an unprecedented degree of belligerence.

LONGSHANKS

Edward ascended the English throne in 1272. At the mature age of 33, he had witnessed the disappointing later reign of his father Henry III, years marked by defeat in France and the humiliating baronial revolt led by Simon de Montfort. Once king, Edward was keen to divert the energies of his barons into war, but the situation in France offered no realistic prospect of success. In any case, Edward appreciated that the questions of Welsh and Scottish independence had first to be resolved, before tackling the re-conquest of the French lands.

THE CRUSHING OF THE WELSH

Edward's military operations against Gwynedd in 1277 were conducted on an unprecedented scale, and designed to fulfil his imperial objectives. Great attention was paid to enforcing public acts of homage to Edward after his victories. Thereafter, the rebels of 1282 were treated with unexpected savagery and accorded the public torture and execution usually reserved for traitors. The massive fortifications erected by Edward's military architect, Master James of St George, cast an inescapable shadow across the Welsh landscape.

The speed and extent of anglicization after 1282 made it clear that Edward was intent on creating a wholly subservient position for Wales within a greater English realm. This limited status was underlined by the bestowal of the title Prince of Wales, now merely honorific, upon his English heir in 1301.

Above: The Plantagenet King Edward I led a ruthless campaign against the Welsh rebels. He kept his new territory secure with a network of fortifications.

TIMELINE	
1282	*Execution of David, last of the Welsh rebels*
1283	*Harlech, Conwy and Caernarfon castles begun by Edward I*
1284	*Wales absorbed into English legal framework*
1297	*William Wallace defeats English at Stirling Bridge*
1301	*Title of Prince of Wales bestowed upon the Plantagenet prince*
1314	*Scottish independence secured by victory at Bannockburn.*

OVERLORD OF SCOTLAND

The failure of the Scottish royal line in the 1280s invited Edward to turn his attention northwards. Edward's preferred solution to the Scottish question was diplomatic. In 1289 he planned to unite the kingdoms through a marriage between his son and Margaret, the heiress to the Scottish throne. These plans were thwarted by her mysterious death in Orkney the following year. As numerous rival claimants to the Scottish crown came forward, Edward used his advantage to force the Scottish nobility to recognize him as feudal overlord of Scotland, then promptly selected John Balliol as king. Edward expected Balliol to accept his role as puppet king with gratitude and support his military operations in France. He was therefore outraged when Balliol negotiated independently with Philip IV of France in 1295.

HAMMER OF THE SCOTS

Edward's response was ruthless. Scotland was to be reduced from a sovereign kingdom to a personal fief. The rich trading port of Berwick was sacked and its inhabitants massacred without exception, an event that horrified Europe. Over 1,500 leading Scots were publicly required to put their seal to an oath of personal loyalty to Edward. The Great Seal of Scotland, the legal symbol of Scotland's independence, was shattered. The records and charters of Scotland were removed to London, as were the Scottish regalia including the Stone of Destiny used in the inauguration of the King of Scots. Scotland's holy relics, including the Black Rood of St Margaret, were scattered. In Edward's correspondence, Scotland was henceforth referred to as a mere lordship rather than as a kingdom. Publicly humiliated and forced to abdicate, Balliol was to be the last King of Scots. Henceforth Scotland would be ruled by an English governor.

SCOTTISH NATIONAL RESISTANCE

Edward's ruthlessness, and the actions of his sheriffs in Scotland, sparked a national revolt led at first by Andrew, Earl of Moray, and William Wallace, a minor lowland landowner. With Edward in Flanders, they defeated an English army at Stirling Bridge in 1297 and Wallace proceeded to raid northern England. Edward was able to crush the Scots the following summer, but only at the cost of suspending operations in France. Once captured in 1305, Wallace met the same fate as Edward's Welsh adversaries. Following Edward's death in 1307, and the resolution of the power struggle amongst the Scottish barons in favour of the House of Bruce, the next phase of Scottish resistance began. Now the experienced warrior King Robert I flew the banners of Scotland. A successful guerrilla campaign between 1307 and 1314 gave Robert the Bruce control of almost every castle in Scotland. In the eye of his people, Robert's crushing victory over Edward II at Bannockburn confirmed that he was the true King of Scots. In the 1330s and 1340s, Edward III continued his grandfather's policy of harrying the Scots, but only succeeded in strengthening their sense of national identity and collective resolve.

Below: At his trial in London, a defiant Wallace rejected the charge of treason against Edward for he had never sworn homage to the English king.

THE BLACK DEATH
1348–51

In the early 14th century Britain enjoyed economic growth, visible in new towns, increased trade and the farming of marginal land. The boom ended in 1348 with the arrival of the bubonic plague – the 'Black Death' – that brought horrific suffering in the short-term and a longer term challenge to the old social and political order.

'SEEDS OF TERRIBLE PESTILENCE'

Following the Italian trade routes from the Black Sea to western Europe, the Black Death reached Britain in June 1348. Melcombe in Dorset was probably the first place in England to be infected, thanks to a merchant crew who carried the disease from Gascony. From there it spread through the West Country, exacting its heaviest toll in Bristol where the town annalist recorded that 'the living were scarce able to bury the dead and grass grew in the High St'. So many priests fell victim to the plague that there were too few to bury the dead and the Bishop of Bath and Wells was forced to permit all Christians, even women, to hear the confession of the dying.

Above: Victims of the bubonic plague became covered in boils and their skin blackened. They faced a gruesome – if mercifully quick – death.

'OUR GREAT GRIEF OF 1349'

The plague moved through central and southern England in the late spring and summer of 1349. By July, it had spread to the northern shires. At Oxford, the local chronicler recorded that 'the school doors were shut, colleges and halls relinquished and none scarce left to keep possession'. At Winchester, the population fell from eight to two thousand. The narrow lanes and cesspools of London provided an especially welcoming environment for the rats and fleas that carried the disease. New cemeteries were opened at Smithfield and Spittle Croft but were soon overflowing. An estimated 30,000 of London's population of 70,000 perished. The rich fled the towns for sanctuary in the countryside, but there was little relief there either. In the village of Crawley in Hampshire the population fell from 400 to 150 and only returned to its pre-plague level in the 1850s.

'THE ROOTLESS PHANTOM'

The Welsh poet Jeuan Gethin, who himself died suddenly in 1349, left a chilling record of the fear that swept across Britain in the year of the plague:

'We see death coming into our midst like black smoke, a plague which cuts off the young, a rootless phantom which has no mercy for fair countenance. Woe is me of the shilling in the armpit...the burden carried under the arms...a white lump...a small boil that spares no one... a burning cinder...an ugly eruption that comes with unseemly haste.'

'SEYNT ANDREW SCHELD US'

In August 1349, the Archbishop of Armagh reported to the Pope that while the plague had carried off two-thirds of the English, the Scots had been miraculously spared. Indeed, the Scots looked on the events of 1349 as divine retribution for all the damage done to them by their southern neighbours. To take advantage of their immunity, a Scots army assembled at Selkirk near the border with the intention of adding to English woes. It promptly contracted 'the foul deth of the Yngles' and the rapid dispersal of terror-stricken troops helped spread the disease throughout southern Scotland. Nevertheless Scottish chroniclers consistently recorded lower levels of fatality than elsewhere in Europe. The cold winter of 1349 may have contained the rats and fleas, and the disease may have travelled less easily through a land in which large settlements were few and far apart. Similarly in Ireland, the Anglo-Irish who lived in towns were badly afflicted, yet the indigenous Irish in the uplands seem to have been spared.

LIFE AFTER THE DEATH

The 'great mortality' faded in the latter months of 1350, but returned in 1361 and again in the 1370s and 1380s. It left a profound mark on English society and its economy. The plagues hit the urban poor hardest, although those workmen and artisans who survived found a greatly increased demand for their services and could demand greater reward. Parliament responded by passing laws to try and contain the rising wages of labourers. Church leaders bemoaned the rise in criminality, especially in London and the larger towns, and lamented the change in moral attitudes amongst the survivors who were determined to enjoy their good fortune. Parliament again responded by passing laws, this time to try and restrain the newly enriched lower orders from wearing the clothes that had once been the preserve of their betters. It was often the middling folk that proved nimble enough to benefit from the economic dislocation. The traditional elites now had to accommodate a wealthier middle class that was quick to question authority and revelled at Chaucer's mocking of traditional values in his *Canterbury Tales*.

Below: Despite prayers and self-flagellation, the plague wiped out large sectors of the population. It led to profound changes in society, particularly among the hard-hit urban workers.

DYNASTIC STRIFE
1450–1499

The kings of England and Scotland had often worn their crowns uneasily. Henry II and Henry III had to make important concessions to their barons. Edward II and Richard II lost their crowns and their lives to aristocratic rivals. However, the War of the Roses was a crisis of a different scale and disturbed the stability of England for decades.

Above: The House of Lancaster was represented by a red rose and the House of York by a white. Both houses were descendants of the Plantagenet kings, embroiled in a dynastic struggle.

THE ROOT CAUSE

The civil war that dominated events in England after 1450 was not unique. France, Spain and Scotland were also riven by factional intrigue at this time. However, the struggle between the houses of York and Lancaster lasted for more than three decades and seriously weakened the government of England. The war stemmed from the deposition and murder of Richard II in 1399 and the usurpation of the crown by his cousin Bolingbroke, who became Henry IV. The new king made good his weak claim to the crown by quashing the rebellions of Owain Glyndwr in Wales and the Percy magnates in the north. The brief reign of Henry V was so successful that the question of the legality of his rule was overlooked. It was only the disastrous years under the incompetent Henry VI that brought the right of the House of Lancaster to govern under scrutiny.

FORTUNES OF WAR

In the first phase of the war, Richard of York pressed his superior claim to the throne, but was defeated at Wakefield in 1460. Richard's son avenged his father at Towton the following year. With the support of the 'kingmaker', the Earl of Warwick, he ruled for the next nine years as Edward IV. When Warwick switched to the Lancastrian cause in 1470, Edward found himself deposed and exiled in Burgundy. Henry VI was briefly restored until Edward returned the next spring and defeated Warwick at Barnet, and Henry's tenacious wife Margaret at Tewkesbury in 1471. Henry was murdered in the Tower of London and Edward ruled cautiously until his early death in 1483. His brother, Richard III, was a brave soldier but a poor politician who failed to build a coalition of support. Henry Tudor defeated Richard at Bosworth in 1485 and sought to unify his realm, but Yorkist pretenders and plots appeared sporadically until the end of the century.

Above: The Lancastrian King Henry VI was imprisoned by Edward of York in the Tower of London and murdered there in 1471.

THE COST OF CIVIL WAR

England was badly damaged by these years of conflict. The battles involved larger armies than any seen on British soil before. The war was also especially brutal, as the public mutilation of Richard of York's body attests, and even contemporaries were shocked by the bloodshed. Government descended into faction, and blood feuds such as that between the York and Beaufort clans disfigured whole regions. As the war lurched from one phase to the next, there was no shortage of English exiles at the courts of France and Burgundy looking for troops and support. Now it was the turn of the English countryside to bear the brunt of foreign-sponsored mercenary armies.

RULERS OF ENGLAND 1399–1485

LANCASTER	*Henry IV 1399–1413*
LANCASTER	*Henry V 1413–22*
LANCASTER	*Henry VI 1422–1453 (falls ill)*
YORK	*Protector Richard, Duke of York, 1453–1455*
LANCASTER	*Henry VI restored to power in 1455–1461 (deposed)*
YORK	*Edward IV 1461–1470 (deposed)*
LANCASTER	*Henry VI restored to power in 1470–1471 (murdered)*
YORK	*Edward IV regains power in 1471–1483*
YORK	*Edward V April–June 1483 (disappears)*
YORK	*Richard III 1483–1485 (dies in battle).*

THE DOUGLAS THREAT

For once, the Scots were unable to take advantage of English disarray, for the Stewart kings had aristocratic difficulties of their own. In the west, John MacDonald Lord of the Isles had ambitions to act as a potentate on a British stage. More persistent still was the challenge from the powerful House of Douglas, which had the tools to catch the kingdom. Their intricate family network ensured obligations and loyalty in every part of the realm, as well as entrance to strongholds like the massive Tantallon in Lothian. In 1400, the most powerful man in Scotland was not the monarch but Archibald the Grim, the Douglas earl who could insult the Stewart kings with impunity from his fortress of Threave. To counter this threat, the Stewarts had to invest heavily in troops and artillery and raise up a new breed of dependable nobles such as the Earls of Campbell. Although the Douglases were decisively crushed in the 1450s, Scottish kings had to be wary of disaffected nobles if they were not to share the fate of James III, defeated and murdered at Sauchieburn in 1488 by an army of his vassals.

Below: James III of Scotland (r. 1460–88) was unpopular for pursuing a policy of alliance with England. He was defeated and killed by an army that included his son, the future King James IV, at Sauchieburn.

POPULATION AND ECONOMY
1100–1400

The High Middle Ages were once seen as a period little affected by social or economic change, where serfs tilled the land unceasingly while feudal lords trained for war. That fanciful picture has given way to a clearer understanding of the dynamism of the medieval economy and the changing society that it served.

HOW MANY SOULS?

The fragmented nature of the surviving sources mean that it is difficult to calculate the population of medieval Britain with precision. Extrapolations from the *Domesday Book* suggest that the number living in England rose from around one million in 1086 to about four million in 1290. Over the same period, Scotland's population is thought to have grown from around 500,000 to about a million by the time of the English invasion in 1296, and there were probably between three and four hundred thousand people living in Wales at the time of Llywelyn the Last in the 1280s. England was therefore the most populous and, by some degree, the richest part of medieval Britain. However, it is useful to remember that around twenty million people lived in mid 14th-century France, and that at times almost half of these were subjects of the English king.

Below: Far from being a phenomenon of the Industrial Age, migration to the towns, especially London, was strong during the Middle Ages. However, the vast majority of the population worked the land.

THE GROWING TOWNS

Until the setbacks of famines around 1315 and the epidemics after 1349, the towns of medieval Britain generally experienced continual and at times rapid growth after 1100. With more than 70,000 souls in 1300, London was unrivalled amongst British towns. The next largest 'English' town was Bordeaux in Gascony, with more than 30,000. York with 15,000 and Bristol and Dublin with around 10,000 were in the next division. Scottish towns were smaller yet, a reflection of the dispersal of the Scottish population throughout the kingdom. The largest burghs in Scotland – Berwick, Aberdeen and fast-rising Edinburgh – each held less than 5,000 inhabitants. With the rise of pilgrimage traffic after 1250, cathedral centres such as Lincoln, Canterbury and St Andrews in Fife grew steadily in size, but the most noticeable growth was in the number of commercial market towns. By 1290 there were over 600 English chartered boroughs and over 2,400 settlements holding markets. However, despite the increasing wealth generated by towns in this period, only around ten per cent of the population of Britain lived in a town setting. Most of our medieval ancestors were peasants.

VILLAGE LIFE

Our received view of medieval rural life as static and unchanging is an inaccurate one, for the period between 1100 and 1400 saw great changes in the British countryside. There was an increased variety in farming practice and new technologies had a beneficial impact on food production. In many parts of England the classic open-field system of arable strip farming was practised, and the communal runrig (ridge and furrow) system was common throughout medieval Scotland. However, medieval landowners and tenant farmers were often quicker to adapt their methods and practices to the prevailing geography and market conditions than some historians have imagined. The rising population before 1350 created demand and strong prices for agricultural products, and so the area of managed land, both arable and pastoral, grew relentlessly. Typical of the agricultural dynamism of the period was the introduction of windmills in the late 12th century. These had many uses, but were especially invaluable in helping to drain the flatter lands of eastern Britain. The substitution of horses for oxen, through resisted in Scotland, allowed farmers to plough faster and over larger acreages. After 1400, the decline in serfdom, and the relative scarcity and high cost of farm labourers, encouraged many landowners to concentrate on pastoral farming, which needed fewer hands.

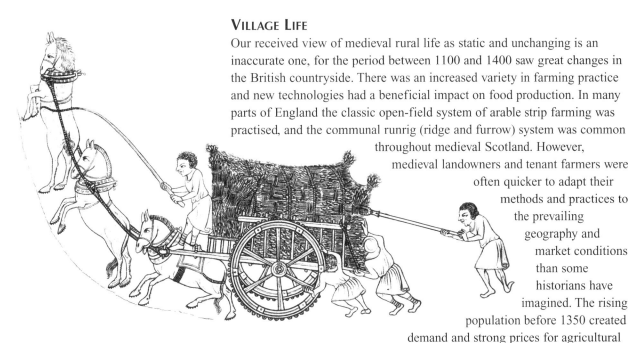

Above: The life of the medieval rural peasant saw many changes between 1100–1400, as farming practices evolved and plague swept through the country.

A GROWING CASH ECONOMY

In the early feudal system, land was granted in exchange for military service or labour services. In England, these obligations were soon commuted into cash payments. By 1150, tenants regularly paid a cash rent to their landlord on many larger estates. Many lords, including the Crown, increasingly preferred money payments with which they could hire specialist troops. Royal officials also preferred obligations paid in cash as tax rather than as acts of service. To oil the growing cash economy, royal mints issued ever-larger amounts of currency and the range of services that could be bought for cash multiplied. In the towns, occupations became more specialized.

WOOL AND TRADE

The export of wool, and after 1375 of woollen cloth, became the single biggest contributor to both the English Exchequer and the Scottish treasury by 1450. Trade links with Europe expanded on the back of the wool trade. Ships from southern English ports did good business in the wine trade with Gascony and Portugal. Eastern ports such as Boston, the leading centre of the wool shipping trade, looked towards the textile markets in the Low Countries while the Scots, despite their political links with France, increasingly traded with Denmark and the Baltic world.

CULTURE AND IDENTITY
1350–1500

The later Middle Ages saw a rise in national sentiment, stimulated by the wars in Britain and France. The international possibilities latent in an earlier, more feudal, period evaporated. The wars also helped the gradual evolution of the English Parliament into a national body.

Left: The third version of the *Magna Carta* issued under King Henry III in 1225, setting out the powers of the monarch and parliament.

KINGS OF ONE NATION

In the 12th century, Henry I of England and David I of Scotland might have exchanged thrones and been happily accepted as king by their new subjects. By the 14th century however, monarchs were already becoming more closely identified with a sense of specific national identity that intensified after 1400. Henry V could not have sat comfortably in 'Dunfermline toun' for long. The English desire to rule all of Britain played its part in promoting Welsh and Scottish nationalism. English nationalism received a similar boost from the wars with France. The Hundred Years War started as a feudal contest for land and title, but ended as a struggle between embryonic nation-states. As a result of losing to France, England was much more insular in 1480 than it had been in 1180, but was arguably more inclined to take an interest in British affairs.

Below: King John (r. 1199–1216), son of Henry II, shown signing the first version of the *Magna Carta* in 1215.

IDENTITY AND LIBERTY

Earlier historians traditionally oversimplified the changing relationship between medieval kings and their subjects. However, by 1450, the idea that a king should consult with his councils and parliaments on important matters stood on slightly firmer ground, even if a powerful and charismatic king with cash reserves could still do as he pleased. The period witnessed the painfully slow and almost imperceptible evolution of Parliament from royal council into a body with a national remit. The Crown lost ground when forced to acknowledge the limitations of royal power expressed in the *Magna Carta* and the *Oxford and Westminster Provisions* of 1258–59. Privileges and responsibilities very gradually accrued to Parliament, such as its 1362 right to agree the levels of duty on wool. Parliament was slowly becoming one of the focus points in the tangled English constitution. The narrative of Richard II's fall from power was played out in a series of parliaments, by turn critical or supportive of the king. Again, long wars often forced impecunious kings to approach Parliament in a reasonably

WRITERS AND IDENTITY

With increased literacy, the written word played a greater part in shaping national consciousness. To counter claims of ancient English overlordship, a school of Scottish historians was encouraged to prove that Scotland had always been a distinct and sovereign nation. Epic literature preserved the glories of Wallace and Bruce, but heroes without poetic representation, such as Andrew Moray, slipped into obscurity. Bards were honoured at the court of the Llywelyns for their propaganda value as much as for their artistic qualities. In England, the triumph of the vernacular over Latin and French was crucial. Chaucer's *Canterbury Tales* and William Langland's *Piers Plowman* were important in the development of an emerging cultural confidence. The anti-clerical and social reformist sentiments in these works, echoing the teachings of Wycliffe and the Lollards, signal the gradual development of a more complex, less deferential society.

Above right: The young Richard II sailed down the Thames to meet the leaders of the Peasants' Revolt, but was unable to land because of their numbers. A later meeting at Smithfield ended in the execution of the rebel leaders.

respectful tone. In the 1320 Declaration of Arbroath, the community of the realm of Scotland even stated that the king was made 'by the due consent and assent of us all' and that the people might jettison a king who abandoned the laws and customs of the kingdom.

THE PEASANTS' REVOLT, 1381

The imposition of a poll tax in 1379 to help fund the war in France sparked riots that spread through England and culminated in the march of a rebel host on London. Manor records were burned and unpopular officials were made to pay for their zeal in collecting tax revenues. The crisis was only defused when the boy king Richard II met the rebel leaders at Smithfield and pretended to meet their demands before rounding them up and executing them.

The rebellion drew its support from a wider spectrum of English society than its name suggests. Although primarily a protest against unjust economic conditions, the revolt was prompted by a wide interplay of concerns and fears. Changes to traditional agricultural practices, the uncertainty of life in the wake of the Black Death and the disappointment and expense of the French campaigns all contributed to the unrest. As a result, the Peasants' Revolt gives us a rare and fleeting glance into the mentality of the ordinary population of medieval Britain, whose lives and concerns are seldom reflected in the surviving records.

TIMELINE

1215	*Nobles impose limits on power of King John through* Magna Carta
1320	*Declaration of Arbroath asserts Scottish independence*
1337–1453	*Hundred Year's War intensifies feelings of English nationalism*
c. 1370	Piers Plowman *written by William Langland*
1375	*John Barbour, the Scottish poet, writes the epic poem* The Brus
1380–1390s	*Geoffrey Chaucer writes* The Canterbury Tales.

THREE RENAISSANCE KINGS
1485–1547

On both sides of the border, Tudor and Stewart kings sought to meet the ideal of the Renaissance prince who governed firmly but wisely and encouraged the arts and sciences to flourish.

HENRY VII (R. 1485–1509)

Henry Tudor inherited a kingdom exhausted by three decades of dynastic feuding. The royal treasury was empty and frequent changes of monarch had debased the office of kingship. Despite his marriage to Elizabeth of York in 1486, Henry's claim to the throne was weak. He was soon challenged by the pretender Lambert Simnel, backed by 8,000 Irish and Continental mercenaries under the command of the Yorkist Earl of Lincoln. Henry's narrow victory at the battle of Stoke in 1487, in which many of his aristocratic enemies conveniently fell, ended the Wars of the Roses.

Above: The marriage of Elizabeth of York to Henry Tudor symbolically reunited the houses of York and Lancaster after decades of war.

STRONG GOVERNMENT

Henry's first task was to put the royal finances on a sound footing. He took a personal interest in the work of his financial officers and by the end of his reign, annual Crown revenues had almost tripled to over £140,000. To secure the peace on which English prosperity depended, Henry's daughters were married into the Scottish and French royal houses. Good relations with France were payback for their help in sponsoring his invasion in 1485, but also ensured that Paris would be less likely to support future Yorkist plots.

STAR CHAMBER

Henry was determined to cut the English nobility down to size. Only the most loyal families were allowed to keep their regional fiefdoms. Justices of the Peace, unpaid magistrates drawn from the lesser gentry, increasingly upheld the king's laws in the shires. Eager to ally themselves with the Crown, these 'new men' were a dependable and relatively inexpensive counterweight to the great magnates. Laws against maintaining large households of liveried men reined back the private armies of the greater lords. Henry also used the court of Star Chamber to speed up cases that were becalmed in local courts, where prominent men could exert undue influence upon magistrates and witnesses. Meeting in secret, the Privy Councillors who sat as judges of the Star Chamber read cases presented as written testimony without recourse to witnesses or juries. There was no appeal against their decisions, even for the most noble of defendants.

Right: Of Henry's succession of wives, only Anne of Cleves (fourth from left) and Catherine Parr (far right) outlived him.

HENRY'S WIVES

Henry's marriage to the Spanish Catherine produced a daughter, as did his union with Boleyn. For giving birth to a son, Henry remembered Jane Seymour as his 'only true wife'. The execution of his second and fifth wives was a sign of Henry's growing despotism as much as his desperation to produce a male heir. Their killings were momentous political events at the tyrant's court, for Boleyn and Howard dragged many friends and relatives with them to the block.

JAMES IV (R. 1488–1513)

Speaking nine languages (Latin, Scots, Gaelic, French, German, Danish, Flemish, Italian and Spanish), James IV of Scotland was the Renaissance prince par excellence. James' commitment to learning was enshrined in the Act of 1496, requiring all freeholders to educate their sons at a grammar school until they had 'perfect Latin'. The king's interest in science resulted in the founding of the Royal College of Surgeons in 1505, as well as the establishment of modern gun foundries and dockyards. His flagship the *Great Michael,* launched in 1511, was the largest European ship of its day, weighing over 1,000 tons and carrying 300 guns. Not surprisingly, after subduing the semi-independent Lord of the Isles with a naval expedition into the western Highlands in 1493, James sat very securely upon his throne.

HENRY VIII (R. 1509–1547)

The reign of this young king began well, for he seemed to enjoy all the virtues expected in a Renaissance monarch. Contemporaries variously described him as athletic, intelligent, pious, well-read and companionable. He was a lavish patron of the arts, particularly music and architecture. Moreover, he inherited a full treasury and a prosperous realm at peace with its neighbours. In time however, Henry's lack of sustained interest in government led to his over-reliance upon his powerful ministers Thomas Wolsey and Thomas Cromwell. Parliament grew significantly in influence during his reign, for the semblance of national assent was needed to legitimize the king's religious and dynastic policies. Henry's need to sire a male heir and his consequent marital difficulties led him into conflict with the Papacy and the Catholic powers of Europe. Religious tensions boiled over into the Pilgrimage of Grace in 1536, an insurrection of northern Catholics unhappy with the break with Rome. Unprofitable wars in Scotland and France in the 1540s bankrupted the English Crown and led to currency depreciation and inflation. Henry's inability to secure his lineage (his only descendants were a sickly son and two daughters), was the greatest failure of his reign and ensured the extinction of the Tudor dynasty.

Below: Despite his reputation as a brutal husband and a despot, Henry VIII was a learned man and a great patron of the arts.

THE ENGLISH REFORMATION
1533–53

Although there had been earlier reform movements, Henry VIII's church reformation was motivated by dynastic rather than religious concerns. His break with Rome was to have serious repercussions throughout the British and Irish Isles and re-defined England's position in relation to the great Catholic powers of Europe.

WYCLIFFE AND THE LOLLARDS, 1350–1450

Calls for Church reform were heard in England throughout the later Middle Ages. One of the loudest voices was that of John Wycliffe, the Oxford theologian who wanted the Church to embrace the poverty of its apostolic origins. Wycliffe especially criticized the papacy and the rich monastic orders. To spread understanding of the Gospel, he also translated the New Testament into English. Wycliffe's ideas resonated in a society that was changing thanks to the growth of trade and the spread of literacy amongst 'the middling folk'. His emphasis upon personal piety and scripture as the sources of salvation, rather than obedience to the Church hierarchy, inspired the popular movement known as Lollardy or as 'mumbling' by its detractors. However, the espousal of Lollard ideas by the leaders of popular insurrections convinced the authorities that church reform would end in social turmoil. As a result, Lollards were persecuted and their leaders burnt as heretics. The movement went underground, but it had helped to prepare the English imagination for the momentous events of the 1530s.

Below: On the Continent, the Reformation under Martin Luther rebelled against the excesses of the Catholic Church, publicly burning a papal warning at Wittenberg in December 1520.

DEFENDER OF THE FAITH

As a social conservative and loyal Catholic, Henry VIII was intuitively hostile to the reformist ideas that blossomed throughout northern Europe in the wake of Martin Luther's 'protest' against the worst abuses of the Church. Henry even promulgated a defence of Catholic tradition and papal supremacy, though the work was probably written by the Catholic humanist Thomas More. A grateful Pope Leo X rewarded Henry's loyalty in 1521 with the title *Fidei Defensor*.

ENGLISH SUPREMACY

Little more than a decade later, Henry was embroiled in a struggle of will with Rome. Henry's urgent desire for a male heir led him to seek the annulment of his marriage to Catherine of Aragon. Pope Clement VII refused, fearful of Charles V, Holy Roman Emperor,

King of Spain, master of much of Italy and Catherine's uncle. Henry's mounting desperation resulted in his excommunication and his rejection of papal jurisdiction over the Church in England. A series of Acts in 1533 and 1534 defined England's clerical independence from Rome. Bishops were to be nominated by the sovereign. Appeals from English church courts could no longer be made to the Pope. By the Act of Supremacy, the monarch became 'the only Supreme Head' of the Church of England. Significantly, England was declared to be 'an empire' in itself, over which no foreign power had sovereignty. England would henceforth find itself in opposition not just to the papacy, but to the Catholic powers of Europe.

Above: In the 1530s, Henry VIII confiscated the land and assets of the wealthy monasteries across England, such as Rievaulx Abbey in North Yorkshire.

DISSOLUTION OF THE MONASTERIES

Laws such as the Treasons Act of 1534 ensured obedience to Henry's new ecclesiastical order. Dissenters were executed, notably Sir Thomas More, the king's old friend and Lord Chancellor who could not bring himself to endorse Henry's actions publicly. Statutes of 1536 and 1539 allowed Henry to dissolve the many monastic foundations throughout England and confiscate their rich assets and extensive lands. This pleased the growing reform faction at his court and should have enriched the royal coffer, had costly wars in Scotland and France not forced Henry to sell out to cash-rich nobles and merchants. As a result, large swathes of England were transferred from ecclesiastical to lay control.

PROTESTANT ENGLAND

Henry's reformation was essentially a 'top-down revolution' and administrative rather than devotional in nature, with Henry largely content to replace the Pope as head of the Church. An official bible in English was published in 1537, a move that encouraged the scriptural reflection favoured by Protestant reformers, but Henry shrank back from more profound doctrinal change. England only became a truly Protestant land during the short and troubled reign of Edward VI (1547–1553). The Lord Protector, Somerset, enforced the use of the *Book of Common Prayer* in 1549 and the use of English for church services. Under the Protectorate of Northumberland, the English Church took an even more radically Protestant form. The outward trappings of Catholic practice, such as clerical vestments, church decoration and the feasts of saints were reformed or abolished. Church doctrine and liturgy reflected the growing influence of the hard line Protestant preachers from Europe who now congregated in London and the larger English ports.

TIMELINE

1380	*John Wycliffe translates the Bible into English*
1534	*Refusal to acknowledge Henry as Head of the Church is made a treasonable act*
1536	*Smaller monasteries brought under royal control and dissolved*
1539	*Publication of the official Great Bible in English*
1549	Book of Common Prayer *introduced into English churches.*

REFORMATION THROUGHOUT BRITAIN
1535–70

The success of Protestantism in Scotland and Wales was an important step towards their eventual absorption within a British state. In Ireland the Reformation seemed successful, but it put down only shallow roots.

IRELAND, 1534–1541

Henry's break with Rome brought an immediate reaction from the Catholic lords of Ireland. A rebellion under the Earl of Kildare invited the Emperor Charles V to replace the heretic Henry as Lord of Ireland. However, once English control had been reasserted, the reformation of the Irish Church seemed to proceed satisfactorily. In 1537, the Irish Parliament recognized Henry's position as head of the Irish Church and agreed to the dissolution of the monasteries. The compliance of native lords was bought with a share of the proceeds. Four years later, the Parliament in Dublin acquiesced in Henry's promotion to King of Ireland. However, beyond the Pale, the bulk of the Irish population remained Catholic, and future Protestant monarchs in London would fear Ireland's potential as a springboard for foreign invasion.

WALES, 1534–1551

The Henrician Reformation was accepted quietly in Wales. The Welsh clergy swore the necessary oaths, and eviction from the monasteries was sweetened for many monks by new posts as parish priests that brought stipends and pensions. As in England, the Welsh gentry were the main beneficiaries when the Crown sold off monastic land. The compulsory use of the English Prayer Books of 1549 and 1552 posed a serious threat to the Welsh tongue, but William Salesbury's unofficial translations of the Gospels and Prayer Book defused the language issue. Thanks to these and later official translations in 1567 and 1588, Welsh made the transition from an oral culture to a printed one. Between 1536 and 1543, a series of Acts tying Wales into the English administrative system similarly met with little resistance. Many regretted the abolition of separate Welsh laws, but Welsh subjects of the Crown were at least now equal in all respects to the English under the law.

SCOTLAND, 1528–1560

The Reformation was more ideological and political in Scotland from the outset. Widespread literacy and links with England and the Low Countries meant that Protestant

TIMELINE	
1535–42	*Wales and England conjoined in legal terms*
1537	*Henry VIII 'replicates' his church reformation in Ireland*
1544–51	*'Rough Wooing' of Scotland by Henry VIII & Protector Somerset*
1560	*Scottish Parliament passes laws to abolish the old Church*
1567	*First translation of the complete Bible into Welsh.*

ideas spread quickly through the burghs of central and eastern Scotland. After the events in England in the 1530s, an international dimension cast its shadow over religious debates in Scotland. The dangerous neighbour to the south was now nominally Protestant, while Scotland's traditional ally France was staunchly Catholic. Reformers looked to London for support, while church leaders such as Cardinal Beaton were firmly in the French camp.

ENGLAND OR FRANCE?

In the 1540s Henry VIII and Protector Somerset tried to force the Scots to accept an alliance with England and forsake their ties with France. Repeated invasions resulted in plentiful booty and military success at the battle of Pinkie, but only strengthened anti-English sentiment. In desperation, Somerset played the Protestant British card, sponsoring pamphlets that encouraged the Scots to throw off the yoke of 'priests and frogges'. Neither propaganda nor intimidation worked. Instead the infant Queen Mary of Scotland was sent to France to marry the Dauphin. Her mother, Mary of Guise, held power in Scotland. A French force of 5,000 men garrisoned the vital port of Leith and French officials held key posts in the Scottish state. Scotland's position as the Catholic ally of France seemed secure.

THE PROTESTANT REVOLUTION, 1560

The switch to Protestantism in Scotland was sudden and, like in England, as much to do with power politics as religious ideals. Many Scots had stopped attending Catholic Mass during the 1550s, preferring to attend private prayer meetings instead. There was widespread support throughout Scotland for the 1557 Covenant that envisaged a reformed Church, and many Scots were horrified by the decision of the Catholic authorities to burn an 83-year-old priest as a heretic. Yet the key event in the Scottish Reformation was the accession of the Protestant Elizabeth as Queen of England in 1558. She was determined to bring Scotland firmly under English control.

Protestant firebrands such as the Calvinist John Knox were soon at work. Knox's Perth sermon against the worship of images in 1559 inspired the first of many Protestant mobs that summer who were intent on 'cleansing' their churches of objects of Catholic devotion. Simultaneously, English forces ousted the French from Leith under the dying eyes of Mary of Guise. As the Auld Alliance with France ended, the Three Estates of Scotland met in 1560 to pass a series of Acts that turned Scotland into a Protestant realm. The authority of the Pope was denied and the Catholic Mass was banned. The following year, the *Calvinist Book of Discipline* set out the strict teachings and practices of the new Reformed Kirk.

Above: The Scottish Calvinist reformer John Knox preached against the 'sinful' worship of images in the Catholic Church.

THE REGIMENT OF WOMEN
1553–1603

In an age when scripture and tradition emphasized the dominant position of men, three women were raised to the sovereign power. They faced a complex mixture of religious and dynastic concerns that flowed from the events of the Reformation.

'BLOODY MARY'

A devout Catholic, Mary had been barred from the succession and declared illegitimate when her father's marriage to Catherine of Aragon was annulled. Despite her attachment to the old Church, the country accepted her accession in 1553 and the plot to put the Protestant Lady Jane Grey on the throne quickly collapsed. Mary's reign was dominated by two aims: to restore the Catholic Church and produce a Catholic heir. Cranmer, the Protestant Archbishop of Canterbury, was executed and replaced by her adviser, Cardinal Pole. Almost three hundred Protestant 'heretics' were burned in the Marian persecution. Popular disaffection increased when she married Philip of Spain in 1554, a union that yielded no children, but sparked fears that England might become a province of the vast Habsburg Empire. In 1558, Mary's support for Spain in its war with France led to the loss of Calais, the last English possession in France. After several false pregnancies, she died unloved at the age of 42. Protestant England rejoiced.

Above: Sometimes referred to as 'the nine day queen', Lady Jane Grey was quickly deposed and sent to the block by the ascendant 'Bloody Mary'.

A REIGN OF TWO HALVES

The Catholic princess Mary Stewart faced a daunting task when she returned to Protestant Scotland from France in 1561. Nevertheless Mary's reign began well. Mary was intelligent, well educated and understood her precarious situation. She wore her religion 'lightly', celebrating the Catholic Mass privately but making no move to interfere with the popular national church. She carefully sided with her Protestant half-brother James Moray against the great Catholic magnates, the Gordon Earls of Huntly, in 1562. Skilful propaganda enhanced her popularity and defused the threat from Protestant preachers. By 1565, Mary, Queen of Scots, seemed secure. Her subsequent downfall stemmed from her need to produce an heir. Her marriage to her Catholic kinsman Henry Darnley, who had Tudor and Stewart blood in his veins, worried Scottish Protestants, who feared a Catholic dynasty. It also alarmed Elizabeth of England, for any issue from this union would have an enhanced claim to the English throne. After 1565, support for Mary evaporated. Darnley's mysterious death in an explosion

TIMELINE

1553	*Catholic Mary I accedes to the English throne*
1555–8	*Marian persecution of prominent English Protestants*
1558	*Accession of Protestant Elizabeth in England*
1561	*Mary Stewart accedes to the Scottish throne*
1567	*Mary Stewart loses control of Scotland and is forced to abdicate.*

and her marriage in a Protestant ceremony to his probable murderer Bothwell scandalized both Catholic and Protestant sections of the nobility. Her reign ended in forced abdication and imprisonment on the island fortress of Lochleven. After a melodramatic escape and a failed coup, Mary fled to England hoping for protection and support from her cousin Elizabeth. There she endured a further nineteen years of imprisonment until the continual rumours of Catholic conspiracies to put her on the English throne finally led Mary to the block at Fotheringhay in 1587.

ELIZABETHAN COMPROMISE

Elizabeth learned from the bitter religious conflicts that had characterized the reigns of her siblings. She herself had almost been destroyed by her false implication in a Protestant plot against Mary in 1554. Her solution was to compromise. As long as her subjects outwardly conformed to her moderately Protestant Church, she did not 'make windows into men's souls'. She herself was practical in religious matters and valued order and stability above doctrinal purity. Her forty-four years as queen gave the Church of England time to settle down into the national imagination and time for Protestantism to become an important element in English nationalism. Attempts to revive the fading flame of English Catholicism, such as the Northern Rising in 1569, were brutally suppressed. By the end of her long reign, only her very oldest subjects could remember the pre-reformation Catholic regime. She equally opposed any moves by Puritans that would have replaced the 'catholic' tone of her church with a more Presbyterian format on the Scottish model.

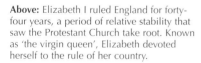

Above: Elizabeth I ruled England for forty-four years, a period of relative stability that saw the Protestant Church take root. Known as 'the virgin queen', Elizabeth devoted herself to the rule of her country.

THE VIRGIN QUEEN

Like all Tudor monarchs, Elizabeth was troubled by the problem of her succession. The example of her sister Mary's alliance with Spain reminded her that marriage to a foreign prince could upset the European balance of power and disrupt the internal security of the realm. Marriage to an English nobleman would also have sparked factional rivalries and divided her court. Elizabeth preferred to encourage a cult of devotion to the idea of the selfless monarch who put the needs of her people before her own happiness as a woman. Her lengthy progresses or tours around her kingdom were an important element in fostering the image of Gloriana. Architecture, music and drama flourished in the service of the State, as did the more ephemeral arts required for staging the appropriate ceremonies and processions that decorated and celebrated Elizabeth's reign.

THE UNION OF THE CROWNS
1503–1603

The existence of a sovereign, independent Scotland had always been a serious problem for the English Crown. Dynastic events after 1503 began the slow process of bringing Scotland within a united Britain.

THE THISTLE AND THE ROSE

In August 1503, James IV of Scotland married the English princess Margaret Tudor at Holyrood Abbey, then outside Edinburgh. Like many of his shrewder ancestors, Margaret's father Henry VII appreciated the importance of securing peace on England's northern border. By contrast, Scottish kings had often used marriage to European brides to highlight Scotland's independence and its links with Continental allies. The much vaunted 'union of the thistle and the rose' cemented the friendship between the two kings while Henry was alive, but after Henry's death in 1509, James was free to revive the 'Auld Alliance'. When Henry VIII invaded France in 1513, James came to the support of the French and marched with a vast army of over 26,000 men to his death at Flodden near Coldstream. Nevertheless he left a son, James V, who carried the Stewart and Tudor bloodlines. James and his descendants had a strong claim to the thrones of both kingdoms.

THE ROUGH WOOING

The low point in relations between Scotland and England came in the 1540s. In 1543, Henry VIII managed to get the Scottish nobles to agree to marry the infant Mary of Scotland to the Prince of Wales. After the marriage, Mary was to be held in England, with Henry acting as Lord Superior of Scotland. With Henry and his English garrisons in charge, Scotland could be held quiet and perhaps slowly absorbed under the English Crown, as Wales had been. However, Henry's plans were too ambitious even for those Scots who favoured the Protestant camp and the Scottish Parliament threw out the marriage treaty. Henry's response was invasion. In 1544, a war fleet under the Earl of Hertford sacked numerous towns in the Forth valley while an English army destroyed the rich border abbeys of Dryburgh, Jedburgh, Kelso and Melrose. Even Holyrood Palace, built by James IV for his English wife, was razed. The invasion was repeated the following year but this 'rough wooing' backfired. The Scots united against

TIMELINE	
1503	*Marriage of James IV to Margaret Tudor*
1513	*Death of James IV at Flodden Field near Coldstream*
1543	*Henry VIII tries to engineer the dynastic absorption of Scotland*
1544	*Hertford's 'rough wooing' or raids into Scotland*
1567	*Mary Stewart's marriage to Darnley produces an heir, James Stewart*
1586	*Treaty of Berwick aligns Scottish and English foreign policy*
1587	*Execution of Mary of Scotland at Fotheringhay Castle*
1603	*James VI of Scotland crowned as King of England*
1604	*James styles himself as King of Great Britain.*

Above: After the death of her first husband the Dauphin in 1560, Mary Stewart married Lord Darnley, with whom she had a son.

their common enemy and, thanks to French support, Henry's plans to forcibly unite the kingdoms failed.

James VI & I

Instead of becoming the Queen of England, in time Mary Stewart became Queen of France, although her brief marriage to Francis II was childless. Her second marriage to Lord Darnley did produce a male heir, whose claim to the English throne was impeccable. James VI was raised as a Protestant by his humanist tutor George Buchanan. In 1586, James took a step nearer the English throne by signing the Treaty of Berwick, promising to support Elizabeth in the event of an attack by Catholic France or Spain. He made only the most feeble protest when his mother was executed in 1587. Two years later, James reinforced his Protestant credentials by marrying the Lutheran Anne of Denmark. The childless Elizabeth made no public pronouncement about her successor, but she paid a generous annual pension to James throughout the last seventeen years of her reign. After her death in March 1603, an Accession Council set aside the weaker English claimants and declared James to be King of England. He and Anne were crowned in July. Significantly, once he had acquired the English throne, James had Fotheringhay Castle razed to the ground and his mother's remains transferred to Westminster Abbey.

The Gunpowder Plot, 1605

After 1603, English Catholics were especially fearful of their zealously Protestant monarch from Scotland. There were several Catholic plots to assassinate James before the famous conspiracy to blow up the Palace of Westminster while the king and the Protestant nobility attended the opening of Parliament. Catholics had been suspected of disloyalty since the Reformation, and after 1605, the celebration of the plot's failure indissolubly linked Catholicism with treason in the Protestant public's mind.

Left: Guy Fawkes, an explosives expert and a key conspirator, has lent his name to an annual remembrance of the failed plot.

Two Kingdoms

In 1604, James styled himself as King of Great Britain, and two years later he approved the design of a Union flag that combined the crosses of St Andrew and St George. Some customs duties on goods traded between the two kingdoms were removed for a time. However, the Parliaments and laws of the two kingdoms remained separate and distinct. Most importantly, their churches differed greatly in liturgy and organization. In Scotland James had often been reminded that he was merely a member of a Kirk run by its local committees and its General Assembly of ministers and elders. In England, he was the Head of an Episcopal church that was his to govern. James greatly enjoyed the increased authority and wealth that flowed from his new status in London, returning to Scotland only once in 1617.

TUDOR AND STEWART IRELAND
1550–1640

The English, and later the British, Crown used planned colonies to try and better control Ireland, but early attempts were half-hearted and only inspired native Irish resistance. The colonization of Ulster was more permanent, thanks to James VI and I who took a personal interest in this first 'British' adventure.

THE FIRST PLANTATIONS

Although the Tudors were monarchs of Ireland after 1541, much of the island was in reality ruled by independent lords who were often Irish and Catholic. Edward VI and his sister Mary initiated a policy of settling English colonists in plantations to extend the area under the control of the royal administration in Dublin. In 1556, the Earl of Sussex was charged with establishing English colonies in Laois and Offally, henceforth to be known as King's County and Queen's County. These plantations would have extended English rule deep into the Irish midlands, but the dispossessed locals resisted fiercely over the next two decades. The settlers were forced back into defensive compounds and were still not safe even after the men of the O'Moore and O'Connor clans were lured to an ambush and massacred in 1578. Failed attempts by Elizabeth to plant a barrier of English colonists in Ulster between the Gaels of Ireland and western Scotland in 1570 also ended in atrocities. When full rebellion erupted in the 1590s, the English colonists in Munster were obliged to abandon their farms and shelter in walled towns.

Above: A section from Ortelius' *Theatrum Orbis Terrarum* (the Theatre of the World), considered to be the first modern atlas, shows England and Ireland in the late 1500s.

THE NINE YEARS WAR, 1594–1603

Later Tudor policies deeply alienated both the Gaelic population and the old Anglo-Irish gentry, who were now excluded from the Dublin establishment on account of their Catholic faith. When Hugh O'Neill, Earl of Tyrone, rebelled in 1594, his army contained many 'substantial' folk who were no longer eligible for government positions. Tyrone's men were also well-equipped and experienced soldiers, who used the heavily wooded landscape of Ireland to great effect. English forces were ambushed and massacred at Clontibret in 1595 and at Yellow Ford three years later, and were defeated yet again at Moyry Pass in 1600.

TIMELINE	
1556	*English plantations founded in Laois and Offally in mid-Ireland*
1570	*Elizabethan plantations in Ulster*
1603	*Irish and Spanish forces surrender after the siege of Kinsale*
1607	*O'Neill sails into exile in Catholic Europe*
1603	*Extensive Protestant plantations in Ulster.*

Tyrone's success encouraged Philip III of Spain to invest money and 4,000 men in the Irish troubles. This foreign intervention spurred London to up the stakes, and a more aggressive policy under Lord Mountjoy turned the tide of events at the siege of Kinsale. The Spanish were discouraged and the O'Neills surrendered in 1603. O'Neill was permitted to keep his lands but quit Ireland with his supporters four years later, when English law was imposed upon Ulster. For the first time, the English administration could claim to control the whole island of Hibernia.

Above: Once the English Crown fully mobilized its manpower and military resources, the Earl of Tyrone had little choice but to lay down his arms and seek an agreement with Governor Mountjoy.

THE ULSTER PLANTATION

In 1603, James VI of Scotland also became King of Ireland. The departure of the O'Neills handed almost four million acres of forfeit land in Ulster to the Crown. James revived the policy of plantation, but on a greater scale than before and with clearer religious and cultural aims. Land once held by the Catholic Church was assigned to the Protestant Church of Ireland. The Protestant lay landowners were banned from renting land to Irish tenants or from selling land to a Gael. The new farming stock of Ulster would be drawn from James' British kingdoms and would be Protestant. Troops who had fought for the Crown against the O'Neills were also given land, but as many of these men were of limited means they received subsidies from the City of London. The place names of Londonderry, Draperstown and Cookston survive as evidence of the influence of the City of London and its wealthy guilds in funding the Ulster project.

THE IMPACT OF PLANTATION

By 1630, there were over 80,000 British Protestant settlers in the six counties of Ulster. Other plantations followed, notably in Wexford and Munster, attracting settlers not just from Scotland and England, but from Wales, 'Huguenot' France and the Netherlands. The settlers quickly set about transforming the economy and landscape of Ireland. The traditional pastoral subsistence economy of the Gaelic clans was replaced with a more commercially managed arable agriculture. The forests were taken for building and shipping while much of the bogland was drained. The old tribal townships gave way to larger planned towns on the English model. The native population remained Catholic, despite attempts at conversion. Many continued as tenant farmers in contravention of the terms of the plantation contract, if only because skilled labour remained scarce.

KING AND PARLIAMENT
1530–1640

After 1530, Parliament evolved into a key element of English government and a powerful partner of the Crown. Tudor parliaments co-operated with government administration, but this consensus came under increasing pressure in the Stewart period.

MEDIEVAL ORIGINS OF THE ENGLISH PARLIAMENT

The Witanagemot or council of senior men provided a source of advice for Anglo-Saxon kings. After 1066, Norman kings ruled as feudal superiors by divine favour, but consulted the nobles and bishops if they wished to secure the adoption of their policies. To legitimize his opposition to Henry III, Simon de Montfort convoked the first elected Parliament in 1265. His principles for identifying borough and county members were broadly accepted by Edward I and his successors. Under pressure to fund his wars in France, Edward III conceded Parliament's right to be consulted about all fiscal levies. However, Parliament's development stalled in the crisis years after 1450, with Yorkist kings and Henry VII preferring to govern through a small Privy Council.

THE TUDOR PARLIAMENT

Parliament re-emerged as a national institution as a result of the break with Rome in the 1530s. Henry VIII desperately needed to legitimize the Reformation and his conception of national sovereignty. New sources of authority were required to replace the old notions of Pope and Emperor. Henry found the perfect instrument in the Act of Parliament or statute made by King, Lords and Commons acting in unison. Henry's supremacy as monarch and head of the Church may have come from God, but the national Parliament was needed to endorse it. Edward VI and Mary both used Parliament to pursue their religious policies. Meeting more frequently from 1529 onwards, Parliament was an important point of contact between the government and the governed, especially as the Commons grew in size and influence. Certain issues prompted friction between Elizabeth and the lower house, notably her reluctance to name a successor. Radical MPs emerged, such as the outspoken Peter Wentworth, who died in a royal prison after breaching

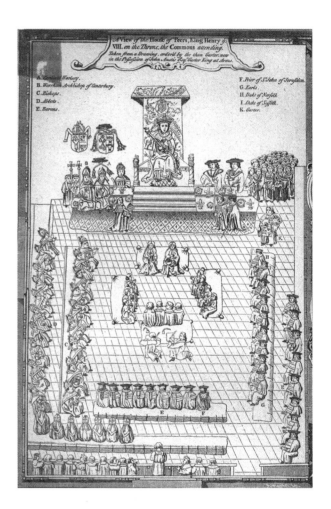

Above: This contemporary engraving shows a meeting of the House of Lords under King Henry VIII, with the Commons in attendance.

Above: The scientist and philosopher Francis Bacon served as Lord Chancellor to James VI & I but was sent to the Tower and fined £40,000 after Parliamentary committees found him guilty of corruption.

the limits of Tudor free speech. However, Parliament's place in the government of England was not clearly defined. It did not meet every year and did not meet at all in twenty-six of Elizabeth's forty-four years on the throne.

PARLIAMENT AND THE STEWARTS

James VI & I had difficulties with his English parliament from the outset. He disliked its control over his revenues and its opposition to his plans for free trade between Scotland and England. For its part, Parliament disliked James' extravagance, his belief in the divine right of kings to rule, and his blatant selling of peerages to raise quick cash. Hostile parliaments in 1611 and 1612 had to be dissolved. A third in 1621 impeached the king's Lord Chancellor Francis Bacon on charges of corruption. Friction between King and Parliament intensified under Charles I, who shared his father's belief in the divine right of kings, was suspected of Catholic leanings and of seeking to gain absolute power. Charles was frustrated at Parliament's unwillingness to vote him the money needed for his wars in Europe. Anger over Charles' foreign policy and his increasingly arbitrary rule sparked disorder in the Commons in 1629. Before its dissolution, this parliament framed a Petition of Rights, stating the liberties of Englishmen under the law and seeking to curtail royal abuses of power such as forced loans, interference with subjects' property and goods and illegal arrest. Charles responded by governing for the next eleven years without once calling Parliament. This had been common enough in earlier ages, but by the mid-17th century many viewed Charles' personal rule as a tyranny. His levying of old feudal taxes such as ship money only added fuel to the growing discontent throughout England.

THE SCOTTISH PARLIAMENT

As in England, the Three Estates of Scotland or Parliament evolved from the medieval royal council. The Estates (prelates, lairds and burgh commissioners) met to consent to taxation, but also influenced a wide range of government activities such as justice, foreign policy and even education – representatives of Scotland's medieval universities sat in the chamber. Unlike England, all elements of the community sat in the same house. As early as the 14th century, the Estates prevented David II from agreeing to an English succession, while parliamentary appointments hostile to the King led to the downfall of James III in 1488. Stronger monarchs such as James IV avoided calling the Estates whenever possible. In the 1630s, a new Parliament Hall was built in Edinburgh at the order of Charles I, but the main beneficiary of these grand new surroundings was the Covenanting regime that took control of Scotland in 1638.

TIMELINE

1530s	*Henry VIII uses Parliament to justify his religious revolution*
1611–2	*James VI & I clashes with his English Parliaments over the royal debts*
1620s	*The Commons grow in authority and discuss foreign policy issues*
1628	*The Commons attempt to define and limit royal power*
1629–40	*Charles I rules without calling Parliament*
1630s	*Scottish Parliament Hall built in Edinburgh.*

THE WAR OF THREE KINGDOMS
1637–49

Unsympathetic royal policies towards the Scottish Kirk in the 17th century prompted a national revolt and a war that spread to all parts of Britain and Ireland. It ended with the victory of Parliament and the execution of the king.

REVOLUTION IN SCOTLAND

In 1637, Charles I resolved to make the Scottish Kirk more like the Church of England. His ritualistic innovations were extremely distasteful to the Calvinist Scots and provoked riots in Edinburgh. The Scots drew up a National Covenant and the Kirk's General Assembly repudiated the 'anglicizing' changes that Charles and his father had implemented. Rather than compromise, Charles tried to coerce the Scots, but was defeated and had to pay them a subsidy of £300,000. To raise the money, Charles was forced to recall England's Parliament in 1640.

THE LONG PARLIAMENT

Parliament now served as an outlet for years of grievance against the king. Seeking to restore the more consensual government of Elizabethan times, Parliament passed Acts to limit the Crown's ability to raise revenue without parliamentary consent and abolished agencies such as the Star Chamber that Charles had overused in the years of his personal rule. Parliament forbade its dissolution without its own consent and decreed that it should meet at least every three years. For his part, Charles was incensed by the execution of his minister Strafford and the imprisonment of Archbishop Laud. A Catholic rising in Ireland and the massacre of English settlers there brought the crisis to a head. Parliamentary radicals such as John Pym did not trust the king with the army that would be raised to re-conquer Ireland. For Charles, control of the army was his fundamental right. In January 1642, Charles entered Parliament at the head of armed men, seeking but failing to round up his most vocal opponents. This attempted coup lost Charles even more moderate support and England drifted towards civil war.

CIVIL WAR IN ENGLAND

In 1642, most Englishmen still hoped for a peaceful solution to the rift between king and parliament. The war began tentatively, for many found it difficult to fight against their god-given king. Charles' hope was to win a quick victory and discourage his opponents. The royalists emerged from the first major battle of the war at Edgehill with a strategic advantage, but failed to exploit it and march on London. In 1643, Charles had further victories, but they were in peripheral areas such as Wales and the west.

Above: Charles I provoked resentment and anger in Parliament with his heavy-handed policies and overspending. His attempt to quell his Parliamentary opponents by force in 1642 led to the outbreak of civil war.

TIMELINE

1638	*Scots sign the National Covenant in defence of their liberties*
1640	*The Long Parliament clashes with the king and his ministers*
1641	*Catholic uprising in Ireland raises fear of royal tyranny*
1642	*First battle between royal and English Parliamentary forces at Edgehill*
1645	*Charles loses the decisive Battle of Naseby in Northamptonshire*
1649	*Charles found guilty of high treason and executed at Whitehall.*

Peace negotiations with the insurgents in Ireland freed up royal troops there, but Parliament's Solemn League and Covenant with the disciplined forces of Presbyterian Scotland brought victory at Marston Moor in 1644. Based at Oxford, and without a navy or access to the major ports, Charles was slowly drained of resources as the war progressed. The king's strongest support generally lay in the margins of Britain in the more traditional societies of western England, Wales and Highland Scotland. These could offer manpower, but were poorer in terms of war materials. By contrast, Parliament could draw upon the more populous areas of England such as the south and east where towns and industry were concentrated. Parliament not only raised and trained the professional New Model Army under Fairfax, but kept it in the field thanks to secure lines of supply and regular pay. At Naseby in 1645, Charles could only muster 7,000 men against a 'roundhead' army twice the size. With his realm reduced to a few isolated strongholds, Charles surrendered to the Scots at Newark in May 1646.

Below: Charles demonstrated great personal courage at his execution on a cold day in January 1649. Royalist supporters later created a cult of martyrdom around his memory.

TOWARDS THE SCAFFOLD

The war between Charles and his subjects convulsed all parts of Britain and Ireland. Irish forces fought in England, Wales and Scotland, while Scots armies interfered in Irish affairs until their defeat at Benburb in 1646. The Scots played a major role in English events. Fighting in Ireland continued almost unabated until 1649, when a new phase of war began with Cromwell's invasion. Despite the long and bloody conflict, many in all three kingdoms still felt a residual sense of loyalty to the king. Charles himself helped to dispel this. After re-securing Scottish support by promising to tolerate a Presbyterian Kirk, he encouraged his supporters to unsuccessfully rise again in July 1648. It was easier now for his enemies to present him as utterly untrustworthy and as an obstacle to peace. Charles was tried for 'treason and other high crimes' and executed at Whitehall in January 1649. About one in four of the English male population fought in the wars and around 200,000 Englishmen died in combat or from disease. In Scotland and Ireland the war was even more bitter, with rich burghs like Aberdeen brutally sacked.

THE AGE OF CROMWELL
1645–1658

With the power of the army behind him, Cromwell rose to power in England. By conquering Scotland and Ireland, he came closer to uniting the British and Irish Isles than any of his royal predecessors.

GOD'S ENGLISHMAN

A minor landowner, Oliver Cromwell served as an uninspiring MP in the 1628 Parliament. In 1642, he recruited a cavalry troop and fought at Edgehill. After conspicuous success in East Anglia and at Marston Moor, he rose to high command in the New Model Army in 1645. He emerged as a major political figure in the period of confusion that settled upon England after the defeat of Charles I. Parliament and the country were split on three key questions: should the Church of England become Presbyterian, what should be done with the Army, and what should be done with the king? Although influenced by the Puritan moral vision, Cromwell tolerated all shades of Protestantism. In early 1647, he was one of the officers that met Charles to try and negotiate a settlement. Later that year, Cromwell also met at Putney with the troops and Levellers (political agitators) who argued for a radical constitution based on manhood suffrage, biennial parliaments, the supremacy of the Commons and an England in which, 'the poorest he…have a life to live.'

Above: The politican Oliver Cromwell regards the corpse of Charles I, whose death warrant he signed.

GOD'S CHOSEN INSTRUMENT

Cromwell came to political prominence when Charles engineered an armed uprising in 1648. Cromwell defeated the royalist forces in Pembrokeshire before marching north to meet a Scottish army, now supporting Charles, at Preston, where he won a convincing victory. After Preston, he grew increasingly disillusioned with Parliamentary squabbling and the king's scheming. Cromwell resisted further negotiations with Charles and came to believe that he should be brought to trial. Cromwell was a member of the court that sat in judgement on the king and signed his death warrant. A Commonwealth or republic was declared in May 1649.

THE CROMWELLIAN CONQUEST OF IRELAND, 1649–50

Two months later, Cromwell was in Ireland. In a nine-month campaign, he conquered much of eastern

TIMELINE	
1647	*Cromwell rises to Lieutenant General of the Parliamentary cavalry*
1648	*Defeats royalist uprisings in Pembroke and at Preston*
1649–50	*Commands Parliamentary forces in Ireland*
1649	*Signs death warrant of Charles I*
1650–2	*Invades Scotland and imposes union with England*
1653	*Sworn in as Lord Protector on 15 December.*

Ireland, taking the key ports of Wexford and Drogheda to facilitate communication and supply. This re-conquest of Ireland was particularly brutal because of the number and experience of Cromwell's troops. A righteously Protestant army had more reason to hate native Catholics than most, for tales of atrocities against their co-religionists in 1641 had been well trumpeted in Protestant pamphlets. By the standards of 17th-century Europe, the massacres at Wexford and Drogheda were exceptional, not in scale, but in the efficiency with which resistors were butchered or rounded up to be sold into slavery in the West Indies.

THE INVASION OF SCOTLAND, 1650–52

The Scottish nobility were shocked by the 1649 regicide and made terms with Charles II, who promised to honour the Kirk. Cromwell marched north to force the Scots to reconsider. After initial stalemate, Cromwell brought the Scots to surrender at Dunbar and entered Edinburgh. Despite this, in early 1651, Charles II was crowned King of Scots at Scone, pinning his hopes on English royalists rising to support a Scottish invasion. However, few rallied to the new king and a dwindling Scottish army succumbed at Worcester in September. Cromwell was now master of both kingdoms and set about unifying them into one state. Lowland Scotland was heavily garrisoned and the Highlands sealed off by a chain of forts. Royalist risings there in 1653 and 1654 were crushed. Scotland was under London control, but the Kirk went untouched and so the Cromwellian regime, though unpopular, went largely unopposed.

THE PROTECTORATE

With Cromwell away on campaign, the purged remainder of the Long Parliament was paralyzed by infighting. When this Rump Parliament proved lukewarm on his plans to unify the three kingdoms, Cromwell – now the power in the land – dissolved it. Its successor, the Parliament of Saints, was equally ineffective in forging an acceptable constitutional and religious settlement. In December 1653, Cromwell assumed the executive power and was sworn in as Lord Protector. An experimental administration of fifteen military districts under 'godly governors' was not popular. Nor was the zeal of the local commissioners, mostly Puritans, who used their authority to enforce strict moral discipline upon the population. Other reforms, such as the introduction of civil marriage and the re-admission of Jews to England, offended the conservative core of society. England had already tired of the republican experiment before Cromwell's sudden decline and death in 1658.

Below: In December 1653, Cromwell was made Lord Protector of the Commonwealth when the Parliament of the Saints collapsed after weeks of factional in-fighting.

THE RESTORATION OF THE MONARCH
1660–1685

Power passed back from the Protectorate to Charles II with little protest and much popular acclaim. Charles offered stability and toleration and there were few recriminations, despite the bitterness of the war and the republican period.

THE FALL OF THE REPUBLIC

The brief government of the second Lord Protector Richard Cromwell fell apart in 1659, due to factional divisions within and between the Army and Parliament. England seemed on the brink of anarchy, but order was preserved by the arrival in London of General Monck, the Cromwellian commander in Scotland, whose disciplined troops had been purged of dissidents. Monck's support ensured a moderate Parliament in which republicans were a minority. Charles II was duly invited to return from exile. There were few demonstrations in support of the saintly Republic. Factional disputes, strict religion, high taxes, European wars – all contributed to the prevailing sense of weariness with political experiment. By 1660, the cause of the turmoil, the tyranny of Charles I in the 1620s, was long forgotten, but the burdens of an overbearing army and Puritan enthusiasm were ever present.

A TOLERANT OUTCOME

Unlike his father, Charles II was a flexible politician who understood the importance of reconciliation. Given the bitterness of the previous decades there was little recrimination in 1660. Cromwell's corpse was exhumed and abused, but most Cromwellians were pardoned. Only the 'regicides' who had signed the 1649 warrant were excluded. Charles made clear his willingness to rule with Parliament and made little protest when old, contentious royal powers of justice and taxation such as the Star Chamber and ship money were not restored. Parliament took care to guarantee that the monarch enjoyed a reasonable income, but not one that would allow him to act too independently. Much of the traditional ruling class was restored to power in the Lords, the Church and the City of London. Lands that had been lost by the Crown and the

THE GREAT FIRE, 1666

In September 1666, the medieval City of London was consumed by four days of conflagration. The old cathedral of St Paul's and eighty-seven parish churches were destroyed, as were over 13,000 houses. Although few deaths were recorded, most of the 80,000 inhabitants of the City area were left homeless.

Above: The Great Fire of London is said to have started in a bakery in Pudding Lane and then fanned out across the city, spread by an east wind.

Above: Charles II entered London on May 29 1660, marking the end of the Protectorate and the restoration of royal rule across the British Isles.

TIMELINE

1659	*Fall of the Protectorate of Richard Cromwell*
1660	*Monarchy under Charles II restored by Parliament in May*
1662	*Cavalier Parliament passes the strict Act of Uniformity*
1665	*Bubonic plague kills approximately 80,000 Londoners*
1666	*Great Fire of London rages from 2–5 September*
1670s	*Catholics excluded from official posts by the Test Acts.*

Church since 1642 were confiscated from their new owners without compensation. However, many smaller royalist landowners who had lost or had to sell their estates in the 1640s and 1650s received little help from the Restoration settlement. Many lost their lands permanently or squandered their remaining fortune in protracted recovery lawsuits.

THE RESTORATION IN IRELAND AND SCOTLAND

After the Cromwellian conquest, large tracts of Ireland had ended up in the hands of Protestant landowners, much of which was confiscated in the mid 1650s from Irish owners who rebelled against the Protectorate. As they were native Catholics, they struggled to regain their land after 1660. The Restoration confirmed the ascendancy of the Protestant aristocracy in much of Ireland. In Scotland, Charles' earlier promises of support for Presbyterianism evaporated once he was back in power. His plans to introduce bishops in 1662 outraged Kirk ministers, who left their pulpits to preach in outdoor services called conventicles. Government repression of these illegal meetings only served to increase resistance to the king's religious policies.

RELIGIOUS REPRESSION IN ENGLAND

There was to be little compromise in the religious settlement in England either. Charles favoured toleration in matters of faith, if only because of his private leanings towards Catholicism and his hope that Catholics would be granted some degree of religious liberty. These hopes were dashed by the 'Cavalier Parliament' of 1661. Fiercely royalist in sentiment, it sought to enforce strict conformity to Anglican doctrine and practices. The 1662 Act of Uniformity forced loyal, moderate Presbyterians to conform or quit the church. Two thousand churchmen lost their livings, often setting up illegal Puritan sects. The Test Acts of the 1670s excluded Catholics and 'nonconforming' Protestants from government office, and adherence to Anglicanism became a requirement of serving on a borough corporation.

THE MERRY MONARCH?

The early years of Charles' reign were marred by the Great Plague of 1665 and the Great Fire of London the following year. War with the Dutch and continuing religious strife in Scotland added to Charles' woes. Europe was overshadowed by the Catholic absolutism of Louis XIV of France and the atmosphere in England grew thick with rumours of conspiracy by both papists and Puritans. Successive ministries collapsed and parliaments dissolved. Nevertheless the restored king generally governed 'lightly' within the limits of his new role as a 'monarch prescribed by Parliament'.

THE SUCCESSION CRISIS
1678–88

The last years of Charles II's reign were tense, for the heir to the thrones of England, Scotland and Ireland was an avowed Roman Catholic and a skilful military leader. Protestants feared for their future under a powerful and autocratic Catholic prince.

THE CATHOLIC HEIR

Although Charles II fathered a score or more illegitimate children, his marriage to Catherine of Braganza produced no legal heirs and his brother James, Duke of York, stood next in the line of succession. James was an experienced soldier who had commanded in both the French and Spanish armies and had shown courage as Lord High Admiral in the naval wars against the Dutch in the 1670s. He also proved an effective, if uncompromising, administrator in the 1680s when he acted as the king's representative in Scotland. James' conversion to the Catholic faith in 1669 was public knowledge, but his daughters and heirs, Mary and Anne, were both raised as Protestants to placate Parliament and national feeling.

THE POPISH PLOT

Rumours of Charles' secret Catholicism created an atmosphere of suspicion throughout the later years of his reign. The flashpoint came in 1678 when Titus Oates, a colourful adventurer of Baptist origin who had lost several clerical livings through allegations of drunkenness and sodomy, claimed to have information about a Jesuit conspiracy to assassinate Charles and place James on the throne instead. The 1605 Gunpowder Plot against the Protestant establishment had never been forgotten in England and Oates' claims unleashed a new wave of anti-Catholic hysteria. Catholics were forbidden to come with 16 km (10 miles) of the capital and rumours circulated that suspicious digging sounds had been heard near the Commons. The magistrate investigating the plot disappeared and was found dead on the outskirts of London, strangled and run through by his own sword. A series of show trials ensued. Fifteen suspected plotters were executed, including James' private secretary, whose only crime was to have corresponded with a French Jesuit acquaintance. The crisis spread to the government and the king's first minister Danby fell from office when his dealings with the Catholic Sun King Louis XIV were revealed.

WHIGS AND TORIES

In the wake of the Popish Plot, English politics polarized on the issue of the succession. Two factions or parties gradually crystallized, each rejoicing in an abusive nickname given by its enemy. The opponents of the Court came

Below: Although a known Roman Catholic, James, Duke of York acceded as James II & VII in 1685 on the death of his brother Charles.

TIMELINE

1681	*Whigs try to exclude James from the Succession*
1685	*Rebellion of the Protestant Monmouth is defeated at Sedgemoor*
1685	*James II suspends Parliament indefinitely*
1687–8	*James attempts to re-catholicize England*
1688	*Birth of a Catholic male heir, James Edward Stewart.*

to be known as Whigs, originally a nickname for the Scottish Covenanters, while Crown loyalists were called Tories from the Irish Gaelic word for an outlaw. Charles, James and their Tory supporters were deeply angered when the Whigs, under the Earl of Shaftesbury, sought to exclude James from the succession and introduced several parliamentary bills to this effect. Charles called no more parliaments after the Exclusion Crisis of 1681, preferring to live off the subsidies that he received from France. An alleged republican plot to murder Charles and James in 1683, as they returned from the Newmarket races, provided an excuse to arrest Whig leaders. Several were executed and others fled into exile. Whigs were purged from office and their centres of power such as the City of London, were subjected to greater royal control.

THE LAST CATHOLIC KING

On succeeding as James II & VII in 1685, the new Catholic king easily dealt with rebellions in western England and Scotland. The leaders of both, the bastard Duke of Monmouth and the Duke of Argyll, were executed. Monmouth's supporters were cruelly treated after their defeat at Sedgemoor and the 'bloody assizes' under Judge Jeffreys were used to emphasize the royal determination to 'extirpate all rebels'. In England, Parliament grew uneasy at the expansion of James' standing army and his commissioning of Catholic officers contrary to the Test Acts, but it was dismissed and not recalled in James' reign. Catholics were favoured for posts in the gift of the Crown. James also pressed ahead with plans to introduce religious equality for all, including Catholics, and charged seven Anglican bishops who dared to protest with sedition. In Edinburgh, James went further, opening a Catholic chapel, school and printing press. The final straw was the birth of

Above: James Scott, Duke of Monmouth fought to take the throne from his uncle at the battle of Sedgemoor in 1685. After losing the battle, it is said that he pleaded with James for his life.

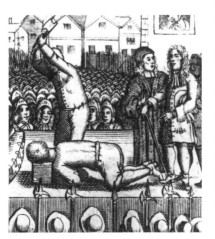

Right: James and his administration were brutal in their response to the uprisings. Rebels such as Monmouth and Argyll were sent to the block.

a male heir in June 1688 to Mary of Modena, now openly satirized as the 'papal mare' by Protestant pamphleteers. The infant James would be raised a Catholic and displaced the Protestants Mary and Anne in the royal line. The Protestant fear of a dynasty of autocratic, Catholic rulers seemed to be coming true and they had only to look across to France, where Louis XIV was vigorously persecuting his Protestant Huguenot subjects, to see their own likely fate.

THE GLORIOUS REVOLUTION
1688–91

The deposition of King James passed off smoothly in England, but many in Scotland and Ireland remained loyal to the 'true king'. Support there for the Stewart cause meant that these were far from bloodless years.

THE LAST INVASION OF ENGLAND

Since the execution of Monmouth in 1685, Whig hopes had centred upon the Dutch stadtholder William of Orange. William was a staunch Protestant and the husband of the Protestant Mary Stewart. Moreover he was the champion of Protestant Europe against Louis XIV. Whig exiles at William's court in Holland encouraged him to invade Britain. However, he was unsure of public reaction to a foreign invasion and waited until he received a formal invitation from leading English nobles. In November 1688, William was hurried across the Channel by a 'Protestant wind' that kept James' fleet bottled up in the Thames. Any doubts that William might have had about the wisdom of invading were dispelled by the warm welcome he received on landing in Devon. Flying banners in support of 'English liberties and the Protestant religion', William gathered additional English forces as he marched towards London.

THE 'BLOODLESS REVOLUTION'

Skirmishes at Wincanton and Reading confirmed that James' English regiments had no stomach for a fight. News reached William's camp that nobles in the north had declared support for him, while Protestant mobs had risen in London, Bristol and Dover against James' Catholic officials. As establishment figures, including James' own daughter Anne, declared for William, James disbanded his unreliable army and was allowed to slip away to exile in France. William seems to have connived at James' flight so there would be no repeat of the events of 1649. A sympathetic Convention Parliament ruled that by fleeing the realm, James had abdicated. William and Mary were invited to reign co-jointly in England and were crowned in April 1689. An Act of Toleration secured broad support for the new regime by guaranteeing religious liberty for most non-conforming Protestants, without challenging the position of the Anglican Church. A Bill of Rights

Above: The fleet of William of Orange, the Protestant pretender to the throne, approaches the shores of Devon.

curtailed the powers of the sovereign and confirmed Parliament's place at the heart of the English constitution. Henceforth England's monarchs would rule in partnership with Parliament. The succession was also settled. Protestant Anne and her issue would rule after the deaths of William III and Mary II. All Catholics, including Prince James Stewart, were barred from the English throne. In a few short months, the political and religious issues that had tortured England since 1603 had been resolved.

CIVIL WAR IN SCOTLAND

The revolution was not bloodless in Scotland. The deposition of the Stewart monarchy threw the divisions between the Presbyterian Lowlands and the Catholic and Episcopalian Highlands into sharp relief. Many Scots could not easily shed their loyalty to the Stewarts. Oaths had been sworn to James, who was not only appointed by God, but the product of a royal house that had ruled Scotland for almost four hundred years. When the Three Estates met in Edinburgh in April 1689, the city was awash with spies and armed supporters of the Stewart and Orange causes. Nevertheless, Presbyterian Scotland selected William and Mary as their new monarchs. William II, as he was titled in Scotland, could be trusted to defend the Presbyterian Kirk, but retaining James as king would have plunged Scotland into war with England. As in England, William ceded significant powers to the Scottish Parliament. Supporters of the old royal house protested against the Orange coup and rode out of Edinburgh to gather their forces. These Jacobites slaughtered a government army at Killiecrankie in Perthshire later that summer, but their charismatic leader John Graham ('Bonnie Dundee') was felled by a musket ball in the moment of victory. The Cameronians, a regiment of zealous Covenanters, stopped the Highlanders' advance at Dunkeld, but the Jacobite threat would haunt Scotland for decades.

Left: Almost 60,000 men fought at the Boyne. James relied on his crack Irish cavalry but they made little impression on William's disciplined musketmen.

BATTLE OF THE BOYNE

James' strongest support came from his co-religionists in Ireland. The Earl of Tyrconnell held Ireland for James and the native population greeted him warmly when he landed at Dublin in 1689 at the head of 6,000 French troops. In 1690, the largest battle of the Williamite War for Ireland unfolded at the river Boyne near Drogheda. The political complexities of the age are highlighted by the fact that Dutch Catholics fought for William while German Protestants stood on James' side. The battle was indecisive, but the discouraged James returned to France, dubbed *Seamus a'chaca* by his abandoned Irish allies. They fought on, only to be wiped out at Aughrim the following year.

TIMELINE

5 Nov 1688	*William lands at Brixham near Torquay in Devon*
10 Dec 1688	*After defeat at Reading, royal forces melt away*
23 Dec 1688	*James allowed to flee to France*
Feb 1689	*William and Mary accede to throne of England*
April 1689	*Scottish Parliament chooses William as its sovereign*
July 1690	*William defeats James at the Battle of the Boyne near Drogheda.*

EXPLORATION AND TRADE
1500–1700

England, and to a much lesser extent Scotland, participated in the expansion of European trade after 1500. By 1700, 'British' settlements existed throughout North America and the East India Company was a major player in the lucrative eastern trade routes.

NORTHERN EXPLORERS

In 1497, the Genoese navigator Giovanni Caboto became the first modern European to land on the continent of North America. Sponsored by Henry VII, Caboto sailed on the Bristol ship *Matthew* and reported 'a new founde land' whose coasts teemed with cod. Other Bristol ships followed and explored the eastern coast of America on an annual basis until Henry VIII stopped their summer voyaging in 1510 for fear of displeasing the Spanish. In the 1550s, the Bristolian Richard Chancellor journeyed twice to Muscovy, reaching Archangel in the far north. Later northern explorers sought a north-west passage around northern America to the Pacific and the spices of the East. In the 1570s, Martin Frobisher made three expeditions to the lands of the Inuit, but these expensive and dangerous journeys yielded little more than valueless ores that Frobisher hoped to turn into gold. After establishing New Amsterdam for the Dutch, Henry Hudson sailed further north for England in 1610. Discovering a vast bay, Hudson believed that he had found a sea channel to the Pacific. Before he could test his theory, his ship was encased in ice for the winter. Hudson was cast adrift in an open boat by his mutinous crew the following spring.

ENGLISH AMERICA

In the 1580s Walter Raleigh organized three expeditions to set up an English colony in North America. Lacking manpower and secure supplies, the settlement at Roanoke Island off North Carolina floundered and Drake had to evacuate the starving colonists in 1586. Although built on a mosquito-infested swamp in 1607, Jamestown in Virginia had the advantage of being at a distance from the powerful Powhatan tribes that had overrun earlier English settlements. Jamestown's main export of sweet tobacco proved popular in London and the colony eventually prospered. Puritan colonies followed in Massachusetts in 1620 and 1630, while English Catholics founded their new world at Maryland in 1634. The Dutch were forced to cede their strategically vital colony of New Netherlands and its bustling capital of New Amsterdam to England in 1674. By 1700, twelve English colonies straddled the Atlantic seaboard. Georgia was added in 1732. More than 200,000 settlers from Britain and Ireland emigrated to North America in the 17th century. However, England's richest possessions

Above: Sir Walter Raleigh, a favourite of Queen Elizabeth I, founded the first English colony in the New World in 1585.

TIMELINE

1497	*Giovanni Caboto sails from Bristol to Newfoundland*
1576–8	*Martin Frobisher explores the coastline of northern Canada*
1584	*English colony established on Roanoke Island in Virginia*
1600	*Charter granted to the East India Company*
1607	*Foundation of Jamestown settlement in Virginia*
1620	*English settlers land at Plymouth, Massachusetts*
1627	*Scottish settlement founded in Nova Scotia*
1630	*Massachusetts Bay colony founded by English Puritans*
1670	*East India Company given quasi-regal rights by Charles II.*

Below: A series of Acts by the newly-restored Charles II granted the East India Company rights hitherto reserved for monarchs.

were in the West Indies, where sugar agriculture and the necessary slave labour were introduced in the 1630s. By 1672, another Jamestown, near Accra in West Africa, gave the English an important slice of the Atlantic slave trade.

THE EAST INDIA COMPANY

Chartered by Elizabeth in 1600, the East India Company struggled at first to win a foothold in the lucrative Indian trade in the face of tough Portuguese competition. Although an English flotilla defeated the Portuguese galleons at Suvali in 1612, co-operation with the Mughal emperor Jahangir proved to be a better foundation for trading success in India. From their factory base at Surat, the Company expanded to Madras in 1639, Calcutta in 1660 and Bombay in 1668. By the end of the century, there were over thirty English trading posts in India dealing in silks, dyes and tea. The Company's formidable naval strength also gained it an entrance to the eastern spice trade and helped establish a foothold in China by 1712. In 1670, Charles II gave the Company quasi-regal rights to raise troops, mint currency, form alliances, and hold courts in its areas of influence. By the early 1700s, the Company operated as a virtually autonomous kingdom within the declining Mughal Empire, winning fortunes for its shareholders and employees alike.

SCOTTISH EXPANSION

The Scots were as keen as other Europeans to grab a piece of the Americas. In 1621, Sir William Alexander was granted a charter to found a Scottish colony in North America. After initial difficulties, Nova Scotia was established by 1627 but abandoned in the 1630s when Charles I gave the colony to France. The real thrust of Scottish expansion was eastwards into Europe. Campveere became the port of entry for all Scottish trade in the Netherlands in 1541. Other Scots merchants went further east into the Baltic, and by 1600 there were Scottish trading quarters in Danzig, Cracow and Konigsberg.

CULTURE AND SOCIETY
1500–1700

The 16th and 17th centuries were marked not just by political and religious crisis, but by significant social, economic and intellectual change. By 1700, England dominated the British and Irish Isles to an unprecedented extent.

POPULATION

In the absence of reliable data, the one incontestable fact about the demography of early modern Britain is that many more people were living on the island in 1700 compared to 1500. Most of these additional people were English. By 1650, the population in Wales had probably struggled back to its pre-plague levels of around 350,000. That of Scotland was less than one and a half million by the same period, but many inhabitants lived in the Gaelic hinterland beyond the reach of the Scottish state. The population of England at the Restoration was about five million. More than half a million of these people were squashed into the burgeoning capital, ten times more than had lived in London in the reign of the early Tudors. Not only had England's population increased, it had significantly outpaced that of the 'Celtic' margins.

AUTHORITY

The various societies in Britain and Ireland remained deeply deferential throughout most of the period 1500–1700. Most lives were played out at a local level where those few with economic, military or spiritual power were clearly and immediately visible by their possession of land or posts in government or the Church. Society remained deeply

IDENTITY AND LITERACY

Far more Britons could read in 1700 than in 1500, especially in areas such as Wales and Scotland, where personal salvation for many had to be found on one's own by reading the Word of God. Contemporaries understood the radicalizing power of the printed page, for governments continued to attempt to control the manufacture and distribution of text throughout the period. One book above all, Foxe's *Book of Martyrs,* with its lurid and lingering accounts of the persecutions under Queen Mary, probably did more than any other to link the ideas of Englishness and Protestantism. In Scotland, the translation of the Bible into English rather than Scots was crucial, for after 1560 God seemed to speak in the power language from down south. As a result, the lowland Scots elite were subtly encouraged to identify with their southern neighbours in ways that helped form a shared sense of British and Protestant identity and paved the way for fuller union in 1707.

Left: John Foxe's *Book of Martyrs*, first published in 1563, was a graphic account of Protestant persecutions, particularly in the reign of Bloody Mary.

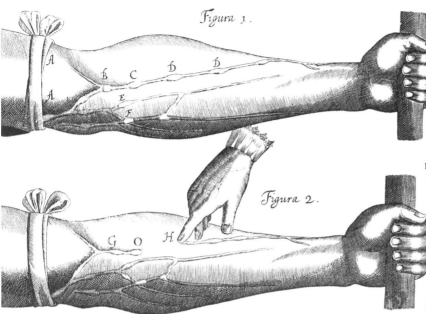

Figura 1.

Figura 2.

Above: William Harvey's discovery of the circulation of blood was based on observation, dissection and experiment.

Below: Thomas Savery's water pump used atmospheric and steam pressure to pump water upwards, an important step towards the development of the steam engine.

conservative and suspicious of change. Opponents of the Stewarts in 1640 and 1688 still voiced their demands for change in terms of the defence of ancient liberties. Many in England wrestled with their consciences before taking arms against Charles I in 1642, whilst many in Scotland faced the same internal struggle in opposing James in 1689. The status and function of women changed little, even under a successful queen such as Elizabeth. Ordinary women remained under the control of their husbands and fathers, and arranged marriage was the norm. Women gained a stronger right of individual conscience from the Reformation but positions of authority in Protestant churches and sects were reserved for godly men. Indeed the abolition of convents under the Reformation reduced opportunities for women to advance themselves in society. Very hard work was the fate of lower class women. They faced even harder treatment if they transgressed social expectations as criminals, prostitutes or witches.

THE SCIENTIFIC AND INTELLECTUAL REVOLUTION

In one particular sphere of life, the traditional role of authority was overturned. In science and philosophy, the prestige of classical and Christian authority gave way to observation, experiment and reasoned speculation. The later 17th century witnessed a flowering of interest in the natural sciences, helped in large part by the foundation of the Royal Society in November 1660. William Harvey's discovery of the circulation of the blood, John Flamsteed's astronomical charts, and the engagement by Isaac Newton and Robert Hooke with all of creation – these were only the highlights of a deepening intellectual curiosity with the physical world. Nor was this merely an academic interest. Thomas Savery used the Irishman Boyle's work on gases in his construction of a water pump that could be used to drain the tin mines of Cornwall. Mechanical looms made their appearance in England in the 1680s. After the religious excesses of the mid 17th century, enthusiasm for religion perceptibly waned at several levels of English society and many were happy to perform the expected outward observances in an increasingly tepid manner. The changing climate helped political philosophers such as Thomas Hobbes and John Locke to construct a distinctly material view of human relationships that owed little to classical precedent and nothing to Scripture.

TOWARDS UNION
1695–1706

After 1700, relations between Scotland and England threatened to deteriorate into war. The government in London pressed for a fuller union that would secure peace and the Protestant Succession.

Above: The Company of Scotland set up the Darien trading post in Panama, which eventually failed due to native resistance to the traders, disease and opposition from London.

ECONOMIC DISASTER

The 1603 Union of the Crowns badly damaged the Scottish economy. Edinburgh's service trades suffered from the loss of the king and his court and Scottish merchants lost their trading privileges in France. England's wars in Europe disrupted Scottish trade in the Low Countries, yet Scots were prohibited from trading in England's overseas colonies. By 1690, the Scots pound, once equal to England's, had dwindled in value to a mere twelfth.

THE DARIEN SCHEME

The Company of Scotland was founded in 1695 'to encourage trade in Africa and the Indies'. When it became clear that the City of London would not tolerate Scottish competition in its areas of operations, the Scots planned a trading post on the Darien peninsula in Panama to control the exchange of goods at the narrowest point of the Americas. The scheme failed for many reasons: the inexperienced settlers of New Edinburgh were surrounded by malarial swamps and attacked by natives and Spanish forces from the outset. However, the Scots who lost their investments in the Company in 1700 remembered that the London Parliament had hindered the Company, and that William had preferred to placate his Spanish allies rather than help his Scottish subjects. Coming after the massacre at Glencoe in 1692, many Scots distrusted William and wanted an end to the Union of the Crowns.

THE ACT OF SETTLEMENT

Despite the attempt to decide the matter in 1689, the succession to the thrones of England, Scotland and Ireland proved an intractable issue.

Mary died in 1694 and William reigned alone until his sudden death in 1702 when his horse stumbled and fell over a mole burrow. Exiled Jacobites throughout Europe toasted the health of 'the little gentleman in the black velvet waistcoat'. William and Mary were childless and were succeeded by Mary's sister Anne. She was 37 years old on her accession and although she had borne seventeen children, none had survived childhood. Anne was the last Protestant Stewart. King James died in France in 1701 and his son James Francis Edward Stewart had the strongest claim to the thrones. As a Catholic however, he was unacceptable and in the 1701 Act of Settlement the English Parliament ruled that the English Crown would pass instead to the safely Protestant rulers of the German principality of Hanover, if Anne died without heir.

THE BATTLE OF PARLIAMENTS

Coming soon after the Darien collapse, the Act of Settlement deeply angered the Scots. The Scottish Parliament responded with a flurry of Acts that defended Scotland's independence from England. Scotland would only accept the Hanoverians on its own terms, would pursue its own foreign policy and would trade with France despite the ongoing Anglo-French war. To the horror of Anne's first minister, Lord Godolpin, this raised the spectre of a Catholic Stewart upon the Scottish throne and a French invasion by the 'back door'. London responded with the Aliens Act, an ultimatum that unless the Scots entered into negotiations for a full union with England by Christmas Day 1705, they and their goods would be considered alien. English troops were transferred from Europe to Newcastle, and rumours of war abounded on both sides of the border. Facing the destruction of their trade with England and a possible invasion by Marlborough's army, the Scottish Parliament agreed to send negotiating commissioners to London.

Below: Prince James Francis Edward Stewart, known as the Old Pretender.

FULL UNION

Thirty-one commissioners from each kingdom gathered in secret in Whitehall in April 1706. The Scots and English met in separate rooms and only communicated with each other in writing. The Queen had approved all sixty-two commissioners and so the broad principles of a Treaty of Union were worked out within ten days. The Scots argued for a federal union that would keep some powers in Edinburgh, but the English demanded a full incorporating union and the abolition of the Scottish Parliament. A supplementary Act secured the Presbyterian form of the Kirk, ensuring that it took little interest in the treaty debates in the Scottish Parliament. Despite fierce opposition north of the border, the Scottish Parliament ratified the Treaty in January 1707 and dissolved itself in March.

TIMELINE

1701	*English Act of Settlement secures the Protestant Succession*
1703–4	*Scottish Parliament asserts its independence from England*
1705	*Aliens Act threatens Scots with trade penalties*
1706	*Commissioners from both parliaments meet in Whitehall*
1707	*Treaty of Union between Scotland and England ratified*
1707	*Establishment of the United Kingdom.*

THE KINGDOM OF GREAT BRITAIN
1707–1714

The Kingdom of Great Britain came into being on 1 May 1707. The Treaty of Union was a genuine attempt to bind two ancient kingdoms that had a long history of enmity, but which also had much in common. Within a few years however, the Union almost broke asunder.

THE TREATY ARTICLES

The Kingdom was symbolized by its new flag combining the crosses of St Andrew and St George. Existing laws in the two countries that went against the Treaty of Union were void, but England and Scotland would keep their distinct legal systems and courts. The Scots accepted the Protestant Hanoverian succession. In theory, both the Scottish and English parliaments were abolished, but the new Parliament of Great Britain sat at Westminster and followed English procedures. The Scots were given 45 seats in the Commons and 16 in the Lords. This was small compared with 513 English MPs and 196 English Lords but was considered a generous representation for the Scots, who would initially pay only a fortieth of the British tax burden. Great Britain was to be a common free trade area, using English Sterling and English weights and measures. The Scots gained access on equal terms to English ports in Britain and in the colonies.

THE EQUIVALENT

Scotland was now part of the new British tax system. This was a shock, for the Scots had little public debt before 1707 and taxes north of the border were low. England, however, had a massive national debt of over eighteen million pounds, largely incurred fighting wars in Europe. The Scots now had a shared responsibility for this debt. To sweeten the pill, they were given several temporary tax concessions on essential items such as salt and the malt used in brewing beer. Furthermore, the English Exchequer agreed to pay a sum of compensation to Scotland known as the Equivalent, fixed at £389,085 and ten shillings. The Company of Scotland was to stop trading, but shareholders were compensated for their losses in the Darien Scheme.

ENGLISH CELEBRATION

The birth of the Kingdom of Great Britain was celebrated with gun salutes at the Tower of London and

Below: Anne, the last monarch of the House of Stewart and the first to reign over the Kingdom of Great Britain. Her rule, from 1702–14, was marked by struggles over the succession.

TIMELINE	
May 1707	*Great Britain formally comes into being on 1 May*
Aug 1707	*Arrival of the Equivalent in Edinburgh*
May 1708	*Scottish Privy Council abolished*
1709	*English Treason Act extended to Scotland*
1711	*Toleration extended to Episcopalians*
1713	*Bill to repeal the Union fails by four votes*
1715–60	*Decline in Scottish economy.*

Above: The Duke of Queensbury presents the Treaty of Union to Queen Anne in London in May 1707.

in St James' Park. Anne spent her first morning as monarch of the new state at a service of thanksgiving in St Paul's Cathedral. It seemed that the ancient threat from the north, and any chance of a Jacobite restoration, had at last been eliminated. The Duke of Queensberry had steered the Treaty through the Scottish Parliament. As he grandly processed through England to take his seat at Westminster, he was feted by crowds and entertained in the great houses of England, much as James VI had been in 1603. A delegation of government ministers met 'the Union Duke' at Barnet and personally escorted him into London.

'A TREATY UNRAVELLED'

Some Scottish nobles soon regretted the Union. The Scottish Privy Council was abolished in late 1707, while a new Treason Act for Scotland in 1709 based on existing English law was in clear breach of the Treaty. Cases lost in the Court of Session in Edinburgh, Scotland's highest court, were appealed to the House of Lords, again a Treaty breach. In 1711, an Anglican clergyman, convicted in Edinburgh of using the English prayer book in his services, was released from prison by order of the Lords. The Tory administration in London granted freedom of worship to Episcopalians in Scotland and enforced a public holiday at Christmas, a feast long reviled by Presbyterians as being of Catholic origin. In 1707 Presbyterians had reluctantly agreed to the Union, thinking their Kirk safe, but by 1715 many were deeply worried by London's interference in the life of Scotland.

SCOTTISH DISAPPOINTMENT

The Equivalent arrived in Edinburgh in August 1707, carried in twelve wagons guarded by dragoons. To the horror of the Scots, only a quarter of the promised compensation was paid in bullion (gold and silver ingots). The rest arrived in the form of paper currency, a novelty that most Scots distrusted. After 1707, the Scots' trade with France declined, though their taste for French brandy and fine silks did not. This, combined with higher British customs duties, led to a rise in smuggling. By 1713, key sections of Scottish society – nobles, merchants, churchmen, lawyers – were deeply unhappy with the Union. A crisis came when the government proposed a new tax on malt, again forbidden in the Treaty. A bill to repeal the Union was brought in and defeated by only four votes in the Lords. For the Scots at least, the Union had got off to a bad start.

THE JACOBITE RISINGS
1708–1746

To the Jacobites, the Treaty of Union was an illegal pact signed by usurper and rebel parliaments. Only the defeat of Jacobitism – and the destruction of its sources of support – would ensure the preservation of the 1707 settlement.

THE INVASION OF 1708

The dissatisfaction with the Union in Scotland greatly encouraged the 'Pretender' James. A substantial French war fleet of twenty ships skirted the east coast of Scotland in March 1708, but bad weather and indecision plagued the expedition. On landing in Fife, there was little sign of enthusiasm for the Jacobite cause amongst the local gentlemen. James fell ill and his French officers headed for home.

Above: The Young Pretender Bonnie Prince Charlie meets Flora MacDonald, the Jacobite heroine who sheltered him during his campaign.

THE 1715 RISING

The second uprising was a more serious affair, for it was backed by powerful forces within Britain. On arriving from Hanover in 1714, the new king George I dismissed Anne's Tory ministers and employed his own Whig men. Disappointed Tories inevitably looked to the Jacobite court in France for potential advancement. One of these, the Earl of Mar, raised the standard of James VIII at Braemar in the eastern Highlands in 1715. He quickly gathered an army of 12,000 men and the support of the important burghs of Aberdeen, Dundee, Perth and Inverness. However, government forces blocked Mar at the indecisive battle of Sheriffmuir near Stirling. Unable to break out of the Highlands, Mar could not link up with the northern English Jacobites who were forced to surrender at Preston. By the time the Pretender arrived at Peterhead in December, the rising was already over and he returned to France.

THE INVASION OF 1719

Spain backed the next attempt to restore the Stewarts, sending a small force to raise the Highland clans and a

TIMELINE	
1708	*French invasion fleet in support of the Old Pretender*
1714	*Queen Anne succeeded by George of Hanover*
1715	*Mar is unable to break out of Highlands after indecisive battle at Sheriffmuir*
1719	*Spanish attempt to restore the Stewarts is unsuccessful*
1745	*Government army in Scotland defeated at Prestonpans in September*
1746	*Jacobites badly defeated at Culloden near Inverness in April.*

Above: The Jacobites were outnumbered and outgunned by the British Government army at the Battle of Culloden in 1746.

larger invasion fleet to invade England. As in 1588, this armada was scattered by poor weather. Two frigates loaded with 300 Spanish troops reached the western Highlands, but they failed to excite much local enthusiasm and were rounded up by Hanoverian forces.

THE 1745 RISING

In 1744, a French invasion fleet was scattered by 'Protestant gales'. Undaunted, the Young Pretender Charles Edward Stewart (also known as 'Bonnie Prince Charlie') sailed to Scotland in July 1745, landing at Eriskay in the Hebrides with only seven companions. Fifty-seven years had elapsed since his grandfather had been deposed and the clans had not forgotten the disappointment of 1715. The risk of failure was high and some clans preferred to sit out the rebellion. Nevertheless by late September, the Young Pretender had gathered an army, captured Perth, defeated the government forces in Scotland at Prestonpans and was holding court in his ancestors' palace of Holyrood. His position was weak, for few in the Lowlands were keen to don the Jacobites' white cockade and important fortresses remained in government hands. With winter closing in, Charles struck out southwards, reaching Derby, a mere 208 km (129 miles) from London, in early December. There was panic in London and the belongings of the royal Hanoverians were flung onto Thames barges as they prepared to flee the city. However, much to Charles' disgust, the exhausted Jacobites turned homeward. Back on home soil, they won a further victory at Falkirk in January, but were pushed northwards by the advance of larger Hanoverian forces. At Culloden Moor near Inverness, the flat terrain was unsuitable for the charge of the Highlanders and government grapeshot won the day.

AFTER CULLODEN

The last pitched battle on British soil signalled the end of the politico-religious conflicts that had bedevilled Britain since the 1530s. The Jacobite threat was over, but that was not clear to contemporaries and the government took strenuous steps to clamp down on the Highlands. The clans were disarmed and the chiefs lost their ancient judicial powers. Work continued on the network of forts and roads that successive governments had been building across Scotland since 1689. In 1748, the Hanoverian government began the construction of its final solution to the Highland problem. Fort George near Inverness took over twenty years to complete and cost the vast sum of £200,000 – well over a billion pounds in modern terms. Capable of holding over 2,000 troops and 3,000 barrels of gunpowder, it was the largest and strongest fortification built in 18th-century Europe. It was the symbol that in the centuries-long struggle to control the island, the south had won.

Below: Following the Jacobite risings, fortifications such as Fort George near Inverness were crucial in suppressing local resistance and maintaining order.

THE RISE OF PARTY POLITICS
1700–1750

By 1700, the Court and Country factions of the Restoration age were evolving into parliamentary parties. Patronage and electoral management held these groups together, as the temper of British politics changed.

WHIG AND TORY

By 1715, the Whig and Tory parties not only had a name but also a sense of collective identity based on their beliefs. Whigs accepted the revolutionary changes of 1688, and stood for the Protestant succession, limited monarchy, the rights of Parliament and toleration for all Protestants including non-Anglican dissenters. Tories were drawn together by older loyalties to the Crown and the Anglican Church. Throughout the early 18th century, the Tories could not shake off their association with the 'old cause' of the Stewarts. The allegation of a secret devotion to Jacobitism, though far from just, kept them out of government office from 1714 until 1760. This was the Whig Age, but their control of central government was balanced by the local powers that many Tory landowners exercised in unpaid but influential posts such as Justices of the Peace.

CROWN AND PARLIAMENT

The reigns of the first two Hanoverian monarchs were crucial in the development of British government. George I spoke little English, was happier in Hanover than in London and was largely content to leave his ministers to rule in his stead. However, he did understand that the Whigs had put him on the throne in 1714, while some Tories were implicated in plots to recall the Pretender. George II detested his father and might have dismissed his father's Whig ministers when he acceded in 1727. However, the Whig supremo Robert Walpole had befriended his wife and George trusted her judgement. Moreover, Walpole was careful to demonstrate his

Above: The Whig minister Sir Robert Walpole is held to be the first unofficial 'Prime Minister' of the United Kingdom.

TIMELINE	
1680s	*Nickname Tory attaches to the Anglican 'court party'*
1680s	*Nickname Whig attaches to the Protestant 'country party'*
1714	*The new king George I prefers Whigs to Tories*
1714–60	*Tories out of power because of their 'Jacobite sympathies'*
1721–42	*Sir Robert Walpole comes to power in wake of financial crisis*
1727	*George II confirms Walpole in power.*

loyalty by recommending an increase of £100,000 in the new king's Civil List revenues. Neither George was much interested in attending Cabinet meetings and so the executive power of the Crown gradually devolved *de facto* into the hands of a first or prime minister. Both kings were content to leave Walpole to master the detail of events and manage the complex web of patronage that sustained the Whig majority in Parliament. Although the king could still dismiss his first minister, even one who held the confidence of Parliament, the seat of executive power inexorably shifted from the monarch to the leader of the Cabinet. Walpole never held the title of Prime Minister, but his long period in power from 1721 to 1742 was central to the development of the premiership.

PATRONAGE

Whig control of the Crown meant Whig control of posts in the armed forces, the Church, in justice and the developing civil service. Only sound Whigs could expect to enjoy successful careers in these professions. Whig control of Parliament rested on their phalanx of 'placemen'. About a quarter of the Commons held minor, untaxing posts in government with generous salaries.

ELECTORAL 'CORRUPTION'

Party managers were also able to control the election of many members in a large number of constituencies. Rotten boroughs abounded where the number of voters was small enough to be bribed. The most notorious examples included Old Sarum in Hampshire, an abandoned medieval earthwork, and Dunwich in Suffolk, a once prosperous woolport that had mostly fallen into the sea. Other members represented pocket boroughs where the local landowner wielded so much influence that he could nominate the members. Often peers in the Lords selected their kinsmen to sit in the Commons and gain parliamentary experience. The Pelham Duke of Newcastle had fourteen Commons seats in his gift. In Scotland, county elections were often decided by 'parchment barons' – lawyers who travelled between hustings with lists of the fictitious voters that they controlled on behalf of their powerful clients. The Septennial Act of 1716 also assisted Whig party managers, for it ensured that the expensive business of a general election was only required once every seven years rather than three.

STABLE GOVERNMENT

Not all products of this system were corrupt placemen, as the 'election' of the able William Pitt as Member for Old Sarum testifies. The system created stable governments and even vigorous Tory oppositions. That stability contributed to the changing temper of British politics during the 18th century. In 1712, the Tories sent the young Whig Walpole to the Tower. On his fall from power in 1714, the Tory Bolingbroke fled for his life to France. By 1750 however, a disgraced Parliamentarian was more likely to be punished by exclusion from the 'trough' of patronage and having to return to his estates.

Above: Although he was a member for the rotten borough of Old Sarum, William Pitt the Elder was an able statesman who rose to be Prime Minister in the 1750s.

Below: Henry Bolingbroke, a Tory minister and Jacobite supporter. Bolingbroke fled the country on the accession of George I in 1714, but later returned to pursue his career in a less volatile environment.

BRITAIN AND EUROPE
1700–1763

By the end of the War of Spanish Succession in 1713, Britain had announced its triumphant arrival on the European stage. In the Seven Years War of 1756 to 1763, Great Britain soundly defeated its competitor for global domination, France.

MARLBOROUGH'S WAR

In 1702, Anne inherited William's struggle against Louis XIV. Fortunately she also acquired the outstanding soldier of the day, John Churchill, Duke of Marlborough, known by his troops as 'Corporal John'. England's ability to forge coalitions and keep them in the field

Above: The Duke of Marlborough won a decisive victory against the French at Blenheim, in modern day Germany.

was also enhanced by the creation of the Bank of England in 1694, giving English and British governments the financial instrument to raise ever-greater war monies. In 1704, Marlborough commanded a European army drawn from seven states. At Blindheim, or Blenheim, on the Danube, he saved Vienna and inflicted the first major defeat that the French had suffered in over forty years. Further battles were won at Ramillies, Oudenarde and Malplaquet in the Spanish Netherlands. Although Marlborough fell from royal favour in 1711, his victories secured the first diplomatic triumph of the new Kingdom of Great Britain. By the 1713 Treaty of Utrecht, Britain gained much of Acadie, the vast tract of French North America that stretched from Quebec to New England. The conquests of Gibraltar and Minorca were also confirmed. By separate treaty, Britain was granted entry rights into the lucrative Spanish slave trade. More importantly, Britain's emerging status as a first rank nation and the decline of French power were implicitly recognized by all Europe.

THE WAR OF JENKIN'S EAR

Preferring stability and prosperity to war, Sir Robert Walpole followed a policy of peace with France for much of his time in power. Proud of avoiding military entanglements in Europe, he is said to have boasted 'Fifty thousand men slain this year in Europe, and not one Englishman'. However, British involvement in the Spanish slave trade sparked trouble in 1739. The

TIMELINE

1704	*Marlborough's first great victory at Blenheim*
1713	*Britain gains much of French North America at Treaty of Utrecht*
1739	*'War of Jenkin's Ear' against Spain*
1740	*War of Austrian Succession leads to Franco-British conflict*
1756	*Austro-Prussian conflict erupts into the Seven Years War*
1757	*Robert Clive defeats the Nawab of Bengal at Plassey*
1759	*The Year of Victories in Canada, the West Indies and India*
1763	*Treaty of Paris confirms British supremacy in North America and India.*

authorities in Spanish America captured a British privateer and, it was claimed, severed the ear of its captain. In due course, Captain Jenkins flourished the pickled and bottled organ in the House of Commons. National indignation forced a reluctant Walpole into a war that began well, with the capture of the silver factory of Portobello in Spanish Central America, but ended in Walpole's resignation.

GEORGE'S WAR

In 1740, war broke out in central Europe between Austria and Prussia. Once the French became involved, Britain and her Dutch allies followed suit. George II himself led an army of British and Hanoverian troops at Dettingen in 1743, the last British monarch to command in battle.

THE WAR FOR THE WORLD

An uneasy peace in Europe was arranged in 1748 and maintained by the ministry of the Whig, Pelham. After his death, a second war between Prussia and Austria erupted in 1756 and the real antagonists, Britain and France, were soon involved. Both nations had amassed a collection of overseas possessions and were rivals for trade, influence and territory in India and North America, so the prize in the struggle between these infant empires was effectively world domination. The war began badly for Britain. In 1756, Minorca and Madras were lost and the able Marquis de Montcalm advanced in Canada. The following year, Cumberland's military inadequacy was exposed in Germany, but this was the turning point in the war. In 1757, a new government formed around William Pitt and Lord Newcastle and news arrived of the astonishing victory of Robert Clive at Plassey in Bengal, where a tiny British and native army of 3,000 had routed an enemy host fifteen times larger.

THE YEAR OF VICTORIES, 1759

Pitt poured men and money into the European war, hoping to keep the French engaged in Europe and 'win Canada on the banks of the Elbe'. The policy bore fruit at the Battle of Minden in August 1759. The Royal Navy's command of the sea won minor victories in the West Indies and West Africa, but also ensured that the French had difficulties in reinforcing their forces in North America. Thanks to Wolfe's daring campaign, Quebec was captured in September. The year of victories ended with the destruction of the French fleet at Quiberon Bay off Brittany. The remaining French possessions in India and the Caribbean were mopped up in 1760. The 1763 Treaty of Paris confirmed that Great Britain had acquired an Empire that stretched from Canada to the East.

Above: George II (r. 1727–1760) was the last British monarch to fight alongside his forces at the Battle of Dettingen in 1743.

THE LOSS OF AMERICA
1763–1783

Britain's problems in North America began in her moment of triumph in 1763. Within twenty years, thirteen colonies had successfully defeated the world's greatest power and won their independence.

THE PRICE OF VICTORY

In the eyes of many colonists, the removal of the French also removed the need for British protection. Many Americans may still have felt themselves to be British, but they were increasingly disinclined to pay for the privilege. The 1764 Pontiac uprising of the native nations of the Great Lakes region indicated that defence was necessary, and London was keen that the colonists should pay their fair share of the costs. However, the colonists resented the taxes and duties imposed between 1764 and 1767 on a range of items – from molasses, glass and tea to legal documents and newspapers. Specific protests against each new burden developed into the general mantra of 'no taxation without representation'.

Above: The Native American chief Pontiac gave his name to the uprising of 1764 against the British occupation of the Great Lakes region.

GROWING APART

American disquiet coincided with George III's attempts to claw back some of the royal powers lost by his father and grandfather, raising fears of a renewed attempt at autocracy. Many settlers had little affection for the Crown in any case, being the descendants of religious refugees from Anglican orthodoxy, or from rebel Scots and Irish stock. The 4,800 km (3,000 mile) Atlantic gap ensured that the colonies were quickly growing apart from Britain, and growing in confidence, with every passing year. This sense of separate identity was accentuated by the clumsy and sometimes brutal response of the British authorities. The 1770 Boston Massacre permanently alienated Massachusetts and many other northern colonists. The 1774 Quebec Act that extended Canada's border down to the Ohio River threatened to seal off any hope of American expansion westwards. The toleration of French Canadian Catholics deeply offended the Puritans of New England. There was no shortage of radicals such as Tom Paine to urge the Americans to take action in defence of their liberties.

THE REVOLUTIONARY WAR

Fighting began at Lexington and Concord in 1775 with the colonial militia pitted against the British regulars. Few expected Britain, with its professional army, experienced officer corps and almost total command of the sea, to have serious difficulty in suppressing the rebel volunteer militias. The different colonies had little tradition of co-operation with each other and the forces of the fledgling Congress were irregular and poorly

Right: Colonists raise the flag of the thirteen United States of America.

TIMELINE

1763	Peace of Paris removes French threat to American colonies
1770	Five colonists killed by British troops in the Boston Massacre
1775	British win an expensive victory at Breed's and Bunker Hill above Boston
1777	British relief forces surrender at Saratoga in New York
1778	French enter Revolutionary War on the American side
1783	Britain accepts the independence of the USA in Peace of Versailles.

equipped. Despite British victory at the first battle of the war at Bunker Hill near Boston in 1775, the depth of American resistance indicated that there would however be no speedy resolution to the conflict. British hopes of dividing the Middle Colonies from the more radical New Englanders evaporated in 1777, when relief forces from Canada were worn down by guerilla action and surrendered at Saratoga in New York. General Washington proved adept at keeping his ill-fed men in the field and American belief in their cause grew as the war developed. British naval power was neutralized by the entry of the French on the American side in 1778 and the Spanish a year later. Britain was now fighting the colonists with one eye on its possessions in India, the Caribbean and the Mediterranean. The war ended in 1781, with the main British force in North America besieged by a much larger Franco-American force at Yorktown in Virginia.

THE END OF THE FIRST EMPIRE

At Versailles in 1783, Britain accepted the independence of the United States of America. The Canadian border east of the Great Lakes was fixed at its present line, so the Americans' door to the West was reopened. The British retained their interest in Canada thanks to Sir Guy Carleton, who skilfully defended Quebec throughout the hostilities. After 1783, an estimated 50,000 British loyalists moved from the USA to make new homes in Canada, helping to found the new provinces of New Brunswick and Ontario. Their arrival, and their hostility to the 'anarchic' USA, provided the manpower and resolve needed to preserve Canada as a British possession. The loss of the American colonies also had consequences for domestic politics in Britain. The king and his Tory ministers were largely discredited. 'Farmer' George's hopes of exercising a more direct interest in national affairs were dashed and he spent more time on his private interests of agricultural improvement and book collecting after the 1780s. The long war in America, coming so soon after the Seven Years War against France, helped to further stimulate the economic changes that were sweeping Britain as the demand for materials continued.

BRITAIN AND THE FRENCH REVOLUTION
1789–1792

The French Revolution was welcomed at first by many in Britain, especially those who hoped for some degree of reform. However, as France slid into terror and war, British views on the revolution polarized and the government began to repress liberal points of view.

THE BLISSFUL DAWN

For over a hundred years, British propagandists had contrasted the virtues of constitutional monarchy with the vices of Bourbon absolutism in France. Not surprisingly then, Britons of all classes and political shades initially welcomed the dramatic news coming out of France in 1789. Tories took pleasure from the discomfiting of an old enemy and from this latest proof of the superiority of the British constitution. Whigs rejoiced in the end of the *ancien régime* and watched Paris carefully to see what could be learned from the French experiment in parliamentary government. Britons of a radical stamp such as William Wordsworth even travelled to France to observe the creation of a new world at first hand – 'bliss was it in that dawn to be alive'. The republican poet Robert Burns also found much fuel in French events for his own unique blend of anti-clericalism and reflection on the inequalities of rank. For a few brief months, most Britons concurred at least briefly with the prominent Whig Charles James Fox that the fall of the Bastille was the greatest and best event in the history of the world.

EDMUND BURKE

One voice stood out against the initial chorus of approval for the French Revolution, that of the Anglo-Irish Whig Edmund Burke. Burke had been sympathetic to the grievances of the American revolutionaries against George III and had been a powerful critic of the failing Tory administration

Above: On 14 July 1789, demonstrators stormed the Bastille prison, freeing the seven prisoners held there and sparking the French Revolution.

THE COMBINATION ACTS

The government was acutely aware that factory workers in the growing industrial towns were especially receptive to radical ideas and calls for action. Political hotheads could be flushed out into the open by *agent provacateurs,* but long hours and low wages meant that many working men had also begun to co-operate in pursuit of higher wages and better conditions. The government's fear of Jacobinism led to the Combination Acts of 1799 and 1800 that made it illegal for workmen to join trade unions.

that lost the colonies in 1781. However, Burke was disturbed by events in France and in his *Reflections on the Revolution in France* of 1790, he correctly predicted that the Revolution would collapse into violent anarchy and military dictatorship. If Burke was the earliest critic of the French Revolution, he was not alone for long, as property holders throughout Britain were increasingly alarmed by the idea that the example of the murderous Jacobins might be emulated on the British side of the Channel.

THOMAS PAINE

Burke's *Reflections* prompted a response in print from the radical pamphleteer Thomas Paine. In 1776, Paine's much-read *Common Sense* had encouraged the American colonists to revolt. Now, in 1791, Paine published *The Rights of Man* to refute Burke's conservative dismissal of the French Revolution. Where Burke had appealed to tradition and authority, Paine drew upon contemporary American and European ideas of the inherent rights of all men. Amongst these was the right of the people to change their government if they so pleased. Paine's ideas struck a chord amongst the middle and lower classes in the new manufacturing towns of northern Britain. Radical Clubs and 'Corresponding Societies' flourished throughout Britain in 1792, with Trees of Liberty planted as acts of solidarity with the French people. The British government was so alarmed by the ideas in Paine's book, and their popularity, that Paine was tried for sedition despite his absence in France.

Above: Unlike Burke, Thomas Paine was an ardent supporter of the French Revolution, a view he set out in *The Rights of Man*.

WAR AND REPRESSION

In January 1793, Louis XIV was guillotined, and France and Britain were at war with each other within the month. The war was ideological from the outset for as George III observed, the existence of the revolutionary government in France threatened the 'foundations of order in every civilized nation'. Now, supporters of the Jacobins were not just politically suspect, but potential traitors. The governing classes throughout Britain were terrified by the spectre of revolution. In Scotland, the reactionary judge Lord Braxfield sentenced the young radical Thomas Muir to fourteen years in the penal colony of New South Wales merely for advocating parliamentary reform. A jittery government suspended Habeas Corpus and arrested known radicals. Thomas Hardy, a cobbler and secretary of the London Corresponding Society was arrested and charged with treason. He was fortunate to be tried under English law and was acquitted, but a Scottish collaborator, Robert Watt, was found guilty and executed.

Below: In January 1793, King Louis XVI of France (r. 1774–92) was guillotined in front of crowds of cheering revolutionaries.

THE WARS AGAINST NAPOLEON
1793–1815

Britain hoped to defeat the French by building coalitions and keeping control of the seas. In 1805, French hopes of invading England were shattered at Trafalgar, but another decade passed before French manpower losses and the British economic blockade finally settled the issue.

THE CAUSE OF WAR

The massacres and executions in France horrified the British public, but Britain nevertheless embarked upon war for strategic reasons. The 1792 Edict of Fraternity, promising to support all nations in their struggle against oppression, seemed targeted at unsettled Ireland. The French capture of Belgium contravened the first aim of British foreign policy – to maintain the neutrality of the Low Countries. French plans to resuscitate Antwerp as a trading centre also threatened to create a rival to London. Britain thus embarked on hostilities that were to last over twenty years.

THE FIRST COALITION

The first phase of the war went badly for Britain. Pitt the Younger hoped to build a European coalition against France, using Britain's financial muscle to bankroll the armies of its allies. By 1797 this policy seemed to have collapsed. Fired with enthusiasm, the armies of revolutionary France swept into Holland and forced the Dutch to abandon their alliance with Britain. Prussia withdrew from the war, while Spain threw in its lot with the French. In 1796, the French Army of Italy swept over the Alps behind its young, charismatic commander Napoleon Bonaparte. France seemed unstoppable on land, while the Royal Navy was hampered in performing its blockading duties by serious mutinies. By 1797, Britain stood alone when her last ally Austria sued for peace.

MEDITERRANEAN STRUGGLE, 1798–1801

With command of northern Italy and a Spanish ally, France controlled the western Mediterranean. French plans to expand into the eastern half of the Sea were shattered by the destruction of Napoleon's fleet by Nelson at the mouth of the Nile in August 1798. In 1799, British naval power kept Turkey and the Kingdom of Naples in the fight and a second coalition was put together. This also collapsed after the French victory at Marengo near Genoa under Napoleon, now First Consul and the absolute ruler of France

TIMELINE	
1798	*Napoleon's Egyptian success threatens British power in the Mediterranean*
1801	*Victory at Copenhagen secures British access to Scandinavian supplies*
1805	*Nelson defeats Franco-Spanish fleet at Trafalgar*
1807	*Orders in Council used to blockade Napoleonic Europe*
1813	*Weakened French forces decisively defeated at Leipzig*
1815	*Final defeat of Napoleon at Waterloo in Belgium.*

that Burke had predicted ten years before. British naval power scored two more successes: at Copenhagen in 1801, and the capture of the strategic gem of Malta in 1800.

THE INVASION YEARS, 1804–1805

The newly-crowned emperor Bonaparte realized that while he could control most of Europe, any hope of long term supremacy required him to crush the 'islanders'. Throughout 1804 and 1805, a vast invasion fleet of barges was prepared at Boulogne. However, before the Royal Navy could be engaged and cleared from the Channel,

Above: The Royal Navy under Lord Horatio Nelson defeated a combined French and Spanish force at Cape Trafalgar in 1805. News of Nelson's death in battle was met with outpourings of grief throughout Britain.

Napoleon's invading army had to be transferred to meet the Austrians and Russians at Austerlitz. His magnificent victory there in December 1805 destroyed Pitt's Third Coalition and despatched the disheartened Prime Minister to an early grave. However, the destruction of the French Fleet at Trafalgar off the Spanish coast in October gave Britain total command of the seas and ensured that there would be no invasion at home. As Admiral Sir John Jervis explained to the House of Lords: 'I do not say that the French cannot come. I only say that they cannot come by sea'.

ECONOMIC WARFARE

In 1806, Napoleon embarked on an economic struggle against British manufacturing power, forbidding his confederates from participating in any trade with Britain. The British responded to his 'Continental System' in 1807 with their Orders in Council which imposed a counter-blockade, stopping all trade between the Napoleonic bloc and the remaining neutral states of Europe. Two years later, the British opened up a new military front in the Iberian peninsula, where Wellington's brilliant campaign tied down French troops that were badly needed elsewhere, especially after the losses of the Russian adventure of 1812. Napoleon marched to Moscow in order to force the Russians to remain within the Continental System. The Russian campaign was a disaster, and he lost an estimated 500,000 men, many to cold and disease. From this point onwards, the arithmetic of resources was against the Corsican genius. A fourth coalition won a crushing victory at Leipzig in 1813, although it was a largely British army that delivered the final victory at Waterloo two years later.

Below: The Battle of Waterloo in 1815 saw the final defeat of Napoleon at the hands of a British-led coalition.

IRELAND IN THE 18TH CENTURY
1695–1800

Growing demands for change after 1775 threatened British control of Ireland's political and economic life. Concerned by the resurgence of Irish national sentiment and the 1798 rising, the government in London united Ireland with Great Britain in 1800.

Portrait of an Irish Chief; drawn from Life at Wexford.

Above: The Penal Laws and the commercial code served to ignite resistance against union in Ireland.

DISCRIMINATION AGAINST CATHOLICS

After 1691, the English and Irish Parliaments passed Acts designed to limit the rights of the Irish Catholic population and ensure the dominance of the Ascendancy, those Protestant Anglo-Irish who belonged to the established Church of Ireland. The Penal Laws were ostensibly designed to encourage Catholics to conform to the Church of Ireland. Beneficiaries were entitled to a larger share of an inheritance if they converted to the established Church and some Catholic lords saved their estates in this way. Overall, the effect of the laws was to reduce the amount of land in Catholic ownership to less than ten per cent by the 1770s. However, there was no mass desertion from the old faith and old ways of life were kept alive by the clandestine Roman clergy and the illegal 'hedge schools'.

THE PENAL LAWS

Under the Penal Laws, Catholics were excluded from the Dublin Parliament, the legal profession and the judiciary. Catholics buying, leasing or inheriting land were subject to legal constraint and they were forbidden to own firearms or a horse suitable for military purposes. Catholics were also debarred from teaching and prohibited from pursuing their studies abroad. The Catholic priesthood was strictly controlled, and some penal legislation was also directed against the dissenting Ulster Presbyterians.

THE COMMERCIAL CODE

In addition to these civil disabilities, the law was used to limit and control the Irish economy. Fearing competition, the Irish cattle trade to England had already been curtailed by the English Parliament of Charles II. In 1699, Irish wool merchants were forced to export their entire output to England, subject to crippling tariffs. The commercial

TIMELINE	
1695	*Penal laws against Catholics passed in Ireland*
1699	*Irish merchants forced to sell output at English markets*
1778	*Volunteer patriotic militias formed to defend Ireland from French invasion*
1780	*Abolition of the commercial code*
1792	*Inspired by the French Revolution, Wolfe Tone forms the United Irishmen*
1796	*Attempted but unsuccessful rebellion in Ireland*
1800	*Irish Parliament abolished*
1801	*United Kingdom of Great Britain and Ireland comes into being.*

Above: After the abolition of the commercial code in 1780, the Parliament in Dublin assumed greater powers of legislation.

code ensured that forestry and agriculture were the prime industries of 18th-century Ireland. The former quickly declined, due to over-felling to meet demand for timber and charcoal. Agriculture was more sustainable and profitable for the increasingly absent Anglo-Irish landlords. By the 1760s, Ireland was a major exporter of salted beef and butter and supplier to the British armed forces and settlers in the colonies. The writer and political activist Swift believed that the combination of legal and commercial discrimination against the Catholic Irish had reduced them to 'a worse condition than the peasants in France'. Not surprisingly, many emigrated to the American colonies.

GRATTAN AND THE IRISH VOLUNTEERS

Although a Protestant, Henry Grattan was an Irish patriot who argued for the legislative freedom of all his countrymen. An able member of the Irish Parliament, Grattan used the crisis of the American Revolution to extract concessions from London. The bulk of British troops in Ireland had been sent to the colonies and there were fears of a possible French intervention in 1778. Volunteer militias of patriotic Irishmen of all religious hue were formed to defend the island and the French were deterred. However, the volunteers were a potent expression of national Irish sentiment. They were also increasingly radical, calling for free and fair trade between Ireland and England. Grattan was able to use the wave of national feeling in Ireland, and apprehension in London, to effect. In 1780, the commercial code was abolished and two years later, the Dublin Parliament was given the power to enact legislation without scrutiny by Westminster.

Above: Pamphleteer and politician Wolfe Tone founded the republican party, the United Irishmen in 1792.

IRELAND AND THE FRENCH REVOLUTION

The ideals of the French revolutionaries found very fertile soil in Ireland. In 1792, the United Irishmen were founded by the republican Wolfe Tone and a number of Belfast linen merchants, to secure a reformed constitution that would guarantee the rights of all Irishmen. The United Irishmen were remarkable in winning over Protestants and Catholic Irish of all classes to join their cause. They also secured support from Paris, which attempted to send an invasion force to western Ireland in 1796. As the situation deteriorated, the Irish government encouraged sectarian attacks by the Protestant yeomanry upon the Catholic population. A rebellion in 1798, in which Wolfe Tone died, was easily suppressed. However, London decided to take a closer interest in Irish affairs and unite the Dublin and British parliaments. Catholic opinion was persuaded to support the Union Bill by the promise of Catholic emancipation. Bribes and peerages were enough to win the support of the MPs in Dublin. The Irish Parliament was abolished, and from January 1801 onwards 100 Irish MPs, 28 peers and 4 bishops sat in the Parliament of the United Kingdom of Great Britain and Ireland.

FEEDING THE NATION
1660–1800

The switch from traditional communal methods of farming to a capitalized, scientific approach revolutionized rural society and the British landscape. Farming was now a business and fortunes were made supplying the growing factory towns.

TOWARDS CAPITALIST FARMING

The period between the Restoration and the Napoleonic wars witnessed unprecedented change in the British landscape. The rising population and rising prices encouraged 17th-century landowners to adopt new farming practices, often modelled on Dutch innovations. By 1650, many English farmers, particularly in East Anglia, had improved their grasslands, begun to use fodder crops such as clover and turnips and were rearing sturdier livestock as a result. In the south of England near London, where returns for investment in modern farming techniques could be better guaranteed, much of the land had already been enclosed by hedges or fences in Tudor and Stewart times. By 1700, there was a prosperous class of substantial tenant farmers and freeholders who had profited from well-managed, concentrated holdings and from producing foodstuffs for the market.

Below: Wealthy landowners throughout Britain encouraged tenant farmers to adopt new, efficient farming techniques during the 18th century.

THE NEED TO CHANGE

Nevertheless, much of southern and central England was still farmed on the wasteful open-field system by villagers who were little more than subsistence peasants. The division of the land into small, scattered strips provided little incentive to change or experiment. Innovative farmers were at the mercy of their neighbours, for there was no way to prevent the spread of weeds and disease from one strip to another, while animals could wander unhindered from pasture to arable land. Traditional land practices also meant that much of the arable land was kept fallow for long periods and ploughable land sat ill-utilized as common grassland or woodlands. Fodder crops were seldom grown so most livestock had to be slaughtered and salted for consumption over the winter. A similar system of subsistence agriculture in Scotland, farming by run-rig or lazy bed, had provided enough food for the medieval population, but was similarly failing to meet the demands of a growing population, as the difficult famine years of the 1690s showed.

ENCLOSURE

The redistribution of the land into compact and manageable holdings entailed both an agricultural and social revolution. Parliamentary approval was required for enclosure, as were land surveys, the preparation of legal title, and the provision of improved farm infrastructure such as drainage, hedging and road building. Enclosure was an expensive process from the outset and the beneficiaries were almost always the richest farmers and landowners who could borrow the necessary capital to improve their new holdings. Once a notice of enclosure was pinned up on the parish church door, many poorer villagers were soon squeezed off both their arable land and the common pastures. Parliament exhorted the Enclosure Commissioners to ensure that the legal rights of all villagers were taken into account, but the very process and the costs of land reorganization meant that many cottars (cottage-dwelling farm labourers) received little or no land in the new landscape. A whole class of lesser farmers either had to sell their land because they could not afford to improve it, or sell their labour to more fortunate neighbours. Many left the land completely and moved to the growing industrial towns in search of work.

Above: Where the old open-field system allowed the spread of weeds and disease between small-holdings, enclosure increased the productivity of farmland.

THE TRIUMPH OF CAPITALIST FARMING

The success of capitalized, scientific farming in the 18th century caught the imagination of the British public, from 'Farmer' George on his Windsor estates downwards. Longer leases provided tenant farmers with an incentive to invest time and energy into their holdings, knowing that they would reap the dividend. The farming pioneer Thomas Coke doubled the lease of an enterprising tenant who had turned marshes into meadows. Machines such as Jethro Tull's seed drill, Small's iron swing plough, and later Andrew Meikle's threshing machine, helped multiply yields and profits. The widespread adoption of scientific rotations that cleansed and nourished the soil increased the amount of productive cropland in use at any given time. Thousands of acres of wetland were drained by digging underground trenches and filling them with rubble before returning the topsoil. Selective breeding and the provision of plentiful fodder crops doubled and tripled the weight of livestock. Innovative breeders, such as Robert Bakewell the sheep farmer and later Hugh Thomas, the founder of the Aberdeen-Angus breed of cattle, were minor celebrities in their day. Artists were commissioned to capture their prize-winning beasts on canvas. Farming societies grew up throughout Britain to stimulate farming improvement through exhibitions, competitions, lectures and publications.

COAL, IRON, STEAM AND COTTON
1750–1830

In the 18th century, industrial production in Britain developed at a rate that many commentators described as 'revolutionary'. New machines and methods of working, and ever-rising demand, turned Britain into an industrial powerhouse.

OUT OF THE DOMESTIC SYSTEM

Before 1700, there were many centres where craft workers in associated trades had long congregated. The guild of Sheffield steelworkers, known as the Company of Cutlers in Hallamshire, was incorporated in 1624 in the reign of James VI & I. Before 1740 however, industrial production tended to be small-scale, with processes scattered around specialist workshops. Most workers hoped to work for themselves, and at their own speed, as independent masters. However, these workshops were too small and had insufficient capital to take advantage of rising demand and technological change. The skilled handloom weavers working in their back rooms gave way to the 'cotton sheds' of the factory age. Later commentators romanticized and lamented the passing of the old craft industries. However workers in the 'domestic' system were often badly underpaid, for 18th-century trade masters were just as keen to keep costs low as any 19th-century factory boss. There were already some larger units of production such as John and Thomas Lombe's silk mill on the river Derwent at Derby, which was employing over 300 workers in a factory setting by 1717.

WATER AND STEAM

Water machinery had long been used in industry, not just to grind flour but to power fulling machines and the bellows and hammers used in metal workshops. Fast-flowing streams played an important part in the first phase of the 18th century industrial revolution. The first water-powered cotton-spinning mill opened in 1771 and was followed by many others such as Quarry Bank Mill at Styal in Cheshire and the New Lanark Mill on the Falls of Clyde in Lanarkshire. Yet the quickening pace of change was such

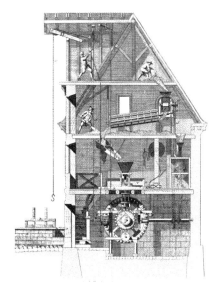

Above: Water mills that harnessed power from fast-flowing streams and rivers allowed quicker, more efficient cotton-spinning.

'THE GREAT CAPITALIST'

The cotton industry advanced thanks to several breakthroughs in spinning and weaving technology. Richard Arkwright combined these in his Derbyshire Cromford mill to produce stronger, all-purpose yarns. Arkwright was quick to see the potential of steam power, installing Boulton-Watt machines in his new mill at Wirksworth in 1780. To use the machines efficiently, his workers were put on twelve-hour shifts. Arkwright's innovations earned him a fortune and a knighthood.

TIMELINE

1733	*John Kay's Flying Shuttle speeds up the process of weaving*
1769	*Arkwright develops the water frame to increase cotton thread production*
1776	*First successful commercial use of the Boulton & Watt steam engine*
1785	*Edmund Cartwright builds the first mechanized power loom*
1815	*Sir Humphrey Davey invents the miners' safety lamp.*

that the first steam-driven mill was built only nine years later. Steam power developed to meet the challenge of draining coal and tin mines as they went deeper underground. Steam was used by Savery's 1698 pump and Newcomen's 1712 engine, which both used atmospheric pressure to raise water but were inefficient and cumbersome. James Watt's improved steam engine, allied to Matthew Boulton's accurately machined cylinders and William Murdock's 'sun and planet' gear wheels, combined to produce a machine that could be used almost anywhere. By 1870, over 100,000 steam engines were at work throughout Britain. Industry was increasingly concentrated above coalfields and thanks to the invention of the powerloom, the early spinning mills on the Pennine hillsides had mostly been abandoned. Nevertheless, water continued to be used well into the Age of Steam. The great waterwheel at the Laxey pit on the Isle of Man was only built in 1854, while the Kilhope lead mine in County Durham installed a water wheel to crush ores in 1866.

COAL AND IRON

In 1700, coal was a domestic fuel in the houses of the rich. By 1850, it was the staple of British industrial might and annual extraction rates had tripled from four to twelve million tonnes. The old methods of bell pits and adit (horizontal) mines had reached their limits by 1700, but deep mines were difficult to work. Humphrey Davey's 1815 safety lamp allowed miners to work in light without igniting the fire-damp, an explosive mixture of air and methane, that was found at depth. After 1795, John Buddle's exhaust pump began to replace the trappers, the infants who squatted all day opening and shutting flaps to push air below. By 1830, steam-powered fans allowed mines to be dug even deeper in search of the 'black diamonds'. Once the Darby dynasty of ironmasters perfected the use of coke to smelt iron-ore at Coalbrookdale in Shropshire, even more coal was needed. Previous ironmasters had used charcoal, even sending shiploads of ore to the Scottish Highlands, where furnaces such as Bonawe in Argyll enjoyed a copious supply of timber. Using coke, and the discovery of 'puddling' or stirring molten ore to release impurities, made quality iron cheaper to manufacture. Vast industrial enterprises appeared across Britain such as the Cyfarthfa Works in Merthyr Tydfil and the Carron Iron Works in Falkirk.

Below: Early miners worked by candlelight at the risk of igniting gases trapped underground. After 1815, the invention of the safety lamp much improved conditions.

THE TRANSPORT REVOLUTION
1700–1820

In Tudor and Stewart times, the packhorse was still the most efficient means of transport in much of Britain and Ireland. By 1820 however, a vast network of canals and turnpike roads had revolutionized the scale and cost of transporting goods.

Below: A tollgate ticket for the Bermondsey, Rotherhithe and Deptford Roads dating from the turnpike era.

THE OLD ROADS

Travelling and transporting goods were major problems in the early 18th century. Long caravans of forty or more linked packhorses were used to carry manufactured goods to market. The fastest way for an individual to travel was still by horse. In 1603, the Earl of Monmouth carried the news of Elizabeth's death to James VI in Edinburgh in less than sixty hours, riding at breakneck speed, and his time was not improved upon until the early 19th century. Both the English and Scottish Parliaments passed statutes empowering local officials to muster labour and materials for road repairs, but these were mostly dead letters. Stone bridges were rare and in much of the country, ferrymen still made a living well into the 18th century by carrying travellers across at fording points on their backs.

THE COMING OF TURNPIKES

Improvements to British roads began after 1660 with the first permitted toll roads. Their success encouraged local businessmen and landowners around Britain to form turnpike trusts with the power to fund improvements from tolls. These new roads were straighter, gated and policed, and many locals resented having to pay to use their accustomed routes, leading to serious riots in Bristol and Yorkshire where gates and tollhouses were destroyed. Nevertheless, the turnpike roads were also much faster, especially after the 1780s when they were built using the Macadam system of cambered layers of crushed stone and gravel in order to minimize water and frost damage. By 1810, there were almost 16,000 km (10,000 miles) of toll road in Britain and over 1,500 daily coach services in and out of London. A massive industry grew up around the country at the hundreds of inn stops which provided changes of horse, new teams of coach drivers and guards as well as refreshments for travellers. Magazines and newspapers from London and other key regional cities now had a distribution system for their products, as had the Royal Mail, which set up an express postal coach service in 1784. The turnpike roads connected the provinces with the capital and allowed villagers in the sleepiest hollow to share in the great events of the nation.

Above: A coach passing through a turnpike at night. The term 'pike' referred to the long bar that would block the way forward until the traveller paid, a system still in use today.

COAL CANAL

The Duke of Bridgewater's 11 km (7 mile) long canal was also built to carry coal from his mines at Worsley to Manchester after 1761. Tourists rode out to marvel at the coal barges crossing high above the River Irwell by aqueduct, but the real wonder of the canal was its effect on the price of coal in the Manchester area, which plunged by over fifty per cent. The Duke became one of the richest men in Britain as a result.

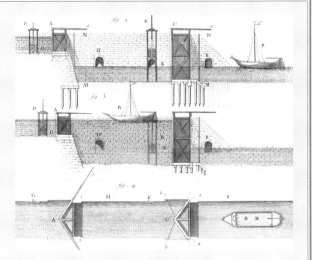

Right: Lock systems enabled canals to be built across previously inaccessible territory, creating a network of waterways throughout the country.

'THE ARTERIES OF INDUSTRY'

The first managed waterways in Britain were short systems of locks and cuts developed along natural rivers. An artificial ship canal was cut from the sea to the inland port of Exeter in 1564, but this venture was less than 3 km (2 miles) long and only 1 m (3 feet) deep. Expensive and of limited economic value, the Exeter Cut attracted no imitators until the changing industrial and demographic pattern of the 18th century made canals more profitable. The 30 km (20 mile) long Newry Canal from Portadown to the Irish Sea was a serious commercial proposition however, making it easier to shift the coal deposits to market in Dublin and England.

THE CRAZE FOR CANALS

The success of the Newry venture encouraged the merchants of Liverpool to fund the Sankey Navigation to the Mersey. This was fully operational and carrying coal at ten pence per ton by 1757. In 1759, the canal engineer James Brindley envisioned a network of linked waterways across England, and began cutting the Grand Trunk canal southwards in 1766. That network was largely in place by 1820, by which time canals had proliferated wherever manufacturers needed access to heavy resources such as coal, iron-ore and clay. However, by the 1790s a number of over-ambitious schemes resulted in canals being built in places where there was no commercial need, or where technical difficulties multiplied costs. By 1830, there were almost 6,450 km (4,000 miles) of inland waterway in Britain and no place in central England and Wales was more than a short distance from a navigable river or canal.

TIMELINE

1555	*Highways Statute makes parishes responsible for the upkeep of English roads*
1660s	*First toll roads in southern England*
1757	*The coal-carrying Sankey Navigation in Lancashire opens*
1760s	*John McAdam develops his system of drained, cambered gravel roads*
1784	*Royal Mail express coaches in service*
1780–1840	*Golden years of stage coaching on the turnpike road system*
1780–1840	*High point of canal system development.*

MORE MOUTHS TO FEED
1750–1850

The population of Britain and Ireland rose dramatically after 1750, even though many chose to emigrate to the new colonies. Although mortality rates were high in the squalid areas of the towns, the overall population trend was rapidly upwards.

THE NUMBERS GAME

Although reasonably accurate population statistics only began with the Statistical Account of Scotland in 1791 and the Census of 1801, one thing is clear. The population of Britain increased relentlessly throughout the Georgian and early Victorian period. Ten million or so British and Irish in 1751 had become over twenty-seven million a century later. Moreover, a far larger number were living in towns and cities. In 1700, about twenty per cent of the English dwelt in large settlements. By 1821, that percentage had doubled. Centres of industry experienced a rate of growth that astonished and concerned contemporaries. Within one lifetime, the market town of Manchester became 'Cottonopolis', with over 300,000 inhabitants. The small university town of Glasgow was transformed – first by the tobacco trade and then by heavy industry – into the Second City of Empire. London grew from around 650,000 in 1750 to almost two and a half million by the time of Victoria's accession in 1837. The older urban centres such as York, Exeter and Bristol also grew, but did so at a slower rate and were soon dwarfed by the big new industrial centres.

THE MALTHUSIAN PREDICTION

Most commentators believed that the rise in population would benefit the economy by increasing the number of consumers and workers. Thomas Robert Malthus, the first British professor of political economy, took

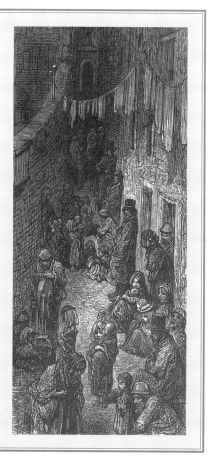

TOWN TROUBLES

The rapid influx of people into urban centres caught the authorities unawares. Sudden and massive overcrowding put an intolerable strain on such urban infrastructure as existed. Open drains and sewers could never cope with the mountains of ordure produced daily in the big cities and few districts had reputable supplies of fresh water. In the poorer areas, poor public hygiene, allied to overcrowded and ill-ventilated slum quarters, were the perfect conditions for the spread of cholera. The disease first reared its murderous head in the port of Sunderland in 1831.

Right: Whilst industrial entrepreneurs grew wealthy, conditions for many of their employees in the urban slums were poor.

TIMELINE

1751	Population of Britain and Ireland approximately ten million
1796	Edward Jenner tests his theory of vaccination
1798	Thomas Malthus predicts overpopulation disaster
1801	First official census of the British population
1831	Cholera arrives in England at the port of Sunderland
1851	Population of Britain and Ireland approximately 27 million.

a more pessimistic view. In 1798, he predicted that the increasing number of mouths would soon outstrip food supplies and provoke widespread famine by 1850. Malthus argued for moral restraint, especially amongst the lower orders, to maintain the population at a sustainable level. His ideas influenced the way that later governments dealt with the problem of the poor, encouraging them to abolish 'outdoor' relief payments to large families and establish the strictly disciplined and sexually segregated workhouses.

FREEDOM AND FERTILITY

After 1750, a flood of agricultural labourers of both sexes left the land in search of work in the new mills, mines and forges of industrial Britain. Many of these urban migrants were in the 15–25 age range and almost immediately found themselves earning relatively high cash wages. Fewer young men had to serve long craft apprenticeships and satisfy guild standards before they could earn enough money to support a family. There were more opportunities to meet potential marriage partners in the towns, and many of the traditional social and religious restraints on the behaviour of the young had been left behind in the smaller rural communities. Many married and bred younger as a result. After 1770, the birth rate in the factory towns of Lancashire and Yorkshire far exceeded that in the more staid market towns of the South and East Anglia.

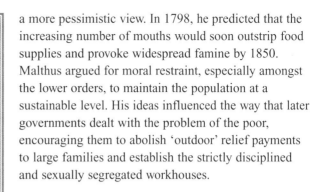

Below: After 1796 Edward Jenner developed a vaccine against smallpox.

SOAP AND SCIENCE

As the canals, and later railways, brought cheap coal to the cities, it became much easier to heat water for bathing, washing clothes and scrubbing homes. The reformer Francis Place (1771–1854) noted that standards of cleanliness amongst the lower orders had much improved in his lifetime, thanks to the abundance of hot water, soap and cotton. After 1770, cotton clothes were cheap and easy to keep clean, unlike the heavy woollens of earlier times that were seldom washed. Advances in the chemical industries transformed soap from a luxury into an everyday product. Andrew Pears began manufacturing a translucent soap in 1789, while the giant St Rollox chemical works in Glasgow produced a range of industrial and domestic bleaches. Cleaner, warmer homes were safer places for infants. Not only were many more people being born – their chances of surviving into adulthood were far higher. Twice as many infants made it to their fifth birthday in 1830 compared with a century earlier. New scientific discoveries helped, particularly the work by the Gloucestershire doctor Edward Jenner into vaccination, which was already reducing deaths from smallpox by 1810.

Deists and Methodists
1700–1800

Religious enthusiasm was not welcomed by many 18th-century Anglican clergymen, for fear of unsettling society. Methodists and some early Evangelical Anglicans took the Gospel to the poorest in the land, while nervous magistrates looked on uneasily.

Spiritual Calm

The Established Church was one of the richest sources of patronage in 18th-century Britain. As such, the Anglican clergy attracted many entrants who were seeking a secure position in society rather than a life of devotion following in the footsteps of Christ. For many, though by no means all, Anglican vicars, their Sunday duties were a necessary interruption to their social rounds, leisure pursuits or at best scholarly interests. Many were deeply aware of how an excess of Puritan zeal had convulsed British society throughout much of the preceding century. As men who valued stability, they preferred the rational and moderate ideas of deist theologians like John Toland whose *Christianity not Mysterious* rejected supernatural elements of faith such as prophecy and miracles. For these believers, deism was a sensible creed that fitted well with the new understandings of the world being revealed by scientific investigation.

Above: Anglican vicars were often deists who argued against supernatural events and miracles, preferring a religion based on rational beliefs.

Griffith Jones

Not all Anglican vicars neglected their flocks in favour of the quiet of their studies. Many were practical and realistic men who took a deep interest in the local schoolhouse and the care of the parish poor. Those who ministered in the growing towns campaigned strongly to curtail the vices of drunkenness and ignorance that afflicted the lower orders.

One of the earliest and most energetic of these Evangelical Anglicans was Griffith Jones, who believed that education was the key to salvation. Rector of Llanddowror in Carmarthenshire, Jones devoted himself to the spread of literacy through his preaching and the circulating school movement. These were schools that stayed in a location for several months before transferring or circulating to the next village or town. In 1737 alone he opened thirty-seven schools. Jones was heavily criticized by some for using Welsh as the medium of instruction in his schools, although that was the spoken tongue of his students.

THE METHODISTS

At Oxford in the early 1730s, the brothers John and Charles Wesley and their friends in the university 'Holy Club' were noted for their disciplined approach to Bible Study, their fasting and their distaste for popular amusements. Their regular behaviour earned them the nickname 'Methodists', which they adopted when they began their missionary activities in the late 1730s. The charismatic preacher George Whitefield showed the way by preaching in the open air to the mining folk of Kingswood near Bristol in 1739. Despite his initial worry that field preaching was sinful, John Wesley soon followed suit. He had no option, for the doors of most respectable Anglican churches were closed to him at this point. Thus John Wesley embarked on a life of mission, travelling many hundreds of miles each year on long preaching tours around Britain to bring the Gospel to the ears of thousands of worshippers. Wesley maintained his exhausting travel itineraries until he was well into his eighties, worshipping with some of the most desperate communities in England such as the coalminers of the north and the workers from the Cornish tin-mines.

ANGLICAN REACTION

The Methodists were not welcomed by other Anglican clerics who disliked their zealous approach and were especially offended by their use of unordained lay preachers to preach and perform pastoral duties. Local magistrates feared the huge congregations of working people who gathered outside towns to listen to Methodist preachers. Crowds in excess of 20,000 were not uncommon. At the time, these were probably the largest gatherings that anyone involved had ever seen or imagined. Wesley and his colleagues were accused of fomenting social unrest and encouraging fanatical religious disturbance. By hinting that these travelling preachers were agents of the Pope or the Jacobites, it was at first easy to stir up gullible mobs, who attacked Methodist preachers and the homes of their known supporters. In time however, this persecution subsided as the good work that the Methodists did amongst the poor, and their own firm moral discipline, came to be recognized and appreciated. Wesley's own godly life – in addition to his itinerant preaching he ran charities, opened chapels and supervised orphanages and schools – was lived wholly within the Church of England, if only just. By the time of his death at the age of eighty-eight, his life's work was already inspiring younger Anglicans and Methodist followers to take a greater interest in improving the lot of the poor and underprivileged.

Below: The Methodist missionaries took to the road, preaching to communities the length and breadth of Britain.

TIMELINE

1696	John Toland publishes his Christianity Not Mysterious
1731	Griffith Jones begins his circulating schools movement
1738	George Whitefield begins his career as a public preacher
1739	John Wesley follows Whitefield's example at Bristol
1740	Wesley founds his first Methodist society
1743	Wesley writes the General Rules to guide the growing Methodist movement
1791	Wesley dies leaving a movement with over 135,000 members.

RADICAL BRITAIN
1815–1820

Britain's war economy was severely affected by the years of peace after 1815. Heavy unemployment and social distress led to radical agitation by working people, but brought a severe response from the government.

SOCIAL DISTRESS

The long wars against France brought mixed blessings for many working people in Britain. War stimulated demand for a wide range of products and provided employment in busy factories. However, it led to higher prices for many daily necessities and increased taxation to meet the government's growing war debts. The price of bread almost tripled between 1793–1815, but the wages of most labourers rose only marginally. Some trades, notably the handloom weavers who found themselves in competition with steam-driven looms, saw their wages in long-term decline. With peace in 1815, government supply contracts dried up, leaving many unemployed at the same time as almost 200,000 servicemen were demobilized and dumped on the job market. Farmers who had expanded their operations on to more marginal land during the war years when grain and meat prices were rising, now retrenched, leaving many agricultural labourers without work. After a short replacement boom immediately after the war, the British economy entered a period of price instability and slump.

THE CORN LAW

In 1815 the Tory Cabinet of Lord Liverpool faced a national debt of nine hundred million pounds that required annual servicing of over thirty million pounds. To help balance the budget, they passed the Importation Act or 'corn law' which prohibited the purchase of expensive foreign grain until the domestic British crop exceeded a set price. The law was meant to protect British agriculture and currency reserves, but it had the result of raising the price of bread and other foodstuffs to unprecedented levels. Speculators made fortunes from high grain prices, while many unemployed people throughout Britain went hungry. The growing sense of grievance throughout the land was compounded in 1816, when the government abolished the wartime tax on incomes that had hit the rich. The national debt would be met from higher duties levied on everyday items such as sugar, tea, beer, tobacco, candles and

TIMELINE	
1815	*End of Napoleonic Wars brings economic distress to workers*
1815	*Corn Law passed to protect British farmers and landowners*
1816	*Spa Fields radical meeting leads to riots in London*
1817	*Manchester Blanketeers march to London but are harassed by the authorities*
1819	*Cavalry attack on reform meeting at St Peter's Fields in Manchester*
1819	*Tory government passes the repressive Six Acts*
1820	*Extremist radicals plan to assassinate the government at Cato Street dinner*
1820	*Week of strikes and protests in Scotland remembered as the 'Radical War'.*

Above: The demonstration at St Peter's Fields in Manchester ended in bloodshed as unarmed protestors were cut down by cavalry troops.

soap. This switch from direct to indirect taxation naturally hit the poorer sections of society hardest. Radical orators found a ready audience for their message that Parliament should be reformed to serve the national interest and not just protect the rich.

AGITATION

Although, or perhaps because, trade unions were banned by the Combination Acts, working men had taken action to protect their livelihoods during the war. Textile workers in Nottinghamshire using the mask of Ned Ludd, a mythical outlaw from Sherwood Forest, had smashed new weaving frames in night raids. In Lancashire and Cheshire, mobs of distressed weavers had attempted to destroy mills that used power-looms. The authorities dealt with these small-scale disturbances quickly and firmly, but they continued to face a succession of threats. A radical meeting at Spa Fields in Islington in 1816 ended in disorder, with armed mobs on the streets of London. The Blanketeers, a massive demonstration march of Manchester unemployed to London in 1817, was designed to petition the Prince Regent for relief and parliamentary reform. The government response was in each case to suspend Habeas Corpus to make it easier to arrest radical leaders and agitators.

'PETERLOO'

As the economic situation worsened in 1919, a huge meeting was organized at St Peter's Fields in Manchester to demand reform. Nervous magistrates ordered the Yeomanry to arrest the radical orator Henry Hunt. In the ensuing melée, eleven demonstrators were killed and over 400 wounded, many by the sabres of the cavalry. This attack on unarmed protestors, some of whom were women and children, earned the ironic nickname of Peterloo. Much of the nation was horrified by these events, but the government responded by passing a series of repressive Acts designed to make it more difficult for the radicals to hold public meetings and publish their opinions. Popular disquiet at these measures receded in 1820, when a plot to assassinate the Cabinet at dinner was exposed. The conspirators were arrested in the act and seem to have been tempted to carry out the plot by a government agent. That same year saw a radical uprising in Scotland in which miners attempted to capture an arms factory near Falkirk and eleven demonstrators were shot dead by troops. The crisis passed over, in part due to improving conditions as the economy adjusted to peacetime demand.

CLEARANCE AND FAMINE
1750–1850

Many Highland Scots emigrated to North America after 1745. Some did so voluntarily, but others were forced out in 'the clearances'. In Ireland, mass emigration followed on from the famines of the 1840s.

TOO MANY MOUTHS?

Despite the disaster of 1745, the population of northern Scotland continued to rise in the late 18th century. However, emigration was becoming a constant factor in Highland society. Tens of thousands of men were taken by the army to form new Highland regiments for the French wars between 1763 and 1815. Others left of their own volition after the bad harvests of the early 1760s, attracted by the fertility and abundance of better land in the colonies. After 1775, Canada became the preferred destination for many Highlanders, as their Catholic faith was rumoured to be unwelcome in New England.

Above: The establishment of sheep farms across the Highlands led to the forced eviction of many small-holders.

THE COMING OF SHEEP

The coming of southern sheep operators triggered the eviction of many small-scale Highland farmers from their traditional farmlands. In the post-Culloden peace, the clan chiefs no longer needed warriors paying rent in military service and in kind. Highland landowners now aspired to join the elites of Edinburgh and London, and for that they needed cash rents. Southern sheep-farmers were happy to offer cash on a scale that no farmer of run-rigs could hope to match. In 1785, one grazing in Glen Shiel was let for sheep at the princely sum of £310. The same land had formerly generated a mere ten pounds from its tenants. In 1826, the entire population of the island of Rum were evicted from their homes and replaced by one farmer with over 8,000 sheep.

Below: Over-reliance on potato crops resulted in an estimated one million deaths in Ireland when the crop failed for three years running.

STRATHNAVER, 1814

The most infamous of the forced evictions occurred in Sutherland, where the Marquis of Stafford evicted 15,000 small-scale farmers to make way for sheep. Stafford offered his tenants land on the coast where they could make a living from crofting and fishing. However, at Strathnaver the evictions were carried out brutally by Stafford's agents. Houses were torched and a woman burned to death. The resulting trial brought the issue to national prominence and won public sympathy for the homeless Highlanders. Nevertheless the clearances continued throughout the 19th century and accelerated after 1850, when wealthy incomers from the south bought Highland estates and cleared them for deer and grouse shooting.

TIMELINE

1760s	*Increased Highland migration to North America and central Scotland*
1780-1840	*Extension of sheep farming throughout northern Scotland*
1814	*Infamous 'forced' clearances in Strathnaver in Sutherland*
1845–6	*Appearance of the potato blight in Ireland and Scottish Highlands*
1846–9	*Serious famines in Ireland and Scottish Highlands*
1850s	*Extensive migration from Ireland to USA.*

KING POTATO

Between 1800 and 1841, the population of Ireland rose from 4.5 to 8.5 million. However, there was little coal or iron in Ireland outside Ulster, so the rising population had to make its living from the land. Restrictions on Catholic ownership of land meant that a system of sub-leasing of farmland had developed. As a result, many rural Irish were forced to farm on tiny smallholdings. In 1840, almost half the farms in Ireland were less than three acres (1.2 hectares) and few Irish farmed more than fifteen (6 hectares). Potatoes were the preferred crop, for they provided twice as much nutrition per acre than cereals. King Potato was the staple ingredient of around four million rural Irish but many families only survived by performing seasonal tasks on the farms of Scotland and western England.

'PUTRID SLIME'

The dangers of monoculture became apparent in 1845, when the Irish potato crop was infested with 'blight', an airborne fungus that withered the plants and turned the tubers into a foul-smelling mush. Three of the four subsequent harvests were also blighted, leaving millions starving and destitute. Government relief measures were temporary, inadequate and slow. Cheap maize imported from America proved to be indigestible without expensive processing. Public relief projects such as building roads provided work, but exhausted men and women who had suffered months of malnutrition. The winter of 1846–47 was especially cold and hit hard upon a weakened population. An estimated million Irish died between 1845 and 1849. Another two million migrated, many to Liverpool, Glasgow and South Wales, though the richer and braver took their chances on the 'coffin ships' across the Atlantic to the United States and Canada. Large parts of rural Ireland were depopulated, and whole communities vanished. Nevertheless, despite the catastrophic human toll, the events of 1845–49 provided fresh ground for a reorganization of agricultural land in the 1860s, and an opportunity to improve food production on a more efficient framework. However, the political cost of the British government's incompetence and delay was to plague Anglo-Irish relations long after the Great Hunger was over.

Below: Up to two million people emigrated from Ireland seeking a better life, many crossing the Atlantic to the New World.

AY 10, 1851.] THE ILLUSTRATED LONDON NEWS. 387

THE EMIGRATION AGENTS' OFFICE—THE PASSAGE MONEY PAID.

THE WORKSHOP OF THE WORLD
1830–1875

During the 19th century, Britain enjoyed a number of advantages that made her the first industrial power. The Great Exhibition in 1851 was a grand statement of British pride in its achievements, but by 1875 that economic supremacy was already under serious threat.

ECONOMIC MASTERY

Thanks to innovative technology, an abundant supply of coal, cheap pig iron and rising demand in its domestic and colonial markets, Britain raced ahead of its European competitors. In the 1820s, British coal extraction was nine times that of France, Germany, Russia and Belgium combined. In 1851, the urban population exceeded the rural for the first time in British history and many of those town dwellers lived in the shadow of a colliery winding-wheel or a mill chimneystack. Industry was also helped by the prevailing 'laissez-faire' attitude of Whig and Tory governments, who were loathe to interfere in industrial matters. As a result, British products dominated the world's markets.

THE GREAT EXHIBITION OF 1851

The civil servant Henry Cole first had the idea of holding an industrial exhibition in London after visiting a Parisian trade fair. He persuaded Prince Albert to lend his patronage to a Great Exhibition of Works and Industries staged in Hyde Park in the summer of 1851. The exhibits were housed within a revolutionary pre-fabricated glass and iron structure, designed by Joseph Paxton and dubbed 'the Crystal Palace' by the satirical magazine *Punch*. Erected in little more than five months, its towering glass halls, packed with over 13,000 exhibits from around the world, captured the imagination of the British public. Thousands flocked to London on the newly completed railway network, often simultaneously taking their first railway journey and first trip to London. The Great Exhibition only lasted for six months before the Crystal Palace was dismantled and re-erected at Sydenham Hill, but in that brief period it attracted over six million paying visitors. The profits provided the foundation for a series of public works such as the Albert Hall and the Victoria & Albert Museum. The exhibition also provided a focus for British pride and the term 'Victorian' began to be used to express national confidence and contentment.

Below: The Great Exhibition of 1851, housed in the Crystal Palace, was a grand statement of Britain's global dominance and her economic and industrial success.

QUEEN VICTORIA

At almost sixty years, the reign of Queen Victoria was the longest of any British monarch. Coming to the throne unexpectedly in 1837, the early years of her reign were dominated by marriage and childbirth. After the death of her beloved Albert in 1861, Victoria became reclusive, but in her latter years, she came to personify a long period of history in which Britain experienced stability, economic growth and imperial success.

BALACLAVA. (Oct. 26th 1854)
"Forward, the Light Brigade!
Charge for the guns!" he said:
Into the valley of Death
Rode the Six Hundred.

Above: The Charge of the Light Brigade at Balaclava, immortalized in Tennyson's poem of the same name, was a military disaster.

CRIMEAN INCOMPETENCE

The fragility of that confidence was quickly exposed when Britain found itself at war with Imperial Russia in 1854. Much of the fighting took place in the Crimean peninsula in southern Russia, but the recent invention of the electric telegraph ensured that *Times* readers could follow the war in the columns despatched by William Russell. The British performance in this modern conflict of trenches, artillery and precision rifles was characterized by inadequate planning and supply, and an incompetent aristocratic command that had purchased its rank. Changing technology was rendering the old structures of British society obsolete, a fact acknowledged by the abolition of the sale of military offices after the futile sacrifice of the Light Brigade at Balaclava.

THE COTTON CRISIS AND THE GREAT DEPRESSION

By 1861, two thousand cotton mills of Lancashire produced over half the world's cotton goods. They were, however, dangerously reliant on raw cotton from the slave-holding southern states of the USA. That supply was turned off for four years by the Union Navy's successful blockade of Confederate ports between 1861 and 1865. Lancashire and the other cotton towns such as Glasgow were plunged into depression with thousands laid off and in need of poor relief at public expense. Surprisingly, there was little disorder. Many of the affected workers sympathized with the Federal North, particularly once the cause of negro emancipation emerged as its key war aim. By 1867 the cotton mills were running again, but like all British industries they were hit by the Great Depression after 1875.

A NEW PLACE IN THE WORLD

British trade was becalmed in the last quarter of the 19th century. Other economies were developing apace, often benefiting from British technology and capital. Wheat and other foodstuffs from the plains of North and South America and the Ukrainian steppes flooded on to world markets. Although this meant that the British industrial worker had access to cheaper food, many farmers were ruined. In other trades, German, American, French, Russian and Japanese industries were now supplying their own internal markets and it became harder to sell British goods overseas. Imperial trade kept British factories busy but by 1890, British supremacy in key industries had been supplanted by more innovative competitors.

VOTES FOR MORE PEOPLE
1832–1884

Throughout the 19th century, the franchise was gradually extended to a wider electorate. Some feared that this would spark revolution – others saw it as a way to manage change gradually.

A ROTTEN PARLIAMENT

Parliament remained unreformed until 1832. Though the British population had risen to 24 million, the electorate numbered only 435,000. A few constituencies – such as Westminster – had relatively open franchises and large electorates. At the other end of the spectrum were the many rotten boroughs. Riots, corruption and drunkenness were the order of the day. Electors expected to be bribed, for they regarded their vote as a property rather than a right. Voting by public declaration encouraged intimidation – even George III sent his retainers down to the hustings in 1784 to pressurize electors thinking of voting for the radical Fox. Elections lasted for days, and as local voting was staggered, it could take weeks before all the general election results were in.

Above: Open elections held at hustings were a scene of riotous disorder, and the focus of bribery and corruption on a massive scale.

REFORM CRISIS

The most glaring absurdity was the almost total lack of parliamentary representation for the industrial towns that contributed so much to the Exchequer. There was little place in a landowners' parliament for the growing middle-class, yet they increasingly held the reins of economic power. Many of these business people were in sympathy with the ideas of the political unions that had sprung up around the country to spread the Reform message. Over time, ideas that had been radical in 1780 – wider franchise, more equal and rational representation, more regular and less corrupt elections – had become accepted middle-class wisdom. In 1831, a new Whig government resolved to reform Parliament. Its first Reform Bill stalled, sparking a general election which the Whigs won convincingly. A second Bill was rejected in the Lords, prompting riots throughout Britain. Public buildings in Bristol and Nottingham were razed by mobs and regiments were alerted to restore order. When the Lords threatened to bring down a third Bill, the Whig premier Grey asked William IV to

TIMELINE	
1832	*First Reform Bill does away with worst electoral abuses*
1867	*Second Reform Act enfranchises all male householders*
1872	*Ballot Act introduces secret voting and does away with the public hustings*
1884	*Representation of the People Act increases the franchise to over 5.5 million*
1885	*Redistribution of Seats Act makes constituencies of roughly equal size.*

create enough new Whig peers to carry the Bill unamended. When the king refused, Grey resigned. The Duke of Wellington was asked to steer a diluted bill through Parliament, but wisely beat a retreat as demonstrators outside his London home demanded 'the bill, the whole bill and nothing but the bill'. Back in power with the king's promise of as many peers as he needed, Grey pushed the Reform Bill into law in June 1832.

MODERATE REFORM

The 1832 Act abolished the worst of the rotten boroughs, which were mostly in the south and southwest of England. Seats in the Commons were allocated to the larger industrial towns in the north and midlands of England and central Scotland, as well as to some burgeoning London districts. The franchise was extended to an additional 217,000 electors. However, this was no revolution. Prosperous middle-class men were absorbed into the national polity, but there was no place for the radicals and working folk who had demonstrated for Reform in the industrial cities. Many felt betrayed by the Whigs and looked for other ways to press for change.

Below: A cartoon depicting Disraeli's success in finally passing his Reform Bill of 1867. The disgruntled Whig Gladstone is shown in hot pursuit.

THE DERBY, 1867. DIZZY WINS WITH "REFORM BILL.'

Mr. Punch. "DON'T BE TOO SURE; WAIT TILL HE'S *WEIGHED*."

A LEAP IN THE DARK

Over the next thirty-five years, agitation for further franchise reform came and went. By the mid-1860s, Prime Minister Disraeli appreciated that the strength of public feeling made further reform inevitable. He hoped to strengthen the Conservative vote and 'dish the Whigs' when he introduced his Reform Bill in 1867. By the time the bill was passed however, progressive Conservatives and Liberals had amended it to include quite lowly town artisans. A million new voters were created, doubling the electorate, but the vast bulk of British adults were still unenfranchised. Nevertheless, it was increasingly clear that the British people could be trusted to have a say in the choice of government without revolution breaking out in the streets.

VOTING IN SECRET

In 1872, public voting on the hustings was replaced by secret ballot, virtually ending electoral bribery. In Ireland, it allowed Irish electors to vote without fear of later victimization by their all-powerful landlords, giving a tremendous boost to the Irish Home Rule movement. In 1884, a third Reform Act brought the county and borough franchise regulations into line, adding another two million householders to the existing three million voters. Seats were allocated on a more rational basis, with many historic boroughs losing their MP. Britain was not a full democracy but many more people had a political stake in the country.

RAILWAY MANIA
1830–1850

After 1830, steam locomotion quickly replaced horse-drawn wagonways, canals and the great coaching services on the turnpikes. The railway was king, and it had a profound impact upon the British economy and way of life.

FROM HORSES TO STEAM

Wooden railways had long been used in collieries and some quarries to help horses pull laden wagons. As early as 1728, the 13 km (8 mile) long Tanfield track carried over a thousand wagons per day from the pits in the Durham hills to the River Tyne. In 1803, the Cornish engineer Richard Trevithick experimented with steam locomotion at Coalbrookdale and at the Pen-y-darren tramway in 1804. By 1814, George Stephenson was building steam locomotives at Killingworth Colliery near Newcastle that pulled loads of thirty tonnes at a steady 6.5 km/ph (4 mph). This success prompted the shareholders of the Stockton to Darlington Railway to appoint Stephenson as their chief engineer. In September 1825, his *Locomotion* pulled thirty-six wagons containing coal, grain and over 500 passengers along the 15 km (9 miles) of track, achieving a top speed of 24 km/ph (15 mph). Following the victory of Stephenson's *Rocket* at the Rainhill trials in 1829, the first permanent passenger service was soon in action. In its first full year of operation, the Liverpool and Manchester Railway carried 445,000 passengers. By 1835, its shareholders were receiving bumper dividends on their investment.

A NATIONAL NETWORK

There was no shortage of investors wishing to sink cash into railways, and the result was a rapid expansion of the network throughout England. The Grand Junction Railway connected the north-west to Birmingham and the Midlands in 1837. In 1841, Isambard Kingdom Brunel completed the Great Western Railway from London to Bristol. In little more than a decade, an embryonic national network had been established throughout England, despite the opposition of farmers, landowners, canal owners, turnpike trustees, innkeepers and

Above: Passenger services came into widespread use in the 1840s. By the 1860s, huge terminals like that at St Pancras were built to manage the burgeoning train network.

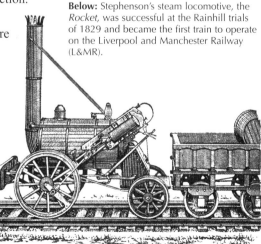

Below: Stephenson's steam locomotive, the *Rocket,* was successful at the Rainhill trials of 1829 and became the first train to operate on the Liverpool and Manchester Railway (L&MR).

Left: The early steam-powered tube trains, despite being smoky and uncomfortable, quickly became the norm for thousands of commuters into London.

UNDERGROUND RAILWAYS

Victorian London's exponential growth made it increasingly difficult to travel around the ever-expanding city. The first underground solution was the Metropolitan Railway, which opened for business in January 1863. Forty thousand passengers travelled on the first day alone, signalling the massive pent-up demand for such a service. By 1884, the inner line network was complete. Initially a steam-powered service, the early Tube was a smoky experience, despite the many vents that carried away the fumes. In 1892, electrification provided a quieter as well as healthier journey.

TIMELINE

1825	Locomotion *used to pull coal wagons from Stockton to Darlington*
1829	George Stephenson's Rocket *wins the Rainhill Trials*
1830	*Liverpool & Manchester Railway opens its passenger service*
1840s	*Railway mania during great age of railway building*
1863	*Metropolitan underground trains operating in London.*

huntsmen who all feared that the railways threatened their interests. By 1870, the length of track in Britain multiplied eightfold and over 400 million passengers were carried annually.

'THE RAILWAY KING'

Railway fever seized Britain in the 1840s. The number of bills before Parliament for proposed new railways rose from 49 in 1844 to 219 in 1846. As had happened in the canal boom, investors rushed to get involved and easily convinced themselves to back schemes that were often uneconomic. The giant of the age was Henry Hudson, chairman of the successful York & Midland line. Hudson used his wealth and his contacts as an MP to build up a railway empire, swallowing up rival companies and merging them into his Midland Railway Company. Hudson fell from grace in 1849 after allegations of corruption, but the rapid development of the railway system throughout Britain owed much to the vision, energy and greed of railway speculators and amalgamators like him.

THE IMPACT OF THE RAILWAYS

Railways were a powerful unifying force throughout Britain. They established one shared national time and provided reliable distribution for all kinds of commercial and industrial products, especially national newspapers and the penny post. Perishable foods such as vegetables and dairy produce were brought to market faster and fresher than in the days of turnpike and canal. Central government could supervise local affairs by sending out auditors and inspectors to check town councils and school boards. Wealthier residents could escape the towns and head for the leafier suburbs. In all parts of Britain, railways provided working class Britons with excursions to the mushrooming seaside towns such as Brighton, Scarborough, Blackpool and Dunoon. By 1875, the wealthier traveller could leave London on a night sleeper and take his breakfast in the Highlands.

UNITE, PROTEST AND STRIKE
1830–1900

Disappointed with the 1832 Reform Act, working class Britons experimented with different types of organization in order to achieve their political and economic objectives.

ROBERT OWEN'S GNCTU

In 1799, the Combination Acts had forbidden working men to join together to negotiate better pay and conditions of service. In the 1820s, after a Parliamentary Commission was set up to examine the matter, the Acts were repealed. This legal change encouraged dozens of new workers' associations across Britain and permitted many existing 'Friendly' and 'Mutual' societies to reveal themselves as trades unions. However, the Welsh radical and philanthropist Robert Owen realized that these organizations were too small and fragmented to achieve much. In 1833 he founded an overarching body called the Grand National Consolidated Trade Union. Many workers and radicals hoped to realize their aims through the GNCTU, which quickly claimed a membership of over half a million and the potential to call a general strike.

THE TOLPUDDLE MARTYRS

The alarmed Whig government encouraged the magistrates in the village of Tolpuddle in Dorset to prosecute six farm labourers who had formed a trades union when their weekly wages were reduced by a shilling a week. The men were accused of swearing secret oaths, a normal and necessary practice amongst trades unionists but illegal since the 1797 naval mutinies. A very harsh example was made of the Tolpuddle 'martyrs', who were sentenced to seven years in the Australian penal colonies. Public outrage eventually forced the government to pardon the men, but the damage was done to the GNCTU, which promptly collapsed. Trade unionism revived in the 1850s but only amongst well-paid specialist workers such as engineers. New 'model' trades unions like the Amalgamated Society of Engineers collected high subscriptions and, as strikes were rare, amassed substantial reserves from which to dispense benefits to members. By the end of the century, despite small

Above: In 1888 the London match girls of the Bryant and May factory called a strike, protesting against low pay, fines and health hazards. The fine system was abolished and the strikers rehired.

TIMELINE

1824–25	*Repeal of the Combination Acts against trades unions*
1833–34	*GNCTU attracts over half a million members*
1834	*Tolpuddle Martyrs condemned for swearing secret oaths*
1839	*First Chartist petition rejected by Parliament*
1844	*Rochdale Pioneers set up a successful co-operative movement*
1848	*Chartist demonstrations in London spark fear of a revolution.*

victories for the London match girls in 1888 and the dockers in 1889, unions for lower-paid workers had made little progress.

THE CO-OPERATIVE MOVEMENT

In 1829, the co-operative supporter Robert Owen set up 'Labour Exchanges' where workers exchanged goods that were valued, not in money, but in the hours taken to manufacture them. More successful was the Rochdale co-operative, started with £28 capital in 1844. The co-operative shop sold quality goods at fair prices and members of the scheme received a share of any annual profits. The Rochdale venture was in part a protest against adulterated foods, such as bread diluted with chalk or plaster of Paris, that were often sold in working class districts. However the 'Rochdale Pioneers' also cared for their members' less material needs, offering a night school, discussion evenings and a library with over 5,000 volumes. Their success was replicated by dozens of co-operative societies throughout Britain.

THE CHARTER

Chartism offered a more directly political avenue for working class dissatisfaction. Thanks to the new railway network, representatives from working mens' associations from all parts of Britain met in Birmingham in 1838 and agreed a common course of action drawn up by the London radical William Lovett. This was the Charter, designed to bring about a more radical reform of Parliament. Chartists wanted the franchise for all men over 21 as a right, secret ballots, the abolition of property qualifications for MPs so that poor men could stand for Parliament, the consequent payment of MPs, equal constituencies and annual general elections to ensure that MPs carried out their electors' bidding. Over a million workers signed the Charter, which was presented to – and rejected by – Parliament in 1839. Three million signed a second Charter in 1842, while a vast demonstration in support of a third Charter in South London in 1848 raised fears of revolution in more conservative minds. Despite these three rejections, most Chartists kept within the law, although some 'physical force' Chartists led by Feargus O'Connor believed that a general strike, or even armed rebellion, would be needed before Parliament granted their objectives.

Below: In 1848, supporters of the Charter demanding enfranchisement and reform of Parliament staged huge demonstrations in London, raising fears of a revolution.

REFORMING BRITAIN
1830–1870

Between 1833 and 1845, the Whigs and Robert Peel's new Conservatives passed a number of milestone Acts. These both established the government's responsibility for social reform and provided a framework for later improvements.

THE PROBLEM OF POVERTY

Inspired by the utilitarian ideas of Jeremy Bentham, who believed that social institutions should be useful, the reforming Whig government of the 1830s began to tackle the ills that had developed in the long years of *laissez-faire*. In much of southern England, large numbers of labourers had been dragged down into the system of poor relief by the well-intentioned but demoralizing payment of wage supplements from the local rates. The system, first applied in the parish of Speenhamland in Berkshire in 1795, had only encouraged labourers to have larger families to gain higher payments. It had also allowed employers to limit wages, knowing that the burden would fall on all parish ratepayers. As a result, poor rates had doubled.

THE WORKHOUSE

After the 1834 Poor Law Amendment Act, able-bodied labourers who applied for relief had to enter the new workhouses, where conditions were made as unappealing as possible to deter the indolent. In these almost penal institutions, the sexes were segregated to prevent further children that would need public care. A strict code of behaviour was enforced upon the uniformed inmates, who endured silent meals of skilly or thin porridge and were set to repetitive hard labour. Life in most workhouses improved after the 1846 Andover scandal which exposed the inhumane treatment which many inmates suffered. However, throughout the Victorian age, fear of the workhouse successfully encouraged labourers to seek employment rather than apply for relief. With the end of the 'Speenhamland' subsidies, employers were also forced to raise wages. In the north, where millwork was more readily available, parish boards preferred to pay unemployed men to carry out useful community work such as repairing roads and laying drains.

TIMELINE

1833	Factory Act begins to improve conditions for child workers in mills
1834	Poor Law Amendment Act puts many poor into the workhouses
1835	New borough councils charged with improving urban conditions
1842	Mines Act prohibits women and children from working underground
1847	Working day in factories effectively limited to ten hours
1850	Factory Act gives mill workers Saturday afternoon off.

THE MINES

Some of the worst conditions were endured in the pits, where children as young as four worked alongside their parents, putting in shifts of fourteen hours or more. The 1842 report of the Royal Commission into the mines horrified the public with its descriptions of the miserable conditions underground. Contemporary images of girls dragging coal barrows along mine-galleries deeply shocked the developing Victorian sensibility. The ensuing legislation brought in a raft of safety measures, restricted children and women to surface work and appointed inspectors to implement the changes.

THE FACTORY

Above: Employees at work in a steel factory in Sheffield. The series of Reform acts led to a reduction in working hours, with half a day's holiday on Saturday.

Social reformers had long been appalled by the long hours and dangerous conditions that mill workers had to endure. Laws passed in 1802 and 1819 sought to limit the hours worked by children in textile mills, but were difficult to enforce in the absence of an inspection regime. The 1833 Factory Act remedied this by appointing factory inspectors charged with ensuring that employers did not hire children younger than nine, and that the new limitations on weekly hours of work, forty-eight for children under thirteen and sixty-nine for teenagers, were respected. Further legislation in 1844 required employers to screen all dangerous machinery and give their younger workers time off for compulsory education. As a result of the efforts of the Ten Hour movement, Acts in 1847 and 1850 reduced the working day for all factory workers to a maximum twelve hour shift with one and a half hours break, and made Saturday afternoons into a holiday. In the 1860s, these improvements were extended to workers in most other industries. Acts such as these required accurate information to be successful, prompting the government to introduce compulsory registration of births, deaths and marriages in England and Wales in 1836.

Below: Housing built up around the factories to accommodate the influx of workers from rural areas. The construction was often shoddy and the slums were a breeding ground for disease.

THE HOME

Rapid industrialization and the need for cheap housing close to the mill or mine meant that accommodation for industrial workers was densely packed and built quickly, often by 'jerry' builders who cut all possible corners. Fresh water and adequate drainage were seldom provided, so many new streets built between 1770 and 1830 were less hygienic than a medieval village. Piles of detritus littered the back yards, attracting flies and vermin, while sewage seeped into the watercourse. In these conditions, diseases such as bronchitis, tuberculosis, typhoid and cholera were common, and soon spread to the districts where the rich resided. Edwin Chadwick's report into the sanitary condition of working class areas led to the establishment of public health boards in 1848. These would eventually work alongside the reformed borough councils, set up in 1835, to improve the infrastructure of the 19th-century town.

God's Work
1800–1900

The 19th century experienced a great revival in piety and faith. This found its most practical expression in the work of Christian missions amongst the domestic poor and 'the heathen' of distant lands.

A Pious Age?

The Victorian Age was one of the most publicly devout in British history. In England, this was in large part due to the influence of Evangelical Anglicans who roused their Church from its 18th-century torpor and encouraged it to take a more vigorous role in the life of the nation. Evangelical laymen were also inspired to campaign against the evils of their day. Their ranks included the anti-slaver Wilberforce and the champion of chimney sweeps Lord Shaftesbury. The tone of Victorian English public life was fashioned by the Evangelical fondness for family prayers, public worship and church-building. The Tractarian or Anglo-Catholic movement transformed the worship of the Church of England, introducing a dash of ecclesiastical colour into the drabness of many industrial districts.

A National Church?

On Sunday 30 March 1851, an ecclesiastical census was taken throughout England and Wales. It revealed that little more than seven million people had attended church that day out of a total population of eighteen million. Of these, only half were Anglican, while the rest attended a myriad of non-conformist chapels. Although the Church of England still dominated public life, it had few members amongst the labouring classes. In the north and large parts of the Midlands, the traditional parish structure had been rent asunder by the rapid urbanization. In many industrial towns, a single vicar was nominally responsible for tens of thousands of souls. It was the non-conformist denominations that were the real spiritual power here, not the established Church. After Catholic Emancipation in 1829, a new Roman Catholic Church evolved, largely to meet the needs of the growing Irish population in Liverpool, Glasgow and London.

The Missionary Impulse

The evangelical desire to spread the Gospel in Africa was connected to the campaign against slavery. British participation in the slave trade was prohibited in 1807, and in 1833 slavery was abolished in all British territories – at great cost to the British taxpayer as slave-owners received over twenty million pounds in compensation. However, African chiefs and Arab slave masters continued in the trade, to the horror of those who attended the public lectures of the London Missionary Society. The young

Above: The missionary David Livingstone penetrated deep into little-explored regions of Africa. He was considered missing for years until the American journalist Henry Morton Stanley met him in 1871.

Right: William Booth, the Methodist preacher and founder of the Salvation Army, receives a warm welcome in Nottingham.

THE PRINCE OF PREACHERS

Charles Spurgeon typified the Victorian preacher. Aged fifteen, his faith was confirmed by his delivery from a snowstorm and two years later he was ordained as a Baptist minister. Spurgeon was a born preacher, whose oratory 'revived' the faith of thousands. His church had to move to larger halls as his congregation expanded. Audiences of 10,000 were frequent, and more than double that number listened to his Crystal Palace sermon in 1857. His Metropolitan Tabernacle in Southwark seated 5,000 worshippers and held another 1,000 standing. Spurgeon was also a prolific writer, and a well-thumbed copy of his sermons was found by Livingstone's deathbed.

missionary David Livingstone began his work in Africa in 1840 with twin aims; to spread the Christian Gospel and find new routes across southern and central Africa. Between 1853 and 1873, Livingstone made three great expeditions – to Lake Victoria, Lake Nyasa and the Nile's source. He hoped that traders would follow in his footsteps, thus creating wealth and raising living standards, so that no tribe would be forced to sell its children in future. There were also missionaries much nearer home. In the Toynbee Hall experiment, university students lived in Whitechapel amongst the poor, performing acts of social work. William Booth's Salvation Army marched into the poorest areas to save the souls of the destitute and minister to their bodily needs.

THE LITERAL TRUTH

Most Victorian churchgoers believed in the literal and historical truth of the Bible, but their faith came under assault from a number of directions. James Hutton, the father of modern geology, had already shown that the earth was immeasurably older than claimed in Genesis. However, his meticulous scientific work *The Theory of the Earth,* published in 1795, made little impact upon the popular mind. By 1850, the work of scientific historians, Bible scholars and archaeologists in Germany had placed the Bible in its context and exposed many of its inconsistencies and later additions. These researches had also largely passed Britain by, thus explaining the public furore that met the work of the biologists Charles Darwin and Thomas Huxley after 1859. Unlike many European societies, the educated British public had not been prepared for the appearance of a rational and materialist explanation of creation and man's development within it.

Right: Charles Darwin's *Origin of Species,* published in 1859, set out his theory of evolution. It prompted a fierce reaction from those who believed in the literal truth of the Bible.

THE BENEFITS OF SCIENCE
1850–1900

In the later Victorian age, a series of scientific breakthroughs revolutionized all aspects of daily life in Britain. Improvements in public sanitation, education and communication heralded the birth of the Modern Age.

LISTER'S SPRAY

Standards of health care improved as medical knowledge increased. Florence Nightingale's school of nursing, established at St Thomas' Hospital in 1860, professionalized the treatment that patients received in the growing number of public hospitals around Britain. By 1854, John Snow was able to offer conclusive proof that cholera, the periodic scourge of London and many other large Victorian cities, was a waterborne disease spread by contaminated water. Stethoscopes were in common use by the 1850s and improved microscopes were beginning to make a contribution to medical research. However, the medical profession was conservative and resistant to change. Desperate to reduce the high post-surgical mortality rate, Joseph Lister developed an antiseptic carbolic spray in Glasgow in the mid 1860s. It was quickly adopted in some Scottish hospitals, yet it was many years before Lister's invention and the theory of bacterial sepsis won general acceptance.

Left: Joseph Lister developed his carbolic spray to stop air-borne microbes from entering wounds. It was used in Prussian field hospitals during the 1870 Franco-Prussian war and saved countless German lives.

PUBLIC IMPROVEMENT

Enterprising town councils could use their new powers and the technology of the age to transform the lives of their citizens. Huddersfield was typical of many. Its new borough council met for the very first time in 1869, and immediately set about building reservoirs and a pipe network to provide clean water. By 1890, the town boasted a steam-powered tram system, a public electricity supply, free schools and imposing civic buildings. London, with four million inhabitants by 1880, lagged behind, unable to cope with the scale of its problems. Thousands of domestic chimneys and hundreds of steam engines added their pollution to the notorious London 'peasoupers' of thick smog. There was no proper sewage system, and little household water before the creation of the London County Council in 1888. Wealthy Glasgow best illustrated the great contrasts to be found in a Victorian city. Its magnificent city centre was built on an unrivalled scale, while the rich districts to the west enjoyed all the advantages of

Below: By the late 1800s, trams were becoming more widely used for urban transportation. Huddersfield opened the first municipal steam-powered tram route in 1883.

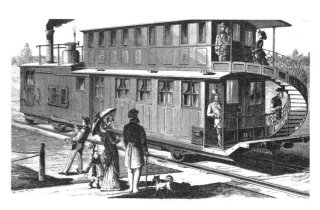

FROZEN ABUNDANCE

In February 1880, the Clyde-built SS *Strathleven* docked in London, carrying its perfectly preserved cargo of frozen Australian mutton. Cargoes of more lamb and butter followed the next year. By the end of the decade, refrigerated ships were bringing in cheap foodstuffs from various colonies around the globe, tying the Empire economically closer as well as pleasing frugal British housewives. The construction of bigger steel ships made refrigerated vessels more economic and by the end of the century the port of London was the busiest in the world. The British consumer of 1900 was also enjoying a wider diet than any of his ancestors.

TIMELINE

1859	*Loch Katrine aqueduct supplies fresh Highland water to Glasgow*
1865–69	*Lister develops his principles of antiseptic care*
1866	*First transatlantic telegraph cable from London to US*
1876	*Alexander Graham Bell demonstrates the telephone*
1878	*Joseph Swan makes the first electric light bulb*
1880	*First refrigerated ships used for long-distance transportation of food.*

Above: Alexander Graham Bell was brought up in Scotland before emigrating to Canada. His studies in communicating sounds electrically led to the invention of the telephone in 1867.

the age, including fresh household water brought from distant Loch Katrine by an ambitious 56 km (35 mile) aqueduct. On the other side of the Clyde, a short walk from the opulent City Chambers, were the squalid slums of the Gorbals, a byword for poverty, filth, destitution and violence.

THE PHILANTHROPIST ENTREPRENEUR

Not all civic improvements were stimulated by government. Energetic Victorian entrepreneurs made fortunes, but often ploughed them back into their communities. William Armstrong was one of the richest men in England, having succeeded as a solicitor, scientist, engineer and arms manufacturer. His hydraulic crane company at Elswick on the river Tyne mushroomed into one of the largest engineering and armaments concerns in the world. Armstrong used his great wealth for public benefit, helping Newcastle to provide a clean water supply and donating parklands for public recreation. His generous donations were used to found schools, including the Newcastle College of Physical Science in 1871, and at his death he left £100,000 for a new public hospital. Every Victorian city in Britain benefited from similar acts of private philanthropy.

TOWARDS THE ELECTRIC AGE

By the end of the Victorian period, someone who had learned to read by candlelight as a child could catch a glimpse of the coming electric future. Improvements in communications were shrinking the planet. A transatlantic telegraph cable linked London to America in 1866, and cables to India were laid in 1870. A few months after Victoria's death in 1901, it was possible to send a telegraph around the globe. The chemist Joseph Swan demonstrated his patent electric light bulb in Newcastle in 1878, and was manufacturing them by 1883. In 1876, Alexander Graham Bell had perfected the telephone and the first London telephone exchange was set up three years later. In 1896, Fort William in the Highlands became the first British town to enjoy electric streetlights, thanks to its giant hydro-electric aluminium smelter that processed bauxite ores brought over from Ireland. All of Britain was being transformed by science and technology.

EDUCATION AND LEISURE
1837–1900

When Victoria ascended the throne in 1837, a significant proportion of her British subjects were illiterate. By 1900 however, a vigorous popular press was one sign of improved national literacy, and of increasing disposable income.

AN UNSCHOOLED NATION

In England, secondary education was largely restricted to those wealthy boys who received a public school classical education. A growing number of 'academies' also offered the middle-classes a practical education in subjects such as science. As in other sectors of Victorian society, charities and private philanthropy provided a service of sorts. Many learned to read in the Sunday schools pioneered by the Anglican Robert Raikes in the 1780s. The Ragged Schools movement provided basic literacy, as well as social help in the form of Penny Banks, Clothing Clubs and Temperance education. Systematic provision only began with the Factory Acts of 1833 and 1844, which forced employers to give their child workers daily schooling. However, most Victorian schools offered a limited curriculum that was delivered in cramped surroundings by untrained staff.

STATE SCHOOLS

Progressive voices had long called for state involvement in education, but it was the industrial and commercial success of nations with school systems such as France, Piedmont and Bismarck's Prussia

Left: The development of the rotary press allowed long reams of paper to be printed quickly, enabling the production of daily newspapers in large numbers.

THE PRESS

In 1841, one third of Britons were unable to read and sign their marriage certificate. By 1900, increased literacy supported a national press that reached most sectors of British society. Stamp duty had deliberately made newspapers expensive in the 18th century but the 'tax on knowledge' was gradually abolished in the 1850s and 1860s. The lifting of duties on paper and on print advertising combined with revolutionary technologies such as rotary presses and mechanical typesetting to produce a cheap, popular press. By 1900, there were thirty-two daily newspapers in London alone, catering for all levels of curiosity. Distribution through the railway network also helped national dailies to build huge circulations. By 1890, the *Daily Telegraph* was read in over 300,000 homes around the country. The half-penny *Daily Mail* appeared in 1896, undercutting its penny rivals and quickly establishing a daily readership of more than 500,000 thanks to its populist and imperialist tone. Sunday newspapers such as the *News of the World* built equally impressive circulations on a diet of sordid court-reports and titillation.

that encouraged British policy-makers to take a greater interest. The 1867 expansion of the electorate also underlined the need to ensure that the nation's citizenry was capable of voting wisely. The 1870 Education Act made schooling compulsory, though it only aimed to fill in the gaps left by the existing institutions. However, the success of the local school boards led to further improvements. In 1890, board school fees were abolished and the school leaving age was raised in 1893 and in 1899. By 1900, education had become the largest item in the national accounts, even though most English children still attended voluntary schools. In Scotland and Wales, Presbyterian and Methodist traditions had helped to encourage a higher literacy rate. Scotland in particular had a rich heritage of successful burgh and charitable schools, and educational innovators such as Dr Andrew Bell had achieved national prominence. Nevertheless, the 1872 introduction of board schools finally ensured that the vision of the old Scottish Parliament for a school in every parish was fully realized.

SPORT AND SHOPPING

After 1850, many urban workers enjoyed a free Saturday afternoon and could travel cheaply on railway excursions. Sports such as football and rugby, which had their origin in street games, had been codified in the public schools and colleges by that point. In the 1860s, local sports clubs began to proliferate and by 1865, large numbers of players turned these games into nationally organized sports. Vast crowds attended football matches from the 1870s onwards and clubs were soon professionalized. Professional Rugby League broke away from the amateur code in 1895. Thanks to John Dunlop's pneumatic tyres, the 1890s were the golden age

Below: Sports such as football gradually developed from leisure pursuits into professionally organized businesses.

of bicycling. Thousands escaped the town at Saturday lunchtime and headed off to the freedom of the newly romanticized countryside. An alternative Saturday afternoon could be spent in the great emporia that developed in late Victorian city centres. The Parisian invention of department stores caught on quickly, as the founding dates of Jenners in Edinburgh (1838) and Delany's in Dublin (1853) testify. Whiteleys in Bayswater was the first purpose-built department store in London. At its peak in the 1890s, it employed 6,000 staff who lived in company dormitories in the few hours they were not at work.

IRISH HOME RULE

1798–1893

The failure to solve Ireland's land problem led not just to famine, but to years of agitation and violence. Eventually Gladstone grasped the nettle and prepared to grant Irish Home Rule.

THE LIBERATOR

The failure of the 1798 United Irishmens' rebellion convinced the lawyer Daniel O'Connell to look for a non-violent way to abolish the Protestant Ascendancy. His Catholic Association collected penny subscriptions for its campaign to abolish the civil restrictions on Catholics and repeal the Act of Union. Despite being elected for County Clare in 1828, O'Connell was unable to take his seat in Parliament. Fearing insurrection in Ireland, Wellington put aside his own conservative views and convinced enough Tory peers to pass the Catholic Relief Bill in 1829. Catholics now had the vote, but only if they met high property qualifications. Wellington hoped this would ensure Ireland returned moderate representatives to Westminster.

THE FENIANS

After the famines of the 1840s, men of a more violent stamp came to the fore. The armed rebellion of Young Ireland fizzled out in 1848, but the Fenians, an Irish-American brotherhood, presented a greater threat to order. Fenian attempts to liberate their imprisoned colleagues in Manchester and Clerkenwell by force were seen as shocking terrorist outrages. In Ireland, the three Fenians executed for the murder of a policeman in 1867 were remembered as the Manchester Martyrs.

DISESTABLISHMENT

Irish Catholics had always resented having to pay for the upkeep of the established Anglican Church of Ireland. The payment of tithes had been reduced in 1839, after the outbreak of exceptionally bloody skirmishes between tenants and constabulary remembered as the Tithes War. However, the issue was a lingering religious grievance that William Gladstone hoped to defuse in his first ministry. The Church of Ireland was accordingly disestablished in 1869. A Land Act the following year aimed to provide evicted tenants with compensation for improvements they had made to the land, but it failed to provide a guarantee of fair rents and security of tenure. The growing number of evictions from smallholdings led to a wave of brutal outrages in the countryside by an increasingly desperate peasantry.

Below: Often described as 'the uncrowned king of Ireland', Charles Stewart Parnell was the founder of the Irish Parliamentary Party.

TIMELINE	
1828	*Daniel O'Connell elected to Westminster but unable to take his seat*
1829	*Wellington persuaded to support a bill for Catholic emancipation*
1886	*Liberal party badly spilt over Irish Home Rule Bill*
1890	*Parnell disgraced by revelations of his affair with Mrs Kitty O'Shea*
1893	*Gladstone's second Home Rule Bill defeated by the Lords.*

Above: The Irish National Land League staged demonstrations against the forced eviction of tenants due to changes in agricultural practices.

THE UNCROWNED KING OF IRELAND

By the 1880s, the Irish countryside was on the brink of revolution. The world depression and the influx of cheap American grain made it impossible to sustain the traditional ways of farming in Ireland. Landowners had no option but to modernize their estates. As the number of evictions of small tenants rose however, so did the criminal acts carried out by 'moonlighters' taking their revenge on their former landlords. More effectively, the Irish Land League organized rent strikes and boycotts if landowners refused to accept its estimate of the value of each holding. Landowners and land agents who evicted tenants, such as Captain Charles Boycott in County Mayo, found themselves isolated and ignored by the local community, unable to purchase goods and services. In Parliament, Charles Stewart Parnell transformed the loose Home Rule League into the well-funded and highly disciplined Irish Parliamentary Party, in many ways the first modern British political party. At the head of this block of over eighty nationalist Irish MPs, the impressive and resolute Parnell set out to delay and obstruct all legislation until the problems of Ireland were resolved. However, Gladstone's attempts to negotiate a settlement with 'Ireland's uncrowned king' in 1882 were ruined by the shocking assassination of the Irish Secretary and his assistant, stabbed to death in Dublin's Phoenix Park by a shadowy nationalist organization known as the Invincibles. Public outrage at the murders, for which many in Britain blamed Parnell, made it impossible for Gladstone to maintain his conciliatory approach to Ireland.

THE HOME RULE BILLS

In his third ministry, Gladstone was dependent upon the eighty-six nationalist votes in the Commons. A Home Rule Bill was duly introduced in 1886. It proposed to devolve authority for all domestic issues to Dublin, reserving only defence, foreign policy and external trade agreements to Westminster. The issue split the Liberal party apart and the Bill fell by thirty votes. The incoming Conservative government attempted to control Ireland rather than placate it, using a new Crimes Act to deal with the violence in the Irish countryside by trying offenders without a jury. By the time Gladstone returned to office in 1892, Parnell had fallen from power and died as a result of the exposure of his longstanding affair with Kitty O'Shea, the wife of a fellow Irish MP. Gladstone presented a second Home Rule Bill but it was again voted down in the Lords. As the century ended and Ireland smouldered, a solution to its problems seemed no nearer than in 1800.

THE BRITISH RAJ
1780–1900

British power in India was confirmed by the defeat of France in 1815. A period of expansion and modernization culminated in the Indian Mutiny of 1857, which deeply affected Anglo-Indian relations.

CROWN AND COMPANY

After 1763, the East India Company's Governor-General held sway over more 'subjects' than many European princes. In 1784, Pitt sought to regulate this situation by appointing a Cabinet minister to oversee Indian affairs of a political nature. There was still great scope for an individual to make a mark in India. Lord Cornwallis successfully held the reins in India when Sultan Tipu of Mysore launched a sudden attack on the British possessions in there 1790. Agents of revolutionary France encouraged Tipu to renew his war against the hated British in 1798, when Napoleon was in Egypt musing over his plans to march on India in the footsteps of Alexander. Richard Wellesley created a coalition of native rulers and destroyed Tipu's army at Seringapatam in 1799. This victory was momentous, for the acquisition of the rich southern sultanate of Mysore made Britain the leading power in India. Wellesley also initiated the policy of controlling native potentates by placing a British Resident or 'adviser', with a detachment of Company troops, at their courts.

Above: Sultan Tipu, known as the 'Tiger of Mysore', who repeatedly launched attacks against the East India Company during the late 1700s. He was eventually defeated at Seringapatam in 1799.

OPEN INDIA

By 1823, the East India Company had ceased to trade and was wholly occupied in administering its territories. India was open to all British manufacturers and its economic importance encouraged British administrators to take a more forceful attitude towards local difficulties. The belligerent Gurkhas of Nepal were defeated in 1816, becoming valuable allies thereafter. In 1819, the power of the scheming Marathas chiefs of central India was broken. In the following decades, the British concentrated upon eliminating 'unacceptable' aspects of local culture such as the Hindu funeral practice of suttee (the self-immolation of widows).

Below: The Gurkha warriors of Nepal served as mercenary troops to the East India Company and became valuable allies of the British in India.

TIMELINE

1784	*British government begins to take greater control of Indian affairs*
1799	*British forces win major victory over Tipu of Mysore at Seringapatam*
1816	*Gurkhas defeated and Nepal made a protectorate*
1848–56	*Lord Dalhousie modernizes the infrastructure of British India*
1857–58	*The great mutiny prompts a British rethink on how to govern India*
1858	*East India Company abolished and full British Raj established.*

Above: The Great Indian Peninsular Railway ran from the imposing Victoria Terminus in Bombay. The railway network was key for the British Raj in maintaining control of their Indian possessions.

WESTERNIZATION

Lord Dalhousie, Governor-General between 1848 and 1856, realized that holding India also required 'policies of improvement'. Over 6,500 km (4,000 miles) of metalled road were therefore constructed, a postal and telegraph system was established and the first railway began in 1853. The Great Ganges Canal was completed, and a system of anglo-vernacular schools and technical colleges was planned. However, Dalhousie's most contentious policy was the 'doctrine of lapse', whereby the lands of native princes who died without heir became British possessions. Inevitably, the speed and extent of Dalhousie's changes inspired native resentment and opposition.

THE MUTINY, 1857–58

In May 1857, a number of Indian troops at the Meerut army base near Delhi refused to use rifle cartridges that had been greased with 'unclean' pig and cow fat. Anger at the harsh treatment of the dissenting men was aggravated by rumours that Hindu and Muslim troops were to be forcibly converted to Christianity. A group of mutineers released the imprisoned men, marched on Delhi and proclaimed an elderly Mogul prince as Emperor. The uprising spread out along the Ganges valley to Lucknow, Cawnpore and Jhansi, gathering support from elements in Indian society who felt threatened by Dalhousie's policies of westernization. The British contingent at Cawnpore – including over two hundred women and children – surrendered, and was massacred. In Lucknow, the British garrison resisted siege until it was finally relieved in September. Once loyal troops had been despatched from the unaffected regions of central and southern India, the fate of the mutineers was never in doubt. The mutiny was avenged mercilessly – innocent Indian civilians were slaughtered wholesale when Delhi was retaken – before wiser counsels prevailed.

THE RAJ

In 1858, the East India Company was abolished and the Crown took full control of the sub-continent. British troops would henceforth make up one third of regimental strength and artillery was carefully held in British hands. A more permanent legacy of the mutiny was mutual distrust between the native and British populations. After 1858, the British kept at a greater distance from their subjects and the position of Indians and Anglo-Indians in society was carefully prescribed. However, the British had learned one important lesson. The policy of annexation stopped and the many existing native principalities were left with a degree of independence.

AFRICAN ADVENTURE
1800–1900

Britain increased its African holdings after 1875 in the 'scramble for Africa'. However, its involvement in the far south of the continent led to wars against the native Zulu nation and the Boer farmers of the veldt.

AFRICAN SCRAMBLE

In 1800, Britain's few possessions in Africa were former slaving posts on the river Gambia and the Gold Coast. Sierra Leone, a territory for liberated slaves founded by abolitionists, became a Crown colony in 1807. More territory on the Gold Coast was gradually acquired while the southern Cape was ceded to Britain after Napoleon's downfall. However, although British explorers and missionaries ranged over the 'Dark Continent' throughout the 19th century, the government was reluctant to acquire more African responsibilities. Britain's hand was forced after 1875 by the scramble of several European powers to create colonial empires in Africa. Chartered companies were the preferred tool for extending British influence in Nigeria, Kenya and Uganda, until Crown protectorates were established in the 1890s.

Above: The Zulu chief Cetshwayo approaches British troops with a peace offering after suffering defeat at the Battle of Ulundi in July 1879.

ZULU WARS

In southern Africa, the British had to contend with the formidable Zulu nation. Under its capable King Cetshwayo, Zululand was an obstacle to British plans for South African confederation and local British officials provoked a conflict in January 1879. At Isandlwana, the British invasion column of 1,200 men was almost completely destroyed by the disciplined *impis* or Zulu brigades. However, the Zulus' lack of effective firepower was exposed later the same day at the mission station of Rorke's Drift, where a small contingent of mostly Welsh troops held out against 4,000 warriors behind makeshift fortifications. The Zulu threat effectively ended at the brief and bloody rout at Ulundi in July. Now British attention was focused upon the Boers, farmers descended from mostly Dutch settlers who had migrated northwards from Cape Colony in the 1830s and 1840s to escape British rule.

Above: President of the Transvaal, Kruger clashed with the British after the mass migration of gold prospectors to the Boer lands in the 1880s.

KRUGER AND RHODES

Two men symbolized the forces at play in southern Africa after 1880. Paul Kruger, President of the Transvaal Republic, was determined to keep the Boers free from Britain and maintain Boer ascendancy within their own lands. However, his ideal was threatened by the discovery of rich gold reserves in the low hills of the Witwatersrand in 1886. In the ensuing gold rush, thousands of mostly British prospectors set up camp in settlements that soon mushroomed into the town of Johannesburg. Although Kruger needed revenue from the gold industry, he was determined that the influx of *Uitlanders* or foreigners would not change the Transvaal. The incomers were denied citizenship and the only legal language was Afrikaans. The miners were charged extortionate rates for essential services such as railway freight and dynamite. These policies outraged Cecil Rhodes, Prime Minister of the Cape Colony, a founder of the De Beers diamond company, and a dynamic imperialist who dreamed of a British Empire in Africa stretching from the Cape to Cairo. Rhodes' planned Uitlander rising against Kruger's regime in 1895, known as Jameson's Raid, was a disaster and he was disgraced. However, it created a climate of suspicion that aided the outbreak of war when the Uitlanders appealed to the Crown for protection in 1899.

TIMELINE

1875–1900	*European powers scramble for African colonies*
1879	*Zulu war ends with Battle of Ulundi*
1886	*Discovery of gold in the Transvaal*
1895	*Jameson's Raid fails to spark an Uitlander rising against the Boers*
1899	*Boer units invade Cape Colony and Natal*
1900	*Siege of several British settlements*
1902	*Guerilla phase of the Boer War ends with the Peace of Vereeniging*
1910	*Creation of self-governing Dominion of Union of South Africa.*

WAR WITH THE BOERS

With local knowledge and temporarily superior numbers, the Boers besieged the British garrisons at Ladysmith, Kimberley and Mafeking. In the spring and summer of 1900, the British launched a successful counter-offensive, relieved the besieged garrisons and occupied the Transvaal capital of Pretoria. The last organized Boer force was defeated in August 1900, but Boer commandos, or wide-ranging irregulars, fought a guerrilla war for another twenty months. Supported and sheltered by the Boer population, the commandos raided Natal and Cape Colony and damaged the railway network. Fortified blockhouses were built to defend strategic points and over 100,000 sympathetic civilians were 'concentrated' in internment camps to cut off support to the guerrillas. Over 20,000 died of disease before the hungry guerrillas ran out of supplies.

UNION OF SOUTH AFRICA

In the Peace of Vereeniging, there was no revenge against the defeated Boers. Instead they were wooed with promises of future self-government, confirmation of their language rights and generous compensation. Most Boers were happy with the terms that created the self-governing Dominion of South Africa in 1910. Though the majority native population were left unenfranchised, the rural Boers enjoyed disproportionate representation and were guaranteed a majority in the new South African Parliament.

THE BIRTH OF THE WELFARE STATE
1902–1912

At the turn of the century, the governing Conservative administration was more interested in imperial than domestic matters. After 1906 however, a radical Liberal government began to seriously tackle the effects of decades of social and economic transformation.

IMPERIAL JUBILEE

The 1897 Diamond Jubilee celebrated the high noon of Empire. Colonial troops from every continent parading through the streets of London featured on the pages of pictorial supplements in the daily press. The following year, at Omdurman in the Sudan, Lord Kitchener's maxim guns decimated the forces of the Mahdi, a self-proclaimed Muslim 'prophet', and avenged the death of General Gordon at Khartoum. However, the celebrations and victories were quickly forgotten as imperial adventure almost resulted in war with France over the Upper Sudan in 1898 and then degenerated into an expensive and initially humiliating conflict in South Africa. The Conservative government did enact two significant pieces of reform legislation; the Workmen's Compensation Act that helped those injured at work, and Balfour's 1902 Education Act, which laid the foundation for a national system of secondary schools. This Act was designed to improve 'national efficiency' at a time when Britain's economic supremacy had been surrendered to the USA and Germany. It passed responsibility for enforcing standards in all publicly financed schools to county and borough councils.

Above: The new generation of Liberal MPs such as Lloyd George and Winston Churchill gained power in the 1906 elections.

LANDSLIDE

Divided over the issue of Empire trade and tarred with the Boer War brush, the Conservatives were badly defeated in the 1906 election. The new Commons consisted of 377 Liberals, 53 Labour and other socialists and 83 Irish Nationalists. Many in the new Liberal government, such as Lloyd George, Winston Churchill and John Burns, were of a radical stamp, much

TIMELINE	
1902	*Balfour's Education Act*
1906	*Provision of School Meals Act*
1907	*School medical services established*
1909	*First old age pensions paid by the State*
1910	*House of Lords reject the 'People's Budget'*
1911	*Power of the Lords weakened by Parliament Act.*

influenced by the studies of working class poverty made by Charles Booth and Benjamin Seebohm Rowntree. The Victorian reliance upon private charity and local action had not proved enough to stop millions falling below the poverty line. As Churchill argued in 1906, 'the State must now earnestly concern itself with the care of the sick, the aged and children'. This was not simple altruism, for British political commentators were well aware that other industrial societies, especially in Europe, were educating and nurturing their human resources with greater efficiency.

FOUNDATIONS OF WELFARE

The evolution of national systems of education in Britain after 1870 had cast a light upon the effects of poverty on many working class children. Sick and hungry children made poor learners, so school meals and medical inspections were introduced by 1908. Young offenders would now be separated from adult prisoners and reformed in specialist institutions such as the youth prison at Borstal in Kent. A modest old age pension was introduced in January 1909 on a weekly sliding scale from one to five shillings. Measures were taken to increase the help available for injured and unemployed workers, and to assist workers in the 'sweated' trades such as tailoring, where the wages of outworkers were traditionally low. The Chancellor Lloyd George also planned a system of national insurance that would provide support in times of personal difficulty, again based on the successful German model.

The only problem was, that at a time when the defence budget was also rising, how would this unprecedented programme of social reforms be paid for?

Above: Many families had fallen below the poverty line in the Victorian age and child poverty was rife. The new Welfare State aimed to provide a safety net for the struggling poor.

THE PEOPLE'S BUDGET, 1909

To fund its programme, the Liberal government needed an extra £15 million in revenue. It planned to raise this by levying new taxes aimed at the wealthiest and those who owned land. Death duties on larger estates were also increased. Lloyd George's 1909 budget set up a political and constitutional clash between the Commons and the Lords, the preserve of the propertied classes. At the height of the crisis, George V agreed to create sufficient Liberal peers to carry a Parliament Bill that would curtail the traditional blocking powers of the Lords. The Liberals won national approval for their programme in a tight general election and the budget was passed. The 1911 Parliament Act fundamentally altered the relationship between the elected Commons and the hereditary Lords. In the same year, the old Chartist demand for payment of MPs, to allow men of all ranks to stand for election, was finally enacted.

PREPARATION FOR WAR
1900–1914

Since the Crimean War in the 1850s, Britain had avoided alliances and conflict in Europe and had busied itself in its colonial affairs. However, as Europe divided into hostile camps, Britain's imperial isolation no longer seemed to be an option.

THE GERMAN BOGEYMAN

The diplomatic and press reaction in Europe to the Boer War revealed that Britain had few friends on the Continent. British public opinion was especially incensed by Germany's public noises of support for the Boer rebels. Germany had long since replaced France as the main European threat in British eyes. Victory over France and unification in 1870–71 had made Germany the dominant power in Europe, a position cemented by its triple alliance with Austria and Italy in 1882. German military strength alone was no threat to British interests, but the rapid expansion of the German navy after 1898 was a direct challenge to Britannia's rule over the waves. Nor, by 1900, could German industrial superiority be denied, particularly in the new vital industries such as chemicals. The new cheap daily press stoked popular suspicion of 'Kaiserist Germany' and played upon the increasingly widespread feeling that British power had perhaps passed its zenith.

Above: Sensationalist novels such as William Le Queux' *The Invasion of 1910* played on the British public's fear of Germany's growing fleet based at the ports of Wilhelmshaven and Kiel.

ENTENTE

An agreement with Japan in 1902 helped secure British interests in the Far East and allowed the government to concentrate attention upon European matters. After a successful state visit to Paris by Edward VII in 1904, Balfour's Conservative government reached agreement with France on issues of mutual interest in North Africa. This 'entente' was strengthened at the 1905 international conference at Algeciras in Spain. The British reached an understanding with France's ally, Russia, two years later. These new relationships with continental powers fell far short of a diplomatic or military alliance, but British military and naval staffs increasingly shared information with their counterparts in St Petersburg and Paris. Such activity was a clear signal to Berlin that Britain was likely to be in the opposition camp in any future European struggle.

TIMELINE

1882	*Triple Alliance of Germany, Austria and Italy*
1904	*Entente Cordial between Britain and France*
1906	*Launch of HMS* Dreadnought
1911	*Eighteen 'dreadnoughts' commissioned*
1914	*4 Aug British declaration of war against Germany.*

ARMY REFORM

Between 1763 and 1900, Britain acquired the largest Empire in history but, outside India, it held sway with a relatively light hand. However, the small forces that policed the colonies now seemed inadequate when compared to the vast armies of millions under construction in Europe. After 1906, the Liberal Secretary of War Haldane created the rapid deployment Expeditionary Force, a contingent of seven divisions totalling over 90,000 men, with their own autonomous field services. Traditional county yeomanry units and volunteers formed the core of the new Territorial Force that could also be assembled quickly for overseas deployment in reserve support. An Officers' Training Corps was established to foster military skills in a British population that, brief outbursts of imperial jingoism aside, had never warmed to the army life.

DREADNOUGHT!

The British response to the modern German fleet assembling in its North Sea ports was HMS *Dreadnought.* Launched in 1906, this new class of battleship was fast, able to outgun its rivals and effectively made other ships of the line, and other navies, obsolete. After hesitating – for fear of provoking tension in Europe – the Liberal government commissioned eighteen Dreadnought class ships in 1911. In 1912, the bulk of British ships in European waters were withdrawn from the Mediterranean, ceding the main responsibility there to the French. This strategic decision helped to ensure that a German attack upon France would directly threaten British lines of naval communication with the Empire east of Suez.

Below: The speed and firing range of the British Dreadnought battleships marked a new standard in naval defence.

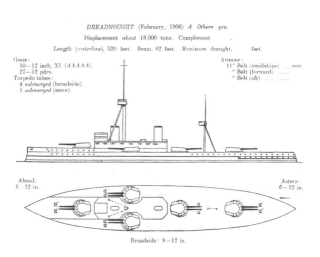

AUGUST 1914

When continental Europe slipped into war in the summer months of 1914, Britain still had no formal military obligations to France and Russia and many were reluctant to commit to a major European conflict. However the German plan to advance on Paris through Belgium spurred Britain's traditional response to any attempted 'great power' dominance in the Low Countries. British support for Belgian independence had been enshrined in the Treaty of London of 1839. On 2 August, Sir Edward Grey promised to help defend the French channel ports and demanded that Germany respect Belgian neutrality. When no such undertaking was received from Berlin, Britain declared war on 4 August 1914.

THE GREAT WAR
1914–1918

The Great War was unprecedented in scale and cost. This total war affected not just the men at the front, but all sections of British society.

INDUSTRIAL WAR

In the opening weeks of the war, the British Expeditionary Force marched to assist the French at Mons and the Marne, but was a tattered remnant by the time the trench line reached the Channel in early December. In 1915, the grim realities of industrialized war set in; barbed wire, bombardment, poison gas, mines, shell-shock, trench-foot, slaughter and everywhere rats and mud. A new volunteer army responded to Lord Kitchener's call to arms and was duly culled at Ypres and Loos. As the likely duration of the war became more apparent in 1916, conscription was introduced. Those who objected were punished and ostracized. Those who fell at the Somme were later characterized as 'lions led by donkeys' and the British command undeniably made many mistakes, notably failing to understand the new technologies of war quickly enough. Nevertheless, the British Fourth Army that launched into the decisive battle of Amiens in August 1918 was a well-equipped, battle-hardened fighting force, supported by 535 massed tanks and many of the RAF's 22,000 aircraft along a 65 km (40 mile) front.

Above: In the battlefields of France, poison gas was used for the first time in the history of warfare. Elementary masks were developed to protect troops.

DISTANT FRONTS

The 1914–18 war ranged across the globe. As the Western Front settled down into grim stalemate in 1915, Winston Churchill suggested striking at the soft underbelly of the Axis powers by invading the heartlands of Ottoman Turkey. However, blunders in executing his daring plan condemned the ANZAC (Australia and New Zealand Army Corps) and British forces to months of murderous exposure on the narrow beaches of Gallipoli. There was more success in Mesopotamia and the Middle East, where British forces eventually wore down Turkish resistance, thanks in part to the charismatic scholar-warrior T E Lawrence who roused the Arabs against their Ottoman rulers.

Above: The cause of female enfranchisement was much helped by the Great War, when women were drafted to work on the Home Front and 'proved their worth' beyond the domestic sphere.

THE WAR AT SEA

Before the war, the yellow press had imagined a titanic clash of dreadnoughts, but the deadly conflict at sea was to prove far less glamorous. In the first months of the war, British control of the northern sea-lanes was secured and the Royal Navy settled down to the grim job of blockading Germany. British strategists were acutely aware that control of the seas, and the war, could be lost in an afternoon of open sea battle. When the British and German fleets did finally meet off Danish Jutland in 1915, British ships took the heavier hits, but it was the Germans who retreated to their ports. Henceforth the German war effort at sea was submarine and aimed at cutting off the supply of food and raw materials to Britain. German U-boats were so successful against the supply ships bound for Britain that the Cabinet considered surrender in 1916. The U-boat menace was finally overcome by the convoy system, helped by technical advances such as hydrophones and depth charges.

HOME FRONT

The impact of the 1914–18 war was felt everywhere, a point rammed home to the residents of southern England who experienced bombing raids by Zeppelin air ships. As in the military, civil volunteerism was replaced by state compulsion. The government took unprecedented powers through the Defence of the Realm Act to mobilize the population. Women were drafted into the vital munitions and electrical industries while others served in auxiliary services and nursing organizations. The initial success of the German U-boats led to food shortages and compulsory rationing. In rural areas, schoolchildren were sent home to work on the farms. Taxation rose inexorably, as did government interference in daily life. Luxuries such as alcohol were restricted, the clock was altered to save daylight and propaganda in posters and songs were inescapable.

THE IMPACT OF THE WAR

In stark terms, the war cost almost a million British and Empire lives, as well as thirty-five billion pounds. A generation was lost and scarred and Britain was materially and spiritually exhausted. It was no coincidence that British society was increasingly secular after the war, for many survivors of the trenches had little further use for organized religion. Many looked for comfort in cults such as spiritualism or dreamed of a better future through utopian socialism. The war also sponsored advances in new technologies such as radio and aviation that had profound consequences for post-war society.

THE PEACE OF VERSAILLES, 1919

After winning the patriotic Khaki Election of 1918, Lloyd George met with the American and French leaders to draw up the peace settlement. In the negotiations at Versailles in early 1919, key British interests were at stake.
- The Empire was preserved and enlarged
- Britain became responsible for Tanganyika, Iraq, Palestine and South West Africa
- British naval supremacy was restored
- By default, Britain emerged as the leading player in the League of Nations.

These diplomatic successes masked the fact that Imperial Britain, like France, had been exhausted by the Great War and was sinking to the rank of a secondary power.

SLUMP
1920–1938

The economic changes prompted by the Great War sharpened regional differences in the British economy. Technological industries prospered in the inter-war years, but traditional manufacturing industries endured years of slump.

FIT FOR HEROES

In the election of December 1918, the 'Welsh wizard' who had led the country to victory was returned to power. Many voters were inspired by Lloyd George's promise of a land fit for returning heroes. Confidence in the economy was high, for the war had transformed British industry. Food production had risen as farmers ploughed up marginal land to take advantage of guaranteed crop prices. Wartime had made it easier to bypass union opposition and management lethargy to introduce American techniques of mass production and automatic machine tools, breeding a new generation of experienced engineers and operatives. New industries such as electronics, aviation and car production mushroomed, but government direction had largely planted these 'industries of the future' in southern and central England. The old industrial centres in northern England, Scotland, south Wales and Northern Ireland enjoyed full employment during the war, while demand for coal, steel and textiles was high. However, they represented the Victorian economy and after a brief 'replacement' boom between 1919 and 1921, factory gates began to close.

COAL SLIDE

The slump in international trade after 1921 led to unemployment and strikes. Working people increasingly looked to the Labour Party for leadership, but Labour's brief governments of 1924 and 1929–31 lacked the time and the resolution to solve Britain's economic ills. Government policies such as wage subsidies seemed to be mere tinkering, and many workers in the struggling coal industry believed that nationalization was the answer to their needs. The return of German Ruhrland coal to world markets in 1925 led to a severe slump in demand for expensive British coal. A Royal Commission into mining under Lord Samuel suggested a compromise of reduced wages and longer hours in return for investment in new machinery and better conditions. This was unacceptable to the miners, who chanted their slogan 'Not a minute on the day, not a penny off the pay' all the way to the Trades Union Congress. On 3 May 1926, workers in many industries responded to the TUC's call for a General Strike.

Above: Lloyd George, who served as an energetic War Premier from 1916–18, represented Britain at Versailles and was voted back into office in the immediate aftermath of the war by a grateful British public.

Right: Crowds milled outside the Stock Exchange in New York in the chaos of the 1929 Wall Street Crash.

GENERAL STRIKE

The strike lasted a mere nine days and was never the harbinger of communist revolution that some conservatives feared. The TUC abstained from interfering with essential services, health care and food transport. Violent incidents were localized and small scale. The volunteers who manned trains and buses achieved little other than embittering and amusing strikers in equal measure. The fledgling BBC proved its worth to the government, transmitting news and views while the Fleet Street presses lay silent. Stanley Baldwin's well-prepared government kept control of the situation and was quick to make 'sympathy strikes' illegal in 1927. The strike left a bitter memory in working class minds however, long after the BBC's twee portrayals of impromptu cricket matches between strikers and scabs (strikebreakers) were forgotten.

THE GREAT DEPRESSION

Britain was quickly caught up in the aftermath of the Wall Street Crash as foreign bankers withdrew their Sterling deposits, forcing the government to devalue the pound in September 1929. Attempts at restricting foreign imports only prompted reciprocal action by other governments and deepened the crisis. By late 1931, almost three million were unemployed in Britain, many of them in the older industrial areas. Single-industry towns such as shipbuilding Jarrow and ironworking Merthyr were especially badly hit. The National Government did little more than introduce wage cuts and the hated 'means test', designed to limit public expenditure. Nothing symbolized the downturn in the old economy more than Order 534, the vast Cunard liner that sat unfinished on the stocks at Clydebank from 1931 to 1934. Its launch as the *Queen Mary* only came once Hitler was in power and a new economic cycle was underway.

VOTES FOR WOMEN
1897–1928

By 1900, the case for women's suffrage had won many supporters, but neither sympathy nor the militant actions of the WSPU (Women's Social and Political Union) brought results. However, the contribution of women to the war effort brought a partial reward in 1918.

NEW STATUS

After 1860, the restricted status of women was changed by several pieces of landmark legislation. Divorced women enjoyed increased rights, while all married women gained greater control of their own property by 1882. After 1872, most British girls had an elementary education, and by the 1890s increasing numbers were studying at college and entering the professions. Physicians such as Sophia Jex-Blake and Elsie Inglis were pioneers in their field, but many women were forging careers in teaching and nursing by 1900. The invention of the typewriter and the telephone created new kinds of jobs and opportunities for women to earn a degree of social and financial independence. Women's political rights were also changing. Propertied women gained the right to vote in School Board elections in the 1870s. After 1884 they could also vote in district and parish elections. Women had begun to participate in Britain's developing democracy, but they were still excluded from the Parliamentary franchise. To many educated women and their supporters, this seemed an indefensible injustice.

CAMPAIGNING MOVEMENTS

The first suffrage campaigners were wealthy, well-connected women who used their access to powerful men to argue their case. The defeat of John Stuart Mill's 'feminist' amendment to the 1867 Reform Bill showed the limitations of that approach. Small local women's suffrage societies developed throughout Britain and were amalgamated into a National Union in 1897. By 1914, the NUWSS (National Union of Women's Suffrage Societies) had a membership of almost 100,000 and was capable of organizing street demonstrations that brought the large cities of Edwardian Britain to a halt. Although its leaders were mainly middle class, the NUWSS actively recruited members amongst the women millworkers of Lancashire and Lanarkshire. In the 1906 election, it forced the Liberal Party to take the suffrage question seriously by threatening to run its own candidates against unsympathetic Liberals. The Women's Freedom League attracted a number of socialists and exhorted its members to withhold payment of their rates and boycott the 1911 census. Men who supported

Above: Emmeline Pankhurst, a founder of the Women's Social and Political Union, was repeatedly arrested for militant behaviour. She died in 1928, shortly after women gained the vote on equal terms with men.

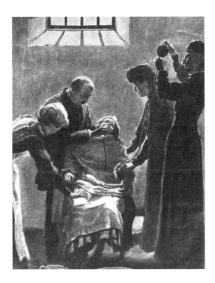

Above: Militant suffragettes who went on hunger strike while in prison were force fed until the 'Cat and Mouse Act' of 1913, which provided for their release when they became too weak and their rearrest once they had recovered.

'the cause' formed their own organizations. The Northern Men's Suffrage Federation petitioned Prime Minister Asquith in 1913 and when he refused to meet them, they staged a raucous protest in the House of Commons. Some women formed anti-suffrage societies and campaigned for the status quo, arguing in their pamphlets that women were not suited by temperament or biology for a life outside the home. Although their numbers were few, these women expressed conservative views that were probably held by the bulk of British society of both genders.

SUFFRAGETTE 'TERROR'

After 1903, the Women's Social and Political Union, a militant splinter group, began its programme of radical action. The Prime Minister was twice assaulted on holiday and the Home Secretary Winston Churchill was pelted with eggs. Places of male recreation such as golf courses, football pitches and cricket wickets were ransacked. Letters in pillar boxes in business and banking areas were destroyed with paraffin and corrosive acids. Portraits of the king were slashed with knives and the royal pennants on the greens of the king's own golf course at Balmoral were replaced with flags in WSPU colours. In 1913, Emily Davison made the ultimate sacrifice for the cause, throwing herself under the hooves of the king's Derby runner. The government responded by monitoring and arresting WSPU leaders. Hunger strikers were released to recuperate and then re-arrested when stronger. By 1914, the militants had alienated public opinion and women's suffrage was no closer.

WOMEN AND WAR

Suffrage organizations reacted in different ways to the outbreak of war. Many in the WSPU, including two of the three militant Pankhursts, dropped their suffrage work and began to beat the patriotic drum – the WSPU paper *Suffragette* was renamed *Britannia*. However, Sylvia Pankhurst campaigned for peace, and many suffragettes supported the Women's Peace Crusade. Most British women of all classes got involved in the war effort, impressing former opponents such as Asquith who remarked 'How could we have carried on the war without them? I find it impossible to withhold from women the power and the right of making their voices directly heard.' In 1918, the Coalition government extended the vote to two million women over 30. Equal franchise with men was achieved ten years later.

TIMELINE

1882	*Married Women's Property Law*
1874	*London School of Medicine for Women established*
1897	*National Union of Women's Suffrage Societies founded*
1903	*The radical WSPU splits from NUWSS*
1909	*First suffragette hunger strike by Marion Wallace Dunlop*
1909	*Introduction of forced feeding in prisons*
1910	*Failure of Bill that would have enfranchised women*
1913	*Cat & Mouse Act allows authorities to re-arrest 'reinvigorated' hunger strikers*
1913	*Death of Emily Davison at the June Derby*
1918	*Women over 30 enfranchised*
1928	*Franchise extended to younger women over 21.*

IRISH INDEPENDENCE
1900–1948

In 1914, civil war almost erupted in Ireland but was postponed by events in Europe. The 1916 Easter Rising presaged the bloody events of the 1920s that gave birth to the Irish Free State.

ULSTER ALONE

In 1910, the Liberal government needed the support of the Irish nationalist MPs at Westminster to curb the power of the Lords. In return, the Irish demanded Home Rule. As the third Home Rule Bill proceeded through Westminster in 1912–13, Ulster Unionists pledged to resist Dublin rule. Under Sir Edward Carson, they prepared to form a provisional government, amassing 80,000 volunteers and importing arms from Europe. Southern nationalists retaliated by forming the Irish Volunteers. To contain the crisis, the government ordered a naval squadron to Belfast and put its troops in Ireland on alert. However, many officers in the British Army in Ireland were strongly Unionist in their sympathies. To the government's horror, in March 1914 officers of the Cavalry Brigade stationed at the British Army HQ south of Dublin, indicated that they would resign their commissions rather than ride north and fight the Ulstermen. Although they could not rely on the Army in Ireland, the government pressed on with the Bill, risking civil war. An emergency conference in July failed to reach a settlement, but Irish affairs were suddenly overshadowed by the startling news of Balkan war and mobilization across Europe.

EASTER 1916

Unionists and moderate nationalists agreed to suspend discussions for the duration of hostilities and Catholic and Protestant Irishmen volunteered to fight the Kaiser. By supporting the British war effort, Irish parliamentarians lost ground to more radical, republican groups such as Sinn Fein, who saw the war as an opportunity to overthrow British rule by force. Members of the revived Irish Republican Brotherhood planned a rising in Dublin in Easter 1916, but the Royal Navy intercepted the German cargo ship bringing munitions. Nevertheless, republican patriots took control of key points in central Dublin – including the General Post Office – and announced the creation of an independent Irish Republic. Despite being outgunned, the patriots held out for six days of fierce fighting. After martial courts, the British military authorities executed sixteen republican leaders, and almost 1,500 republicans were interned. Nationalist Ireland was

Above: Sinn Fein volunteers in uniform guard the roof of Liberty Hall on the first day of the revolt of Easter 1916.

Below: James Connolly, effective Commander in Chief of the Easter uprising, was executed by a firing squad after it failed.

TIMELINE

1914	Home Rule Bill passed but postponed by outbreak of WWI
1914	Curragh Camp mutiny
1916	Easter Rising in Dublin
1918	Sinn Fein 'Ourselves Alone' win election in Ireland
1919–21	IRA wages guerrilla war against the British
1922	Partition of Ireland comes into effect
1937	Independent Republic of Eire established
1949	Ireland formally leaves the British Commonwealth.

Above: The revolutionary leader Michael Collins addresses a Dublin crowd on the day the Irish Free State was launched in 1922. He was shot and killed in the subsequent civil war.

appalled by the treatment of the '1916 martyrs', and support for their cause was reflected in the overwhelming electoral victory of Sinn Fein two years later.

OURSELVES ALONE

Refusing to take their seats in Westminster, Sinn Fein set up its own Parliament in Dublin, the Dail Eireann, and attempted to establish its authority throughout Ireland. The Irish Republican Army under Michael Collins made it impossible for the British to govern by targeting police and other officers of the Crown. IRA military organizations waged a guerrilla war of independence from January 1919 to July 1921, killing over 600 British personne but taking even heavier losses. The British responded by using paramilitary forces, dubbed the Black & Tans on account of their uniform. The Black & Tans quickly gained a reputation for brutality, and their readiness to execute republicans without trial alienated moderates in Ireland and Britain. The Irish war degenerated into a bloody round of atrocities and reprisals. In the elections of May 1921, Sinn Fein won every seat outside Ulster bar one. British commanders in Ireland despaired of restoring order even with vastly increased forces that a war-bankrupted Britain could little afford. It was clear that Ireland needed a political rather than a military solution.

PARTITION

Ulster Unionists had much to gain from Lloyd George's suggestion of partition, for they could expect to dominate the North and escape Dublin rule. For nationalists, the loss of Ulster was a heavy price to pay for securing control over the rest of the proposed Irish Free State. Hard line republicans rejected the Partition Treaty outright. The new Ireland was baptized with blood spilt in a two-year civil war between rival nationalist factions. In 1937, links to the British Crown were severed by the declaration of an independent Republic of Eire, a situation finally acknowledged by Britain in 1948. A year later (1949) the Republic of Ireland left the British Commonwealth but, to its great advantage, joined the European Economic Community in 1973.

THE ROAD TO WAR
1930–1939

During the 1920s, Britain played a leading role in the newly created League of Nations. However, in the more troubled atmosphere of the Fascist Age, more traditional diplomatic skills were employed to buy time for re-armament.

COLLECTIVE SECURITY

With the absence of America, Russia and Germany, Britain and France were the most influential powers in the League of Nations. The weakness of this peacekeeping body was exposed as early as 1923, when the invasion of Greek Corfu by Fascist Italy went unpunished. Nevertheless, successive British governments in the 1920s and early 1930s supported the League and its principles of collective security. In the positive atmosphere of the period, Britain was happy to accept the limits on its fleets outlined in the 1922 Washington Naval Treaty and to join in the reaffirmation of Germany's Versailles borders at Locarno in 1925. In the darker days after 1930, British governments were too concerned with domestic problems to fully appreciate the disaster unfolding in Manchuria – where the League failed to stop Japanese aggression – or fully grasp the implications of the collapse of the World Disarmament Conference in 1933.

THE ITALIAN THREAT

In the early 1930s, British strategists were vexed by the rise of Fascist Italy, which threatened British influence in the Mediterranean. Fascism, which many imagined to be the ideology of the future, even impinged upon domestic considerations, as Oswald Mosley's black-shirted British Union of Fascists seemed to be attracting support from disgruntled elements. Matters came to a head in 1935 when Mussolini invaded Abyssinia, the last independent state in Africa. The League of Nations eventually imposed its ultimate weapon of sanctions upon Italy, but these excluded oil and other strategic materials. Like the French, the British hoped to use the crisis to win over Mussolini as an ally and the British government allowed Italian ships access to the Suez Canal. The exposure of a plan to cede large parts of Abyssinia to Italy, concocted by the French and British foreign ministers, caused a public furore in 1935. It also exposed empty British rhetoric about the value of the League and signalled that Europe had returned to traditional methods of great power diplomacy.

Above: In the 1930s the old democracies of western Europe were overshadowed by the rise of two rival ideological states – Nazi Germany and Soviet Russia.

TIMELINE	
1932	*Manchurian Crisis reveals weakness of League of Nations*
1935	*British and French hypocrisy over Abyssinia exposed*
1935	*Britain signs naval pact with Nazi Germany*
1936	*Hitler re-enters the demilitarized Rhineland*
1938	*Hitler annexes Austria*
1938	*Britain sacrifices Czechoslovakia at Munich*
1939	*Hitler invades Poland.*

Right: Neville Chamberlain, British Prime Minister 1937–40, pursued a policy of appeasement with Hitler.

RHINELAND, ANSCHLUSS AND SPAIN

A greater danger to European security was now emerging in Germany where Hitler, as often promised, had begun to tear up the Versailles settlement. Britain had tacitly encouraged him in this by agreeing to an increase in German naval strength in June 1935, contrary to Versailles. When Hitler remilitarized the Rhineland in 1936, some like Lord Lothian took solace in the view that he was entitled to 'enter his own backyard'. Similarly, to many British commentators, Hitler's annexation of Austria in 1938 seemed entirely in keeping with the political and cultural destiny of Mitteleuropa, although it had been expressly forbidden at Versailles. German and Italian intervention in the Spanish Civil War was also overlooked, for many conservatives preferred the possibility of a stable right-wing Spain under Franco to the Republic with its links to Stalinist Russia.

MUNICH APPEASEMENT

As Hitler's ambitions became clear in the later 1930s, Chamberlain's government sought to appease the Führer by granting his 'reasonable' demands. The British government was acutely aware that public opinion in Britain was resolutely opposed to military invention over central European matters. Chamberlain, himself deeply committed to avoiding war as a result of his experiences in 1914–18, flew three times to Germany to meet Hitler during the Sudetenland Crisis in September 1938. Chamberlain also knew that Britain was not ready, both in terms of morale and materiel, to challenge the Nazi war machine. At the Munich conference, Chamberlain succeeded in averting war in Europe. However, he did so by sacrificing democratic Czechoslovakia, the child of the Versailles Peace Treaty, which lost its defences on the German frontier and much of its industrial potential.

Below: German troops marched into Poland on 1 September 1939, triggering the start of the Second World War.

BACK TO WAR

In March 1939, Hitler revealed his contempt for the western powers by marching into the remainder of Czechoslovakia. Chamberlain reluctantly began to put Britain on a war footing, doubling the Territorial Army and guaranteeing Polish independence from German aggression. In August 1939, Hitler's pact with Soviet Russia gave him a green light to invade Poland. When he did so on 1 September, Britain honoured its commitment to the Poles two days later.

ALONE
1939–1941

The Second World War began in earnest for Britain in the spring of 1940. Within a few short weeks, much of western Europe fell into Hitler's hands and Britain was left to fight on alone.

PHONEY WAR

As in 1914, a British Expeditionary Force was quickly despatched to France, but the war in western Europe would have to wait until Hitler had finished off the Poles and secured his eastern border with Soviet Russia. This was the Sitzkrieg, seven months of inactivity in which the Allied and German forces sat patiently along the fortified Maginot and Siegfried lines. At home, British children evacuated in September were back home for Christmas when the expected terror from the air did not materialize. Hitler specifically ordered the Luftwaffe not to bomb British cities, still hoping to encourage the pacifist elements in the British establishment. However, British bombers won the 'confetti war', by dropping propaganda leaflets over Germany. For the passengers of the SS *Athenia,* sunk by a U-boat on the first day of the war, and for the 833 crewmen of HMS *Royal Oak* lost in October, the war was far from phoney. On mainland Britain however, cars driving during the blackout were the most persistent threat to life.

BLITZKRIEG

In April 1940, Hitler occupied Denmark and Norway to secure his supplies of Scandinavian iron-ore. British failure to defend Norway led to Chamberlain's replacement by Winston Churchill on 10 May 1940, the same day that Hitler launched his lightning war in the west. With a decisive superiority in tanks and aircraft, the Wehrmacht swept through the Netherlands and Belgium. Avoiding the static Maginot Line, German panzers pushed through the Ardennes and raced across France to the Channel. The BEF was cut off from the bulk of the French army and had no option but to make for the port of Dunkirk and home. For nine days and nights, a flotilla of ships of all sizes braved bombardment and air attack to carry off almost 340,000 British and French troops. Once in England, these demoralized men were dispersed by railway and deposited in squares and parks throughout Britain. When France surrendered on 25 June, Britain was left alone to face Germany and its new opportunistic Italian ally.

THE BATTLE OF BRITAIN

The appointment of the belligerent Churchill as Prime Minister dashed Hitler's hopes that Britain might surrender rather than fight on alone. Hitler began to plan an invasion, but crossing the Channel required total air

Above: Boats of all types were despatched over the Channel to rescue the allied soldiers stranded on the beaches of Dunkirk.

Right and below: The Prime Minister Winston Churchill praised the role of RAF pilots in the Battle of Britain with his famous words 'Never in the field of human conflict was so much owed by so many to so few'.

"NEVER WAS SO MUCH OWED BY SO MANY TO SO FEW" THE PRIME MINISTER

supremacy. From July to September 1940, the Luftwaffe and RAF battled for control of the skies above southern England. The conflict was one of gradual depletion of industrial and human resources. British factories could churn out 450 new fighters a month, but pilots were much harder to replace. RAF losses in late August and early September exceeded those of the Luftwaffe and the situation was critical. The turning point came in mid September, when the RAF inflicted just enough losses on the Germans to force them to reconsider their tactics. By then, over 730 pilots had been lost or seriously wounded. Nevertheless the RAF still held the daytime skies. Henceforth, the Luftwaffe concentrated on bombing London and other industrial cities at night. The main thrust of the Blitz lasted from September 1940 to May 1941 and there were few nights when German squadrons were not at work above London or other key targets such as Liverpool, Coventry, Hull, Bristol and Plymouth. Despite the horrors inflicted on the civilian population, British morale was maintained and industrial production in affected cities was quickly restored. Over a million Britons served in the civil defence forces as wardens, rescuers, medical workers, special police and fire fighters. The 'few' won the battle in the skies but it was a vast civilian legion that ensured eventual victory on the ground.

TIMELINE: BATTLE OF BRITAIN

July 1940	German planes attack shipping in the Channel
13 August	Luftwaffe begin their 'Eagle' attack on Fighter Command
20 August	Churchill makes his speech praising 'the few'
Late August	Fighter Command almost overwhelmed by Luftwaffe attacks
7 Sept	Goering switches his emphasis to civilian bombings – the Blitz
15 Sept	Germans suffer heaviest losses in the air war over Britain
17 Sept	Hitler postpones Operation Sealion, the planned invasion of Britain
1 Oct	Heavy losses force the Germans to switch to night bombing only
May 1941	Coventry badly damaged by heavy bombing.

GLOBAL WAR

Initial British success against the Italians in North Africa receded when Rommel's Afrika Korps pushed the British back towards Egypt in 1941. British forces in the Balkans were spread too thin to resist the German onslaught in Yugoslavia and Greece in April. The German conquest of Crete by airborne invasion a month later exposed British shipping in the eastern Mediterranean to attacks from the air. As U-boats wreaked havoc in the North Atlantic, there was little cheer for blitzed Britain until the sudden news from Russia in June, where Hitler had launched 'Operation Barbarossa' against the eastern Soviet Union. Hitler's attack in the East provided Britain with an ally, albeit one whose armies were crumbling and in retreat until 'General Winter' (Russia's notoriously cold winter weather) came to their aid. As the situation in Russia stabilized, even more heartening news came from Pearl Harbor in Hawaii.

THE GRAND ALLIANCE
1942–1945

The coming together of Soviet Russia, the USA and the British Empire against common enemies was an uneasy alliance, but their massive reserves of manpower and production ensured final victory in 1945.

TOWARDS VICTORY

Britain's coalition with Russia and America did not guarantee victory but the combined manpower and resources of the Allies made it less likely that the Axis powers could win. Before Allied fortunes began to turn, there would be further failures by British command, notably the humiliating surrender of Singapore in 1942 which irrevocably damaged British standing in the Far East. Shipping losses in the Atlantic reached record levels in 1942 and it was well into the following year before the Allies' technological superiority through Asdic (sonar), hedgehogs and squids (anti-sub mortars), and radar began to tell on the U-boat packs. With the seas more secure, the western allies were able to deliver victories in North Africa, Italy and eventually in north-west Europe, while Germany slowly bled to death on the Eastern Front.

INDUSTRY AT WAR

As in 1914–18, resources and production were paramount in the 1939–45 struggle. Britain became a fully centralized industrial state, far more so than 'totalitarian' Germany, with almost all planning decided by the War Cabinet and the Ministry of Production. The hard-learned lessons of the Great War were quickly remembered and the British population was mobilized and militarized quickly and efficiently. The inter-war slump industries were in demand again and thousands did their bit for the war in shipyards, foundries, munitions works or in the mines. From the outset, the propaganda of the Ministry of Information reminded every Briton that the war would be won as much by switching off unnecessary lights, taking shallow baths and rehashing leftovers as by any act of heroism at the Front. The suggested welfare reforms in the 1942 Beveridge Report and the 1944 Butler Education Act gave British servicemen and workers an encouraging glimpse of the sunny uplands beyond eventual victory.

THE BOFFINS

The war created a new and unlikely hero – the boffins or scientists who could win technological advantages over the enemy. After initial difficulties, Watson-Watt's radar eventually helped the RAF to locate incoming

Above: Propaganda posters from the Ministry of Information reminded Britons to be resourceful and do their bit to help the war effort.

TIMELINE

June 1941	*Soviet Union attacked by Nazi Germany*
Dec 1941	*USA attacked by Japan*
Feb 1942	*Fall of Singapore to the Japanese*
May 1943	*Allied fleets begin to win the Battle of the Atlantic*
June 1944	*Return of Allied troops to northwest Europe*
May 1945	*Victory in Europe*
Aug 1945	*Victory over Japan.*

bombers. However, the less glamorous work of R V Jones to distort the Luftwaffe's navigation beams probably did as much to defeat the German threat in the skies. Engineers adopted the recent invention of plastics to make dozens of cheap, light parts for aircraft, ships and tanks. Pre-fabricated 'mulberry' harbours and PLUTO, the pipeline under the ocean, provided instant landing places and abundant petrol for the armies that poured into Normandy in 1944. British physicists such as James Chadwick, the refugees Sir Rudolf Peierls and Otto Frisch, and the metallurgist Cyril Smith all made important contributions to the development of the atomic bomb.

Above: Following the suicide of Hitler and the surrender of the German forces, a weary but elated Winston Churchill declared Victory in Europe on 8 May 1945.

Below: Enola Gay, the American B29 bomber that dropped the atomic bomb on Hiroshima on 6 August 1945.

VICTORY IN EUROPE

Some Allied strategists expected Nazi Germany to fall by Christmas 1944 and the US authorities printed dollar style marks for use in a defeated postwar Germany before the setbacks at Arnhem and the Ardennes. These were the last moments of triumph for the Wehrmacht in the West. The German war effort was haemorrhaging men and materials on the eastern Front and Hitler's secret weapons, the V1 flying bomb and V2 rocket, had caused alarm, but relatively little damage. The RAF and USAF had reduced most German cities and industrial plants to rubble. The Rhine was crossed in March 1945 as the Red Army closed on Berlin. Hitler's suicide on the 30 April, two days after Mussolini's execution by partisans in Milan, prompted the unconditional surrender of German forces in north-west Europe to Field Marshal Montgomery on 4 May. Four days later a formal armistice was signed at Rheims. Churchill, the first great voice to warn of the dangers of Nazism, declared Victory in Europe to the exhausted but elated British and took his place alongside Pitt and Lloyd George as one of Britain's greatest war leaders.

VICTORY OVER JAPAN

However, the war was not over, as the troops in the 'forgotten' Fourteenth Army in Burma knew only too well. Victory at Kohima and attention to supply and communication gave General Slim's forces the edge over a tenacious Japanese foe. With the capture of the port of Rangoon, the Allies were ready to roll back the Japanese conquests throughout South-east Asia. Preparations for a costly invasion of the Japanese heartlands were underway, when the news of the atomic obliteration of Hiroshima on 6 August broke to a war-weary and relieved Britain. The Soviet declaration of war upon Japan and a second atomic bomb at Nagasaki three days later forced the reluctant Japanese to surrender.

THE AGE OF AUSTERITY
1945–1951

Many British troops in the Second World War believed they were fighting for a better world. In 1945 they voted Labour so it could implement its radical manifesto.

A BRAVE NEW WORLD

The British Armed Forces in the Second World War were the best educated and most fully enfranchised in the nation's history. Many servicemen had enjoyed a secondary education and most were literate. As the war progressed, the old quiescent and homogenous officer corps was replaced by a wider range of men drawn from all parts of 'civvy street'. They knew their time in uniform was temporary and wanted to know why they and their men were fighting. In periods of monotony between action, servicemen keenly attended discussions and talks hosted by their education officers. Dog-eared paperbacks from Penguin and the Left Book Club were avidly read in camp and under decks. The Atlantic Charter and the Declaration of the United Nations added a social purpose to the war effort. The struggle was not just against Hitler and his like, but was for rights such as freedom from fear and want. In Britain, these lofty aims were translated into practical terms by the 1942 report on social reform chaired by Sir Edward Beveridge. It called for a comprehensive post-war system of social security and heath care. His report was a bestseller and its proposals were much discussed on radio programmes such as *The Brains Trust*. Junior officers who were close to their men knew the result of the 1945 General Election long before the ballot boxes were opened.

LABOUR LANDSLIDE

Central planning had won the war and now it could win the peace. Churchill had led Britain to victory, but he was tainted by the memory of the Tories' dismal interwar record on mass unemployment and slum housing. The Labour leader Clement Atlee had won many admirers as Churchill's efficient wartime deputy. Attlee's own reserved personal manner reassured electors that a vote for Labour and its welfare plans was not likely to be the first step towards Bolshevik excess. As the votes were slowly gathered from around Britain and from theatres of war around the globe, it was clear that Labour had won a substantial mandate for change from the British people.

NATIONALIZATION AND SHORTAGE

Between 1945 and 1951, Labour took the Bank of England and the power, iron, steel and railway industries into public control. National Boards selected by government would henceforth run these key sectors of the

Above: The Labour leader Clement Attlee was voted into power in a landslide defeat over the Conservatives, becoming Prime Minister of Britain from 1945–51.

WELFARE FOR ALL

In 1946, National Insurance was extended to all adults, with weekly contributions pooled and returned to the sick and unemployed. Maternity and death grants were issued to ease the difficulties many families experienced at these critical moments in life. Family allowances were also paid to mothers. The destitute could apply for National Assistance. Despite opposition from many in the medical profession, Aneurin Bevan oversaw the creation of a National Health Service that provided care to all – regardless of income. Attlee's historic government ensured that the State would

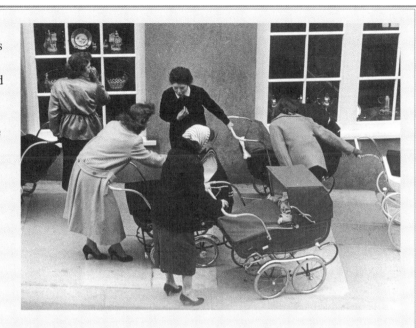

Above: The climate of optimism in the period after the war led to a rise in birth rates across Britain, dubbed the 'baby boom'.

meet its responsibilities to care for the nation 'from the cradle to the grave'. It could not house the nation though, for construction skills and materials were in short supply. Reconstruction in the damaged cities was especially slow. Thousands of young, demob-happy, married couples were already busily producing the post-war baby boom, but knew that it would be many years before their name reached the top of the council housing list. Some squatted in abandoned military camps but most found a room with relatives and saved for a residential caravan or dreamed of entering one of the new 'pre-fabs'.

economy in the interests of all. However, there was little worker participation of the old Soviet kind and many workers saw little difference apart from the new sign at the works gate. Much of the money to pay for capital investment in these basic but neglected industries came from the US Marshall Aid programme. The products of Britain's factories were too valuable to be sold at home. They were needed to earn foreign revenue and reduce Britain's balance of payments deficit. The Chancellor Sir Stafford Cripps exhorted British industry to 'export or die'. Wealthier British consumers were deterred from buying luxury goods such as cars by purchase taxes as high as 66 per cent and restrictions on borrowing money. Clothing, furniture and many foodstuffs remained rationed in Labour's command economy. There were difficulties in distributing essential commodities – coal was scarce in the freezing winter of 1946–47 and the cost of living went up when the pound was devalued in 1949. An American returning to Britain in 1951 would have thought the country was still at war.

THE END OF EMPIRE
1919–1970

The 1945 Labour government was keen to exit from India as quickly as possible. After Suez, the wind of change swept through the African colonies as the Union flag was lowered across the Empire.

THE COMMONWEALTH

In 1914, imperial Britain looked to its Dominion lioncubs, Australia, New Zealand, South Africa and Canada, to fight alongside the Motherland. By the end of 1917, the leaders of the Dominions sat in the War Cabinet, an acknowledgement of their military importance and the fact that they had become sovereign nations, as their independent membership of the League of Nations also signified. In 1931, their evolution from colony to nation was recognized in the Statute of Westminster. Henceforth the Dominions were members of the British Commonwealth, an association of former colonies linked by historic affection to the Crown. Significantly, Chamberlain's Cabinet in the later 1930s was not sure if the Dominions would be willing to sacrifice their young men for Britain a second time.

INDIAN DISOBEDIENCE

The 1919 India Act offered some authority over health, education and agriculture to the Legislative Council, but reserved real power over policing, justice and finance to Crown officials. The nationalist Congress condemned these limited proposals, triggering violent demonstrations. When an Indian crowd defended their right to assemble, General Dyer's order to fire resulted in over 350 deaths and 1,200 wounded. Dyer believed he had averted rebellion and civil war, but liberal opinion in Britain was horrified. The Labour Party committed itself to end British rule in India and feted Mahatma Gandhi when he visited Britain in 1931.

NIGHTMARE AT MIDNIGHT

By the time Atlee was able to honour Labour's promise to India, the subcontinent was dissolving into civil strife between Hindi, Sikh and Muslim, with over 4,000 killed in one riot in Calcutta in 1946. Muslims under Ali Jinna had evolved their own plan for a separate Islamic state. Under instructions to expedite a rapid British withdrawal from India, Lord Louis Mountbatten, the last British Viceroy, managed to get agreement for partition by bringing independence forward by a year. The new India and Pakistan came into being at midnight at the

Above: The Indian leader Mahatma Gandhi encouraged the tactic of peaceful civil disobedience as a means of gaining independence from British colonial rule.

TIMELINE	
1919	*Massacre at Amritsar in Punjab with over 1600 killed or wounded*
1931	*Statute of Westminster acknowledges sovereignty of white Dominions*
1947	*Creation of India and Pakistan*
1956	*Suez Crisis in Egypt*
1957	*Independent Ghana emerges from the old colony of Gold Coast*
1960	*Macmillan makes his 'Winds of Change' speech in South Africa*
1965	*White Rhodesia declares 'unilateral independence'.*

Above: Lord and Lady Mountbatten, the last British Viceroy and Vicereine of India, who oversaw the partition and independence of India and Pakistan in 1947.

Above: The apartheid regime in South Africa provoked strong opposition in Britain. PM Harold Wilson banned arms sales to South Africa and there were widespread boycotts of South African goods.

start of 15 August 1947. However, millions were caught on the wrong side of the new borders drawn up by the Boundary Commission and had to cross hostile territory in search of safety. An estimated 200,000 – from all religions – were the victims of Britain's hasty flight from imperial responsibility.

SUEZ

Colonel Abdul Nasser came to power in Egypt in a coup in 1954 and saw himself as an icon of leadership for nationalist movements struggling everywhere against the fading European empires. By nationalizing the Suez Canal in 1956, Nasser threatened Britain's communications with the Far East. Britain responded by sending troops into Egypt in conjunction with French and Israeli forces. This provoked a howl of condemnation at the United Nations in New York. Prime Minister Eden's actions alienated many of Britain's diplomatic friends in the Commonwealth and beyond, particularly the Americans who had been left in the dark. Although a military success, the adventure ended in sudden ceasefire and a humiliating evacuation. Suez underlined Britain's new position in the post-war world. Its days as a great power were over and it could not act independently to defend its interests without being sure of American support.

WIND OF CHANGE

Within the decade 1957–67, the vast majority of Britain's possessions gained their independence, as a tide of nationalism swept through the colonial world. The number of Commonwealth members rose in this period from ten to twenty-seven. Ghana was the first black state to emerge in the process of decolonization that quickly erased British pink from the African map. In his landmark speech in 1960, Macmillan acknowledged that the days of colonial rule were over. There were only two problems – Rhodesia and South Africa – where white minorities were determined to hang on to power. The Afrikaner government in South Africa hoped to do this through its elaborate system of apartheid or 'separate development'. White Rhodesia unilaterally declared its independence from Britain in 1965. The Labour Prime Minister Wilson responded by banning arms sales to South Africa and prohibiting all British trade with Rhodesia. Both issues claimed an elevated place on the British political agenda for decades. Establishing majority rule throughout southern Africa was to take years of international sanctions, civil unrest and sustained guerrilla action.

BRITAIN IN EUROPE
1945–2005

Slow to react to the realities of the post-war world, Britain missed out on the opportunity to influence the new Europe from the outset. Britain's relationship with Europe continued to raise fundamental questions about national identity.

FIRST STEPS

After 1945, a number of western European states began to explore the idea of closer co-operation. Some, like Italy and Germany, were seeking to secure their new democracies, while others like France were looking to find ways to contain a resurgent Germany in the future. All hoped to accelerate and enhance the process of economic reconstruction. Winston Churchill gave his blessing to these goals when he called for a United States of Europe in 1946. Churchill also chaired The Hague conference in 1948 that gave birth to the Council of Europe a year later, which Britain joined as a founder member. However, Britain differed from the advocates of greater integration in many ways. It had not been occupied in the two world wars, nor had it suffered as much devastation. It still saw itself as a major world power that could make its mark in the world alone – or at least in conjunction with the Commonwealth. It also believed that it enjoyed a special relationship with the United States. Britain's contribution to Europe would be made through transatlanticist bodies such as NATO (National Atlantic Treaty Organization) and the OECD (Organization for Economic Co-operation and Development).

Above: Winston Churchill meets Princess Juliana of the Netherlands at The Hague Congress of 1948 where he repeated his call for increased European co-operation, first made at Zurich two years ealier.

THE TREATY OF ROME

Britain sent observers to the 1955 Messina Conference that considered the next steps towards deeper integration. It was also initially involved in the negotiations that led to the 1957 Treaty of Rome, but withdrew when the extent of European ambition became clear. Britain therefore missed out on the opportunity to shape the future European Economic Community and found itself excluded from a neighbouring tariff-free market of over 200 million people. The British hastily cobbled together an alternative European free trade area (EFTA), that did not have the implicit aims of further social

TIMELINE

1951	*European Coal and Steel Community – first step towards Euro-integration*
1957	*The Common Market established by the Treaty of Rome*
1957	*Original members of EEC - France, Germany, Italy and BeNeLux*
1973	*UK, Ireland and Denmark join the EEC*
1975	*British membership confirmed in a national referendum*
1981	*Greece becomes the tenth member*
1986	*Portugal and Spain admitted*
1990	*Admission of Austria, Finland and Sweden expands EEC to 15 states*
2004	*Accession of an additional ten states to the renamed European Union*
2007	*Accession of Bulgaria and Romania brings EU to 27 member states.*

and political integration that underpinned the EEC. With only 90 million members in seven geographically scattered countries, it was a poor substitute for access to the 'Common Market', which was already forging ahead in terms of growth and standard of living.

MEMBERSHIP

Harold Macmillan was quick to realize that Britain's future really lay with Europe and instructed Edward Heath to negotiate entry. This was vetoed in 1963 by de Gaulle, as was Harold Wilson's attempt to join in 1967. De Gaulle felt that the 'Atlanticist' British were not fully committed to the European ideal and were insufficiently *communitaire*. Entry was possible after de Gaulle's departure from the scene, but a third application revealed mixed feelings in both main political parties. Britain was joining a club that had made its own rules over two decades and these ran counter to long-cherished British practices and the interests of British farmers and fishermen, not to mention suppliers of cheap foodstuffs throughout the Commonwealth. Nevertheless the Treaty passed through the Commons on an open vote, and Britain, led by Edward Heath, joined the EEC in January 1973.

SCHISM

The European issue and the continuing integration of the EEC raised questions about British destiny that transcended party boundaries. In the 1970s Labour was badly split, with the Left and the trades unions calling for exit. The Labour government elected in 1974 was divided throughout its five years in office. Further harmonization and integration embodied in the Maastricht Treaty of 1993 split the Conservatives and their schism over Europe helped keep them out of power after 1997. Celtic nationalists such as the SNP initially opposed European entry until the success of small EU members such as Ireland and Denmark became impossible to ignore. Anti-Europeans looked to Mrs Thatcher to champion their cause and were cheered when she negotiated a rebate in Britain's budget contributions. However she followed in Macmillan's pragmatic footsteps and signed the 1987 Single European Act. British nationalists who feared living in a federal European superstate were forced to create their own party, UKIP (United Kingdom Independence Party), which gained almost 17 per cent of the vote in the 2004 European elections but failed to make an impact in the following general election.

Below: The seat of the Council of Europe in Strasbourg, France. The Council includes 46 member states who are not all members of the European Union.

CONSENSUS AND CONSUMERISM
1951–1975

Following the Second World War, Britain experienced two decades of rising living standards. However, serious underlying industrial weaknesses were obscured by the cheap glamour of the 1960s.

GOLDEN YEARS?

From 1953 to 1970, unemployment was low, real wages increased by 20 per cent and living standards steadily improved, markedly so for many working class families. Labour's austerity measures were dismantled and private industry, helped after 1955 by the new television advertising, set about meeting the needs of the domestic consumer. Both main political parties were committed to full employment and social welfare, creating a political consensus that was called 'Butskellism' by the press who saw little difference between the policies of the Tory Chancellor Butler and his Labour shadow Gaitskell. Yet there were fundamental problems in the British economy. Recurring balance of payments crises forced Harold Wilson to devalue the pound by almost 15 per cent in 1967 and ban tourists from taking more than £50 out of the country. Industry was bedevilled by low productivity and wildcat strikes, for which rigid management and restrictive trades union practices were often equally to blame. The economy of the south and Midlands periodically overheated but the provinces lagged behind. Britain prospered after the war, but compared with the surging economies of the EEC, its meagre performance merited the nickname 'sick man of Europe'.

CAR CRASH

The motorcar was the iconic product of the age and by the early 1960s, owning one came within the reach of many more British families. Much of England was quickly linked by a motorway system that, at first, offered freedom and mobility to all. Yet by 1975, almost half the cars on British roads were foreign built and the once proud British car industry was in serious decline. Three of the four main car groups were American-owned, but it was the build quality of European and Japanese imports that posed the greatest threat to British producers. British car plants struggled with a complex set of interconnected problems; old machinery and methods, inflexible management and an antiquated trades union structure. The saga of Hillman Imp cars typified the age. Rather than expand their successful

Below: A young woman in an MGB convertible, Britain's best-selling sports car, introduced in 1962.

Ryton plant near Coventry, the Rootes Group were forced by the government to build a new factory in the unemployment blackspot of Linwood near Glasgow. The workforce there had no experience of building cars and components from Midland suppliers had to be shipped up to Scotland at great expense. After a reasonable start in 1963–65, the project eventually fell apart in a welter of strikes, poor sales and crippling warranty claims.

THE SIXTIES

In 1960, the baby-boomers reached adolescence. American teenage culture had already reached Britain in Presley's rock 'n' roll years, but 'pop' reached its apotheosis in the sixties, thanks to unprecedented youth spending power. As the decade unfolded, pop culture developed from naïve, commercialized fandom into cult rebellion and an explosion of sexual and narcotic experimentation that some experienced and many wistfully longed for. If most watched the sixties on their television sets, Britain was indeed becoming a more permissive and less judgemental society. The laws against abortion and homosexuality were relaxed in 1967 and theatre censorship ended the following year. The contraceptive pill had a profound effect on sexual mores. Prescribed only to married women at the start of the decade, by 1970 it was routinely given to single girls. However, the sixties were not simply about consumption and hedonism. Grammar school and college-educated youth also experimented with a range of exotic ideologies and beliefs, from Maoism to Buddhism. Student sit-ins and demonstrations railed against the Vietnam War, South African apartheid and the British deployment of Polaris nuclear missiles in 1968. Horror at the pollution caused by the Torrey Canyon supertanker disaster off Cornwall in 1967 helped promote rising public interest in environmental conservation.

Above: During the 1960s greater spending power triggered an explosion in pop culture and leisure pursuits, and the widespread availability of the contraceptive pill resulted in greater sexual freedom.

CONCRETE UTOPIA

High-rise flats came to dominate the British urban landscape as local government set about remodelling city centres and so-called slum areas with a vengeance. Councils gained additional subsidies from Whitehall the higher they built. The new villages in the air, using cheap pre-fabricated building systems, seemed to be the solution to Britain's persistent housing problem. Contrary to television documentaries that concentrated upon the alienation and practical difficulties that some experienced, surveys repeatedly showed that most tenants liked their 'flats'. Yet the modernism of Le Corbusier did not always transfer well from southern France to Britain. Sir Basil Spence's 1962 award-winning but damp-ridden project at Hutchesontown in Glasgow was demolished just three decades later. The collapse of Ronan Point in Newham in East London in 1968 signalled the end of the dream of building a new Britain in concrete.

THATCHER'S BRITAIN
1979–1997

Mrs Thatcher propelled British party politics rightwards and recast the British economy by reducing union power and government interference.

WINTER OF DISCONTENT

The later 1970s were years of drift. Two decades of economic decline culminated in rampant inflation and rising long-term unemployment. In 1976, the Labour government had to surrender Britain's accounts to the external supervision of the International Monetary Fund in exchange for a £2.3 billion loan. The trades unions rejected wage restraints and called their members out on strike throughout the winter of 1978–79. Pickets outside hospitals, tales of the unburied dead, and rats scuttling in mountains of uncollected rubbish on the streets of London made powerful television and headlines. Consensus Britain had failed and the poster slogan 'Labour isn't working' swept Mrs Thatcher into power with a comfortable majority.

PRIVATIZATION

The new administration believed that the roots of Britain's decline lay in the socialist economic foundations laid down in Atlee's time. Government had to be reduced and much tighter control of the money supply and public spending exercised. Daughter of a shopkeeper and wife of a businessman, Mrs Thatcher believed that the British people had to be set free from government and unions and be allowed to keep more of their earnings. The portfolio of industries and properties under state control was systematically privatized. By selling assets such as Britoil, British Telecom and British Airways on the stock market, the government hoped to create a property-owning democracy. Similar motives inspired the selling of council house stock to long-term tenants at attractively discounted prices. Critics argued that the main benefactors were speculators who cashed in on the 'sell-offs' and that a few private investors now owned assets that had once nominally belonged to the whole nation. Nevertheless, international confidence in Britain strengthened, bringing in foreign investment and restoring the position of the City. Inflation was eventually squeezed out of the system but at the cost of unprecedented numbers of unemployed workers and bankrupted firms. Government subsidies were few and those enterprises that could not survive were sacrificed in order to create a leaner business sector.

Above: Margaret Thatcher, Prime Minister 1979–90, became known as 'The Iron Lady' after setting out her unwavering position on the Cold War in 1976.

TIMELINE	
1975	*Mrs Thatcher replaces Edward Heath as Tory party leader*
1979	*Conservatives returned to power after Labour's 'winter of discontent'*
1982	*Falklands War against Argentina in the South Atlantic*
1984–85	*Mrs Thatcher takes on and defeats the National Union of Mineworkers*
1989	*The 'Poll Tax' introduced into Scotland*
1990	*Mrs Thatcher resigns from office after failing to win support from her Cabinet.*

UNIONS

In 1983, Mrs Thatcher cashed in on the public jingoism that followed victory in the brief but deadly Falklands War, winning a massive majority that was owed above all to the professionalism and sacrifice of the British Armed Forces. Now she had the mandate to take on the unions. The miners had defeated Edward Heath's Conservative government ten years earlier but carefully amassed coal stocks and the vast gas and oil reserves coming ashore from the North Sea gave Mrs Thatcher a much stronger hand than her predecessor. Violent clashes between police and pickets throughout the year-long strike made for disturbing television. Eventually, Tory resolution broke the NUM, which splintered as the strike-weary men returned to work. Within a year, the British coal industry had largely disappeared – all but fifteen pits were closed. Banning secondary picketing and requiring unions to ballot before striking gave individual union members greater power and reduced the influence of extreme Marxist and Trotskyite entryists, whom Mrs Thatcher condemned as 'the enemy within'. British industry entered a period of relative calm that attracted foreign investors such as the carmaker Nissan, which opened its highly successful Sunderland plant in 1986.

COLD WARRIOR

For her hostility to the West's policy of *detente* in the Cold War, the Soviet Defence Ministry dubbed Thatcher 'The Iron Lady' in 1976. She revelled in the nickname and found her ideological soul mate when President Reagan was elected in 1980. When the Soviets deployed their long range SS20s in eastern Europe, Thatcher permitted the USA to site their Tomahawk Cruise and Pershing missiles on British soil despite massive protests by peace campaigners such as the Greenham Common Women. She was quick to appreciate the significance of Mikhail Gorbachev's rise to the Kremlin in March 1985 and his attempts to reform the stagnating Soviet Union through *glasnost* (openness) and *perestroika* (restructuring). One of the longest serving Prime Ministers, she was still in power as the Cold War ended and could claim to have played a key role in helping bring about Soviet downfall after 1989. Her reputation for inflexibility served her well in foreign affairs but contributed to her eventual downfall. She failed to grasp the depth of hostility to her 'poll tax' reform of local government finance or the extent to which the European issue was splitting her party. Nevertheless, she recast British politics and subsequent governments had to work well within the parameters that she set.

Below: A disgruntled pensioner demonstrates against Thatcher's unpopular Community Charge or 'poll tax', one of the factors contributing to her downfall in 1990.

MULTICULTURAL BRITAIN
1948 ONWARDS

The arrival of 'New Commonwealth' immigrants after 1948 caused unforeseen difficulties and prompted periodic rethinks about how this radical change in British society could best be managed.

AFTER THE WINDRUSH

Like all members of the New Commonwealth, the 500 Jamaicans on the SS *Empire Windrush* who landed at Tilbury in 1948 carried British passports. Theoretically, almost a quarter of the world's population shared their right to live in Britain, but the consequences of this were overshadowed by the desire for cheap labour. In the 1950s, the annual number of immigrants averaged over 30,000, rising to over 100,000 in 1961. At this point the Conservatives responded to growing public anxiety and introduced a Commonwealth Immigration Bill. This reduced the number of immigrants through a voucher system, limiting entry to those with specific skills and qualifications. Social conservatives thought that this legislation was already too little too late, while liberals concurred with Labour MP Hugh Gaitskell that this was 'a shabby Bill'. Once back in power, Labour took the first steps towards outlawing the 'colour bar' by passing the 1965 Race Relations Act. It became illegal to refuse access to public places such as restaurants, hotels and pubs on grounds of race. Although the 'No Irish, No Blacks' signs came down from the windows of boarding houses, the Act did little to stop prejudice in the areas of employment and housing.

Above: Jamaican immigrants disembarking from the SS *Empire Windrush* in 1948.

RIVERS OF BLOOD

In 1968 Labour introduced a second Race Relations Bill to outlaw racial discrimination in a broader range of areas. On 20 April the controversial

Above: In 2001, violent riots erupted in Bradford, Burnley and Oldham in the north of England, signalling the discontent in many ethnic communities.

Conservative thinker Enoch Powell publicly attacked the Bill, which he believed would encourage immigrant communities 'to agitate and campaign against their fellow citizens' in demand of further special legal consideration. The classicist Powell's allusion to 'the River Tiber foaming with much blood' caught the attention of the media and the imagination of many anxious members of the 'indigenous' population. Wolverhampton's postal system collapsed under the weight of messages of support for their local MP. London dockers went on strike and Smithfield Market workers drew up a petition of support when he was dropped from the Tory Shadow Cabinet. Some election experts claimed that Powell's stance on the immigration issue helped Edward Heath win several key marginal seats in his surprise 1970 election victory. The Left now had a racist bogeyman to vilify, while British nationalist groups had a martyr and proudly sported badges with the cross of St George and the slogan 'Enoch was right'. Powell himself saw some justification for his fears in the race riots that erupted in Brixton, Toxteth and Handsworth in the 1980s.

THE IMMIGRANT EXPERIENCE

The sheer variety of individuals and communities that settled and developed in Britain after 1950 makes it difficult to typify their experience. Thousands of Irish and West Indian nurses found rewarding careers in the National Health Service in the 1960s. Asians from Kenya and Uganda, victims of Africanization in those lands, arrived in Britain destitute but quickly became powerful players in British commerce. However, Asian textile workers who settled in the mill-towns of northern England suffered as much as any native worker from the alarming shrinkage of Britain's manufacturing base after 1970. Those with poor English and poor general skills often found themselves in low paid, unattractive jobs and gravitated towards rundown inner-city areas in Birmingham, Bradford, Leicester and Nottingham. By 1990 urban Britain had become a multi-racial society on a scale unimaginable two generations previously. Although many of immigrant origin were visibly rising to more prominent positions in British life, others felt themselves to be victims of a deep-rooted systemic prejudice, described as 'institutional racism' in the 1999 Macpherson Report into the police handling of the murder of a black schoolboy.

MULTICULTURALISM?

As in much of western Europe, the prevailing approach of the governmental elite to the presence of so many distinct ethnic and cultural groups in Britain after 1970 lay in the ideology of multiculturalism. This promoted equal status for all cultures in Britain. Social liberals hoped that this would foster increased interculturalism. Critics feared the creation of ethnic ghettoes that would weaken national unity. Their fears seemed to be justified by the radicalization of elements within Britain's Muslim community that became more visible after the 2001 riots in Bradford, Oldham and Burnley. The suicide bombings of 7 July 2005, in which four Muslim Englishmen murdered 52 commuters on the London Underground, marked a new phase in thinking about how to manage the problem of British ethnic diversity. In 2006, the New Labour government was redefining British identity in terms of 'essential values' such as history, tolerance and the rule of law that were part of Britain's traditional 'monocultural' heritage.

TROUBLES IN NORTHERN IRELAND
1968 ONWARDS

Decades of discrimination against Catholics in Ulster sparked a civil rights movement in the 1960s. Badly handled by the Parliament at Stormont and the security forces, the situation deteriorated from protests into armed struggle.

ORANGE ULSTER

The 1922 partition of Ireland created a Protestant State of Ulster in the North. However, unionists were acutely aware that 'their' province was also home to a large Catholic population that hoped for Irish reunification. Unionist political control was maintained by gerrymandered boundaries that ensured majorities in Ulster's Stormont Parliament and in local councils. Control of the streets was guaranteed by the B-Specials, an armed part-time police force composed of loyalists that was deeply distrusted by the Catholic community. Discrimination in favour of unionists in employment and housing was the rule. Of the 10,000 workers in the Belfast shipyards, less than 400 were Catholic. County Fermanagh had a Catholic majority, but the bulk of council houses built between 1945 and 1968 were allocated to Protestant families. Nevertheless, many Catholics in Ulster reluctantly accepted their status as second-class citizens because of the province's prosperity relative to the Irish Republic and their advantages from sharing in Britain's Welfare State.

CIVIL RIGHTS

The Troubles had their origin in the civil rights movement in 1967 that attracted support from young students at Queen's University, Belfast. Twenty-five thousand people took part in the first civil rights march from Coalisland to Dungannon in August 1968 that was consciously modelled upon similar protests by activists in the American South. A march in Derry in October ended with the world's media capturing scenes of police beating young demonstrators. The situation deteriorated, as Catholic youths from Derry's Bogside exchanged rocks and petrol bombs for police CS gas. Protestant rioters in Belfast burned Catholic homes. British troops were sent to Ulster to keep the peace, but it was the

Above: After clashes between Protestant and Catholic residents, British soldiers were sent to patrol the streets of Belfast in 1969.

TIMELINE	
1967–68	*Beginning of 'the Troubles' in Northern Ireland*
1969	*Escalation of civil disorders in Belfast and the Bogside in Derry*
1969	*British troops deployed in Northern Ireland*
1972	*Thirteen killed in Derry on 'Bloody Sunday'*
1994	*Ceasefire declared by the IRA and loyalist paramilitary groups*
2001	*The IRA begins decommissioning its weapons.*

Provisional IRA (Irish Republican Army) that seemed more capable of defending Catholic areas such as the 'no-go' Free Derry. The British Army squandered the initial goodwill it received from the Catholic population through its use of CS gas and rubber bullets. In 1971 the Troubles intensified, when 226 men accused of political violence were interned without trial in the H-blocs at Long Kesh camp. Only two of the interned were Protestant. On 30 January 1972, remembered as Bloody Sunday, thirteen civilian marchers protesting against internment died when the Parachute Regiment barred the way. Northern Ireland erupted. On 21 July, 300 people were injured as twenty-two bombs exploded in Belfast city centre. London was forced to suspend Stormont and impose direct rule.

SUNNINGDALE AND THE LONG WAR

In 1973, the British and Irish governments met with nationalist and unionist parties to try and reach a political settlement. The agreement reached at Sunningdale in Berkshire was an ambitious attempt to force the unionists to share power with the nationalist community. It provided for an Assembly, a cross-community Executive and a Council of Ireland to encourage cross-border co-operation. The agreement was too demanding for most unionists. Most pro-Sunningdale unionists lost their seats in the 1974 general election and were replaced by hard-liners. The Protestant Ulster Workers' Council organized a general strike in May 1974 that paralyzed the province and wrecked any chance of implementing the settlement. After Sunningdale, the Provisional IRA pursued a 'long war' of sporadic attacks in Ulster and on the British mainland, most famously bombing the Grand Hotel in Brighton during the Conservative Party conference in 1984. Between 1969 and 2001, more than 3,500 people died as a result of the Troubles. Of these, over 1,800 were civilians, and 125 were killed on the British mainland.

THE BELFAST AGREEMENT

Although paramilitary activity and atrocities continued in the 1990s – twenty-nine died in the Omagh bombing in 1998 – the 1990s saw movement towards a political settlement. In August 1994, the Provisional IRA declared a ceasefire and the main loyalist organizations followed suit six weeks later. Talks between the main parties including Sinn Fein led to the 1998 Belfast Agreement that restored self-government to Northern Ireland on the basis of power sharing. The Executive and Assembly were suspended in 2002 as a result of continuing distrust over the question of decommissioning of arms. By 2005, this seemed to have been resolved. The issue of policing the province fairly and in a manner that both communities could trust still lay at the heart of Ulster's problems. In 2001, the tainted Royal Ulster Constabulary was replaced with a new Police Service of Northern Ireland that was committed to recruiting Catholic officers. Sinn Fein finally announced its acceptance of the PSNI in late January 2007, opening a way forward for the return of devolved government to Northern Ireland.

Above: In 1984, the IRA bombed the Grand Hotel in Brighton where Mrs Thatcher was staying during the Conservative Party Conference.

NATIONALISM AND DEVOLUTION
1934 ONWARDS

The merits of Scottish and Welsh Home Rule were debated from the 19th century onwards. Nationalist pressure on Labour led to the re-establishment of a Scottish Parliament in 1999. To meet Welsh aspirations, a National Assembly was set up in Cardiff.

HOME RULE FOR SCOTLAND AND WALES

The Liberal party, and early Labour groups, long expressed support for some degree of Home Rule for the 'Celtic nations'. A Scottish Home Rule Bill was presented in 1913, only to be derailed by events in Europe. However, the disillusionment felt after the Great War and during the years of slump led to a resurgence of nationalism in the 1920s and 1930s. Plaid Cymru, the National Party of Wales, was founded in 1925, drawing its support from the rural north and west where a feeling of separateness was nourished by the Welsh language and the tradition of religious nonconformism. In 1934 a number of Scottish nationalist factions coalesced into the Scottish National Party but, despite winning its first seat in 1945, it made little electoral impact for a long time. Instead, the Scottish Covenant Association kept the issue alive, collecting two million signatures in support of a Scottish Assembly in 1950. Underpinning these developments was a sense that Scotland and Wales were neglected by Westminster, a feeling exacerbated by the highly centralized policies pursued by Whitehall after 1945.

THE NATIONALIST THREAT TO LABOUR

In 1966 Gwynfor Evans won the Carmarthen by-election for Plaid Cmyru. The following year the SNP took Hamilton. In both cases, the nationalists won safe Labour seats, in part because of a feeling that Labour was taking its core vote in Scotland and Wales for granted. The message for Labour was clear. Although the Conservative Party was ideologically opposed to 'Celtic' independence, it was Labour who had most to lose if the nationalists broke out of their rural hinterlands into the industrialized areas of central Scotland and south Wales. During this first high tide of nationalism in the 1970s, the SNP campaigned on the slogan 'It's Scotland's Oil' and won over 30 per cent of the Scottish vote and eleven seats in 1974. Frightened by the prospect of losing their safe Scottish and Welsh seats, Labour moved quickly to offer Scottish and Welsh assemblies, and referenda were held in 1978. The majority of votes cast in Scotland were for an assembly but a 40 per cent yes vote

Below: Dr Winnie Ewing with actor Sean Connery at the opening of the SNP Congress in 1999.

Above: Queen Elizabeth II visits Wales during celebrations for the opening of the Welsh Assembly in 1999.

requirement meant that the proposal foundered. In Wales, splits within the Labour Party meant that the referendum failed.

DEVOLUTION

The ensuing Thatcher years were resented by many in Scotland and Wales. Relatively few Scots and Welsh voted Conservative – from 1986 to1997 the Secretary of State for Wales did not even represent a Welsh seat – yet Tory policies had a drastic effect upon manufacturing industry in these areas. In Scotland, politicians joined with prominent representatives of civic society in the 1989 Constitutional Convention to campaign for greater democratic accountability through devolution of power from Westminster. The Labour government returned in 1997 was committed to establishing a Scottish Parliament and a Welsh Assembly. The yes vote in the Scottish Parliament referendum won convincingly although the Welsh result was much closer. In 1999, Dr Winnie Ewing, the Hamilton victor thirty-two years before, opened the first session of the Scottish Parliament since 1707.

THE QUESTION OF IDENTITY

These political events reflected deeper long-term changes in British society. Polls repeatedly suggested that the sense of 'Britishness' was fading and was increasingly the preserve of the older generations that remembered the war or members of more recently arrived communities. Devolution naturally encouraged the older national identities, and while a renaissance of Welsh-ness and Scottish-ness was to be expected, the pronounced resurgence of English national feeling after 1997 took many commentators by surprise. The devolution settlement markedly failed to address the problem of reciprocity. English MPs at Westminster lost all say over devolved issues such as education and health that were now Edinburgh's sole concern. Yet Scottish MPs at Westminster could still vote on these matters in an English context. Calls for Scottish MPs to withdraw from the House when purely English matters were discussed carried an undeniable democratic logic but were anathema to Labour which was heavily reliant on its Scottish members. The situation was exacerbated by the number of Scots in the Cabinet, lampooned in the press as the 'tartanocracy'. Calls for an English Parliament grew louder in the press and polls showed a majority of Scots and English in favour of ending the union. Its tercentenary was celebrated with a whimper in January 2007.

TIMELINE

1913	*Scottish Home Rule Bill postponed by WW1*
1934	*Creation of the SNP in a coalition of smaller nationalist groups*
1945	*Election of the first SNP Member of Parliament*
1974	*SNP win over 30 per cent of Scottish popular vote in general election*
1978	*Inconclusive referenda for assemblies in Scotland and Wales*
1997	*Successful referenda for a Scottish Parliament and Welsh Assembly*
1999	*Opening of the devolved Parliament and Assembly.*

THE NEW MILLENNIUM
1997 ONWARDS

After eighteen years out of power, a fresh Labour leadership convinced the electorate that it could be trusted in government. After a vigorous start, the New Labour project ran aground in the sands of Iraq.

Above: The Millennium Dome in east London, designed as part of the Millennium celebrations, stood empty for many years before becoming a privately-owned entertainment venue.

NEW LABOUR

After 1979, four consecutive electoral defeats kept Labour in the wilderness. After 1994, its new leader Tony Blair and his advisers, Alastair Campbell and Peter Mandelson, were conscious of the need to present a palatable image on the television screens of Middle England. Blair succeeded in convincing Labour to drop Clause IV of its constitution, its historic commitment to the Marxist dream of 'common ownership of the means of production and exchange' (Karl Marx, *Das Kapital*). This, and re-branding as New Labour, symbolized a rightward shift. There was to be less dependence on the unions, the ditching of much socialist ideological baggage and the adoption of market-orientated policies that acknowledged the realities of post-Thatcherite Britain. These changes were resisted by the left, but were imposed by tight party management and scrupulous attention to the detail of public presentation that many derided as 'spin' and 'control freakery'. In 1997, with the Shadow Chancellor Gordon Brown exuding a sense of financial prudence, New Labour won easily against John Major's weary and divided Conservatives.

THINGS CAN ONLY GET BETTER

With the youngest Prime Minister since 1812 at the helm, much was expected of the administration. Its first years were marked by a flurry of landmark legislation such as the Human Rights Act passed in 1998, followed by a Freedom of Information Act in 2000. A Scottish Parliament and a Welsh Assembly were established, while a significant advance towards peace in Northern Ireland was made in the 1998 Belfast Agreement. In Blair's second term, the Ulster peace process stalled over IRA decommissioning and costly reforms to the NHS showed little apparent benefit for patients. Although Gordon Brown kept a tight control of public finances at first, and was praised for giving the Bank of England the power to set interest rates in 1997, critics began to point to his 'stealth taxes' and questioned whether the increased spending on public services in New Labour's second and third terms had brought about any tangible improvements.

TIMELINE

1994	*Blair becomes Labour leader after sudden death of John Smith*
1997	*New Labour defeats John Major in general election*
2002	*US government pushes for disarmament and regime change in Iraq*
March 2003	*Largely US and UK coalition invades Iraq in second Gulf War*
2005–2007	*Deterioration of military and political situation in Iraq*
June 2007	*Blair resigns and Gordon Brown becomes Prime Minister*
August 2007	*Collapse of the US housing market triggers a global financial crisis*
2008	*Britain enters the worst recession since the 1940s.*

IRAQ

After the terrorist attacks on New York and Washington in September 2001, Blair quickly identified himself with President Bush's 'war on terror'. His decision to follow the Americans into war against the Iraqi dictator Saddam Hussein in 2003 dominated the remainder of his premiership and consumed much of the government's energy. There was intense opposition in Parliament and throughout the country to Britain's involvement in Iraq. Although Saddam's regime was quickly overthrown in 2003, the lack of a political strategy for postwar Iraq resulted in a chaotic insurgency lasting many years, and British troops suffered many losses.

HANDOVER

Blair's credibility never recovered from the Iraq debacle, and in October 2004 he announced that he would seek a third term but not a fourth. Although Blair's own popularity remained low, Labour defeated the lacklustre Tory opposition in 2005, but with a greatly reduced majority and only 35 per cent of the popular vote. Further criticism of Blair came with his failure to defend the British EU budget rebate, won by Mrs Thatcher in 1984, which was effectively reduced by twenty per cent in 2005. Civil libertarians were appalled by plans to introduce identity cards in the wake of the London Underground bombings of July 2005. Never loved by his own party – despite winning three election victories – Blair resigned in June 2007 and was replaced by his Chancellor of ten years, Gordon Brown.

Below: For years after the invasion of Iraq, British troops continued to try and contain the insurgent factions that arose in the wake of Saddam Hussein's regime.

FINANCIAL CRISIS

In July 2007, a failure of confidence in the United States housing market triggered a financial crisis which soon spread around the world, and Britain was among the countries worst affected. Banks were revealed to have huge capital deficits as a result of over-leveraging and investing in mortgage-backed securities. In September 2007 the Bank of England stepped in to prevent the collapse of the British bank Northern Rock, but this failed to restore consumer confidence and a few days later there was a run on the bank – the first since 1866. Northern Rock was the first of a string of banks to hit financial difficulties and require government bailouts, and in 2008 the country entered a recession. While assuming a leading role on the international stage in tackling the financial crisis, Brown was also criticized for failing to anticipate it during his ten years as Chancellor of the Exchequer.

INDEX